D1191225

CHINA'S AGRICULTURAL MODERNIZATION

China's Agricultural Modernization

THE SOCIALIST MECHANIZATION SCHEME

ON KIT TAM

University of New South Wales, Duntroon

CROOM HELM

London • Sydney • Dover, New Hampshire

© 1985 On Kit Tam
Croom Helm Ltd, Provident House, Burrell Row,
Beckenham, Kent BR3 1AT

Croom Helm Australia Pty Ltd, Suite 4, 6th Floor,
64-76 Kippax Street, Surry Hills, NSW 2010, Australia

British Library Cataloguing in Publication Data

Tam, On Kit
    China's agricultural modernization: the
    socialist mechanization scheme.
    1. Agriculture and state—China 2. Farm
    mechanization—China—Political aspects
    I. Title
    338.1'61'0951   HD2097

    ISBN 0-7099-2478-X

Croom Helm, 51 Washington Street, Dover,
New Hampshire 03820, USA

Library of Congress Cataloging in Publication Data

Tam, On Kit.
    China's agricultural modernization.
    Bibliography:p.
    1. Agriculture and State—China. 2. Farm Mechanization
—Government Policy—China. I. Title.
HD2098.T36   1985   338.1'61'0951   84-29333
ISBN 0-7099-2478-X

Printed and bound in Great Britain by
Biddles Ltd, Guildford and King's Lynn

CONTENTS

LIST OF TABLES AND FIGURES

Figures

ABBREVIATIONS

CCP	Chinese Communist Party
FYP	Five-Year Plan
ha.	Hectare
h.p.	Horsepower
kW	Kilowatts
kWh	Kilowatt Hour
NCNA	New China News Agency
NPAD	National Programme for Agricultural Development
NPC	National People's Congress
SCMM	Survey from China Mainland Magazines
SCMP	Survey of China Mainland Press
SWB	Summary of World Broadcast, Weekly Economic Report by British Broadcasting Corporation

INTRODUCTION

Agricultural mechanization as a policy issue had been brought up more than once after the land reform of the early 1950s, but it never assumed any priority as an immediate aim with intended real national significance. However, after the convention of China's Fourth National People's Congress in 1975, the mechanization of agriculture was fast becoming the focus of China's agricultural development policy. In October 1975, the First National Conference on Learning from Dazhai in Agriculture resolved to make the rapid progress in achieving basic mechanization an important success criterion in this national campaign. Indeed, such urgency was attached to this goal that the agricultural mechanization objective was featured as the basis for the modernization of the agricultural sector and of the whole economy in a series of important national conferences which followed.

The Second National Conference on Learning from Dazhai, which was held in December 1976 and was four years ahead of the scheduled reconvention time, affirmed the priority of rapid mechanization as a central objective for rural development. This was followed up by the Third National Conference on Agricultural Mechanization in January 1978 in which plans were said to be made for the realization of basic mechanization by the year 1980. These national conferences were accompanied by numerous conferences and working committees at the ministerial and provincial levels. Thus, between 1975 and 1978, China appeared to have embarked upon an urgent attempt to mechanize its agriculture in an economy where the agricultural sector provided employment to the bulk of the population. In contrast, during the whole time since 1949, including the preceding Fourth Five-Year Plan period (1971-5), no such urgency was evident and certainly no similar national programme on such a scale with grandiose plans to put the rapid mechanization of agriculture as a national objective had ever been attempted.

What was the background and what were the relevant factors that led to China's decision to make the basic mechanization of agriculture a central objective? While the mechanization objective has been abandoned by the present leadership, subsequent discussions in China may suggest that this reversal of decision is based solely on

1

the consideration of feasibility in terms of the limits of resources and technology. However, was the mechanization objective only an engineering proposition to upgrade the level of technology to achieve better performance in agricultural production? In China's rural industrialization efforts since the 1960s, some western economists saw a viable alternative model for rural development that could offer some lessons to other developing countries. The building of an agricultural machinery industry was very much a part of these efforts. What had been the progress towards mechanization prior to the start of the rather short-lived mechanization campaign in 1975? Could the prevailing economic circumstances lend support to a rapid mechanization programme, and if not what were the difficulties?

To shed some light on these and other related issues, this study investigates the actual experience in mechanization during the Fourth Five-Year Plan period, a period which, as will be discussed, represented in many ways a new stage in China's rural development. The historical perspective and the development approach under which mechanization efforts were exerted during this five-year period, and the mechanism, outcomes and problems these entailed will be examined. The study is not intended to be focused solely on the estimation and reconstruction of input and output figures or on the ideological struggles and social transformations in the rural villages. It is intended to address the issues involved in agricultural development and mechanization through a more integral analysis of the way technological transformation has been linked to China's quest for social and economic development.

In actual fact, while agricultural mechanization could in itself be an important economic objective, it had previously served, and was formalized in 1975, as an equally important instrument to transform the institutional and organizational structures of the rural economy. Indeed, such a transformation was conceived to be a necessary condition for the realization of technical advancement in the sector. The pursuit of agricultural mechanization had thus been the extension and a continuous part of the rural socialization process that began with the land reform programme. The mechanization of agriculture was therefore inseparable from the emphasis which the previous Chinese leaders had attached to the socialist transformation.

This book will adopt an impartial approach in the analysis of the subject. That is, no value judgement will be implicitly made of the economic system per se, although this does not mean that policy and performance cannot be examined against general economic principles, and efficiency criteria defined under the existing conditions and stated objectives. This approach also means evenhandedness in dealing with the assessment of policy orientation of a particular leadership group whether it represents the ruling faction of the time or not. This is particularly important because when there was a major change in economic policy, all policies by the previous leadership group tended to be totally discredited, often without adequate presentation of facts and analysis. At times, past activities were simply not recorded in the official accounts on which observers of the economy, both inside and outside China, very much depended for their evaluation. Since the availability of economic statistics had been poor until the recent relaxation, it is useful therefore to discern carefully the selective accounts presented by one group (i.e. the ruling leadership). Even today, for various reasons, there are still relatively few details of the economic activities during those years of the Cultural Revolution.

There are two main parts in this study. The first part, consisting of the first two chapters, is intended to provide the necessary background and perspectives on China's evolution of development approach towards the rural sector. The second part, from Chapter 3 to Chapter 6, deals with the country's rural development policy and problems as manifested in the actual experience and efforts in the promotion of agricultural mechanization during the Fourth Five-Year Plan period (1971-5).

Chapter 1 examines and clarifies the various objectives and priorities for socialist development in China to provide a better understanding of the associated policy initiatives and reforms that have been attempted. There is also a brief outline of the past performance in agricultural production and of the possible role of a national policy to promote agricultural mechanization. Major changes and shifts in emphasis in the approach to rural development between 1949 and 1970 are discussed in Chapter 2. Through analysis of the policy oscillations on mechanization and collectivization, the underlying theme in the seemingly conflicting developments is probed. It identifies a number of problems that have emerged making the past developmental theme less effective.

There were significant political developments during the early 1970s and the formulation of economic policy reflected them. Chapter 3 traces these developments and explains the characteristics of China's overall direction and approach towards economic development and its policies for agricultural development and mechanization. While the official economic approach was moving towards adopting more economic efficiency criteria in guiding production activities during these five years, the movement was not straightforward. The mechanization of agriculture assumed a secondary consideration in policy priority until 1975.

Trends in the production of agricultural machinery are examined in Chapter 4. In order to understand better the plausible causes of the policy design and the constraints of the prevailing organization of economic activities on such production on a regional level, a number of emerging patterns are identified and discussed. While there was notable growth in the aggregate output of various agricultural machines, the supplies of prime movers, attachments and spare parts were found to be seriously inadequate. Inefficient utilization of machines was widespread. Despite the fact that local manufacturing of machinery was being promoted as an integral part in the pursuit of self-reliance, real progress in this depended essentially on the plans and actions of the central bureaucracy.

Chapter 5 examines the system of control and management. It analyses the then existing general mechanism of material allocation for the supply and production of agricultural machines. The management arrangements under which the experiment in mechanization had been carried out are studied. Whether it was in the flow of inputs for manufacturing or in the distribution of the final products, a centralized approach managed by several levels of government had been maintained. Increasing control over the process provided a basis for the selective introduction of modern inputs on a more comprehensive scale to a few regions. However, after some years of experience with collective ownership of agricultural machinery, no satisfactory system of machine management had emerged. The increasing number of restrictions placed on the activities of the collectives and their members had contributed greatly to that problem.

Since the days of the land reform programme, the Chinese government had been trying to initiate a continuous stream of institutional changes in the rural sector, basically through raising the degree of socialization, in order to ensure that a high level of savings and investment was made by the rural collectives. Chapter 6 discusses the means employed by the government to maintain a desired level of capital accumulation within the rural sector. The role played by the commune system in the financing of mechanization is examined.

The years of the early 1970s signified a time of significant change for China, both in its internal and external conditions. Although changes of a more profound nature are being made since the death of Mao Zedong in 1976, what occurred during those years will continue to exert influence over the future course of the country's development. Indeed, the present reforms and adjustments are in many respects a reaction to the past developments under the new priorities and circumstances.

With new priorities and strategies, the new leadership are devising new policies and replacing old rules. In order to be effective, they must be considered and formulated in the light of the developments and problems that have prevailed in the recent past. Not only is it necessary to reverse or revise past practices that are no longer considered appropriate to the new demands, it is equally important to identify and tackle those basic problems which had caused difficulties and might render the new objectives unattainable if not resolved properly. This study will therefore attempt to provide some insights into these issues. While China had more or less managed to produce sufficient food for its population, and might have for this reason been regarded as exemplifying a successful rural development model, much needs to be clarified before any positive lessons could be drawn from the experience. In any case, it is now evident that an even faster economic growth would have been achievable had some of the obstacles been removed.

Chapter One

CONCEPTS AND BACKGROUND

The development of China's agricultural sector has been studied with interest by scholars since 1949, and many important works have been written on the various economic aspects of the subject (Perkins, 1969; K. Chao, 1970; Schuran, 1969; Kuo, 1972; Walker, 1965; Stavis, 1975). Although the question of agricultural mechanization was really an academic one until the mid-1960s, it seems to have received less attention than it deserves.[1] While a number of studies directly tackle the subject of agricultural mechanization in China, the focus is generally on the technological side of the question (Kuo, 1964, pp.134-51; Chin and Choa, 1962-4, pp.1-9; Khan, 1976, pp.17-26; Nagahiri, 1976; Ishikawa, 1975).

Apart from the fact that agricultural mechanization had not been accorded top priority before 1975, the official blackout on economic statistics since the 1960s has made it necessary to reconstruct various estimates from the fragmentary information available if some knowledge on the Chinese development is to be gained. As long as the Chinese government maintains the policy of not publishing comprehensive socio-economic data, a proportion of the works and efforts by economists studying China will continue to be taken up by estimation and interpretation of basic economic data.[2]

In the early 1970s, the development of local industry, which includes the production of agricultural machinery, has attracted considerable attention from students in Chinese development. For some scholars, local industry is regarded as the realization of bringing industrialization to the countryside (Riskin, 1971; Sigurdson, 1972, 1975; K.I. Chen, 1976).[3]

Studies on local industry have demonstrated the importance placed by China on the adoption of intermediate technology suited to local resource endowments for the purpose of economic development. Increased understanding of the many functions that local industry can assume, including those relevant to the modernization of agriculture is thus gained. However, the preoccupation with the technological aspects of the development in local industry tends to have given less consideration to the demands for changing the structure of the economic system and to the way and the mechanism through which the rural collective framework has actually helped, or obstructed, in the development of local industry. In this way, the question of agricultural mechanization, which really involved more than the output of tractors or irrigation equipment, has thus been treated in a more technical perspective, and has not been studied in relation to the transformation of the institutional and organizational structures of the Chinese economic system.

BASIC OBJECTIVE OF CHINA'S DEVELOPMENT

The study of a nation's economic development and well-being has long been part of the subject matter of economics. Since the Second World War, the growing concern for the underdeveloped economies has led to a process of rethinking and reexamination of the concept and objectives of economic development. Literature on the issue has grown enormously. It is not the aim of the present study to engage in this reappraisal and debate. Different countries, due to their historical circumstances, factor endowments, technological level and political orientation, may have different priorities and policies for their pursuit of economic development. Even within a single country, there are changes in all these elements over time. In China's case, the basic objective has always been the building of a modern socialist economy within a relatively short span of time.

Mao, in his Opening Speech to the First Session of the First National People's Congress in 1954, pronounced that: 'Within the time span of a few five-year plans, from the basis of an economically and culturally backward country, we will build a great industrial nation with modern culture ...' (Mao, 1977-a, p.132). In 1957, when China was on the verge of the Great Leap Forward movement, Vice-Premier Li Fuchun spoke, not without optimism, of the basic objective for China in the next ten years:

> We must continue our socialist revolution to win a decisive battle over capitalism. In terms of our socialist construction, our main task is to build a basically integrated industrial system. Such a socialist economy would incorporate modern industry, modern agriculture, and modern sciences and culture. To accomplish this task, we need about twenty years, starting from the establishment of the People's Republic (Li, 1958, p.24).

As a result of the severe setbacks following the Great Leap Forward, readjustment programme was under way. However, even at that time, the modernization objective seemed not to have suffered any drastic change though the timetable was lengthened (Mao, 1967-a, p.194). In 1965, Zhou Enlai again made a call to turn the country into a 'strong socialist state with modern agriculture, industry, defence, science and technology' in the 'not too distant future' (Zhou, 1965).

The pursuit of modernization for a socialist economy in China has no doubt been the primary preoccupation of the Chinese Communist Party and has been recognized so by most outside investigators of the Chinese economy. Even for the Cultural Revolution, this fundamental commitment to economic development appeared to have remained basically unchanged.[4] However, there are major conceptual and practical problems associated with the objective of attaining modernization, which must be 'socialist' and not any other kind of modernization.

In essence, problems arose when the Chinese leadership, or some part of the top leadership, found that there were conflicting ideas on how to assign relative priority to the pursuit of certain characteristics of socialism and of modernization, at a particular period of time or for some fields of development.[5] The reasons could be many. They might include a belief that the pursuit of one at a certain time might lead to the negation of the other, or a presumption that one has to be pursued first in order to bring about the healthy development of the other, and so on.

In polemical terms, the problem is at times seen as a question of whether 'production relations' should be changed first so as to realize the full potential of the 'productive forces', or that the material base of the economy should be developed first to make subsequent transformation of production relations possible.[6] It is also seen in the light of the struggle between the 'capitalist roaders' and the representatives of the 'revolutionary line', the 'leftist' and 'rightist' deviation versus the 'correct' approach. Western observers also give it various labels such as the 'pragmatist' approach and the 'radical' approach represented respectively by the 'Liuist' and the 'Maoist', etc. Of course, it is no secret that an element of power struggle is ever present, either as part of the cause or as a result.

Nevertheless, as socialism is generally accepted by all Chinese leaders to be a transitory stage to communism, and as China does not wish to follow exactly the way the Soviet Union has developed, a process of trial and error has been inevitable in China's search for her own road to socialism. Hence, in practical terms, policy formulation would have to incorporate some desired characteristics which are perceived to constitute socialist modernization. Difficulties have arisen because of uncertainty or disagreement over these characteristics or the policies needed to realize them.

An underlying concept for China's attempt at socialism has been a desire to control the outcome of economic and social activities. This is ultimately linked to the desire to raise the living standard of the population according to certain patterns of distribution and is inseparable from the aim to attain national power. Translated into practice, China has adopted an economic system with central planning, with a high degree of control over resource allocation and over distribution of wealth and income for the purpose of fast industrialization.

As a result of historical circumstances, internal and external conditions, some basic characteristics of China's quest for socialism over the first twenty odd years have emerged. These include the commitment to develop by self-reliance, to promote the level of socialization and to enhance equity based on a system of central planning. It is sufficient to stress again that the interpretation of each of these characteristics, the relative emphasis assigned to each, and the strategy for their implementation have not remained unchanged over the years.[7] It should also be noted that most of them are really interdependent. For example, it can be argued that, in order to achieve a faster rate of output growth, a high level of savings and investment is necessary for a developing economy such as China's without access to international finance or aid (at least up to the late 1970s). And to obtain the desired amount of savings and effectively turn them into productive investment, control over income distribution (e.g. elimination of property income from private ownership of means of production) and over resource allocation are often seen as necessary and a system of central planning for economic development is thus employed. One favourite way to better facilitate such controls has been, of course, to increase the extent of public ownership in the economy.

In summary, China's basic objective is to build up a modern economy rapidly, based on some perceived fundamental elements of socialism. In many respects, the way that rapid industrialization is to be achieved and the interpretations of the 'demand' of socialism in China are closely related. However, some conflicts between the perceived principles of socialist development and the need for rapid output growth have posed a constant challenge to which a flexible trial-and-error approach has been adopted.

To help understand the various major Chinese policies and concepts relating to the attempt to achieve socialist modernization which are relevant to the present study, brief explanatory notes on a number of such policies and concepts are made in the following section.

EXPLANATORY NOTES ON SOME CONCEPTS AND DEFINITIONS

The purpose of the notes here is to outline official phraseology used in Chinese pronouncements which have direct relevance to this study. Although most of these pronouncements are phrased in political slogans whose economic implications may not be immediately apparent to outsiders, they usually underline quite definite economic thinking and policies.[8] However, it is by no means the purpose of this section to explain all official Chinese terminology nor does it try to establish a comprehensive vocabulary for studying socialist economic systems.[9] The aim here is to facilitate later analysis without having to diverge into lengthy discussion on their meanings each time they appear.

Public Ownership

In essence, all major means of production have until recently been owned either by the 'whole people' through the state, or by groups of individuals. Thus, theoretically, public ownership is made up of state ownership and collective (or group) ownership. As for private ownership, it consists mainly of personal belongings, dwellings and other simple and small tools until the recent reforms. In practice, state ownership encompasses all factories, mines and corporations run by the various levels of the Chinese government, all of which can broadly be termed as state enterprises. Though state enterprises are owned by the 'whole people', each of them would keep their own separate account, and have their own different lines of controlling authorities. Collective ownership mainly entails the ownership of farmland and means of production by groups of individuals who are members of rural collectives. These rural collectives have been organized into the communes with a three-tier ownership system. As this form of rural collective will be discussed later, it is sufficient to note here that the property rights of collective ownership are restricted rights.[10] For instance, though the farmland is 'owned' by the production team or the production brigade (depending on which is the basic unit of accounting in the commune system), they are not allowed to sell land to their own members nor can they freely exchange land with other rural collectives. Hence, this qualified ownership is in reality a custodianship bestowed on the rural collectives by the government.

'Economic Methods' versus 'Administrative Methods'

This dichotomy reflected the different approaches to economic management in China. When economic methods are given ascendance it means that scale economies, specialization of production, market exchange relations, material incentive, profit as criterion for performance, and speed of output growth are generally given greater emphasis. However, administrative methods have tended to favour tighter and more complex economic planning and central controls, preferring economic interactions among enterprises of various types through bureaucratic channels.

Administrative methods of economic management have generally been facilitated by more centralized forms of administration with economic plans having a wider scope and deeper penetration. However, the two approaches are not mutually exclusive in application. Judging from China's experience in the first three decades since the Revolution, the two approaches really represented the relative emphasis in the overall development strategy mix. Both have been tried and promoted at different points in time but both have taken the concept of public ownership of the means of production and the need for central planning as the basis of their operation.

Nevertheless, this dichotomy does carry with it some important implications. For instance, the adoption of economic methods would certainly not help the development of regional self-sufficiency and would also tend to favour faster growth for the more efficient production centres. In terms of regional equality, the net result in the short term is not clear. On the one hand, the reduction of regional self-sufficiency may halt the trend towards increasing inter-region disparity. On the other hand, the shifting of resources to more efficient production centres would definitely aggravate inequality. The net short-term outcome depends on the relative strength of the two opposing forces, on the existence and effectiveness of any government redistributive measures, and on the level at which regional disparity is measured. Since material incentive is stressed or at least more acceptable in economic methods, inter-personal disparity in income is likely to rise, at least in the short run.

There is little doubt that different groups of the top Chinese leadership have had preference for one approach over the other, and such disagreements have also been likened to political struggle between the 'revisionist' and the 'revolutionary' lines. In essence, it is the same dispute over the relative priority for developing productive forces and production relations. In actual fact, however, no approach has ever completely dominated and the actual practice has often been a compromise.

'To Respect and to Realize the Party's Rural Economic Policies'

This slogan was promoted intensively after the abandonment of the Great Leap Forward movement and again in the early 1970s. 'The Party's rural economic policies' have to be viewed in the context of the development of events of the time. With the economic failures following the Great Leap Forward movement, a readjustment programme with cut-backs in many areas of economic activities was carried out. In the agricultural sector, the ill-conceived rush to lift the level of socialization was also corrected. Against this background, a document entitled 'Work Regulations for Rural People's Communes' was drafted by the Chinese government.[11] The document dealt mainly with two problems. First, it attempted to fix and formalize the system of the commune so that economic relations among the communes, the production brigades (which still acted as the basic accounting unit in 1961 but were quickly shifted downward to the production team), the production teams and the commune members could be stabilized. The other problem was to bring about recovery and development in production quickly. The document stressed the need to stabilize the commune system and to give more emphasis to production and to the question of improving commune members' incomes.

In other words, the policy thinking behind this slogan was to promote greater stability and more consistent rules and regulations so that efforts could be concentrated on expanding production. Such a policy was of course compatible with the then prevailing emphasis on using economic methods. Since the Cultural Revolution, many economic regulations had been ignored and violated, principally by various levels of the commune administration and by the government. Cases of arbitrary merging of rural collectives, arbitrary shifting up of the basic accounting unit in the commune system, and the elimination of all private economic activities were reported to have been prevalent. The campaign urging the realization of the Party's rural economic policies was again promoted with vigour in the early 1970s.

THE TECHNOLOGICAL PROBLEMS FOR CHINA'S AGRICULTURAL DEVELOPMENT

According to Chinese economist Xu Dixin, in 1963, agriculture supplied 40 per cent of industry's material inputs and 80 per cent of light industry's material inputs. In addition, about half of the 1963 budget revenue came directly and indirectly from agriculture.[12] (Xu, 1961, p.45). In the 1970s, agricultural population accounted for 80 per cent of the total population.[13] Agriculture in 1973 still provided 40 per cent of industry's material inputs and 70 per cent of light industry's material inputs (Ji, 1975, p.7). As in 1963, about half of the state's 1973 budget revenue still came directly and indirectly from agriculture. Approximately two-thirds of the products from light industry were sold in rural villages. Between 1952 and 1973, the tax revenue and profits obtained by the state in light industry were equivalent to three-quarters of the state's total investment on capital construction for the whole industrial sector during the same period (Wu and Chen, 1978, p.23). This result is perhaps not surprising for a country with a large rural labour force working on a relatively small area of arable land. However, over a decade has passed since agriculture was formally recognized by the government to be a bottleneck in China's quest for modernization. Thus, this continued dependence by the rest of the economy on the performance of agriculture is clearly unsatisfactory.

The growth of the economy was therefore severely constrained by this precarious and technologically more backward sector. As agriculture commands the provision of food to the whole population, and to a considerable extent, of materials for industries and of accumulation of investment funds, any disturbances in this sector will have a serious effect on the general economy. It should be noted that while 80 per cent of the population live and work in the rural sector, the share of agriculture in the national product in the 1970s is estimated to be between 20 per cent to 40 per cent only.[14] Hence, labour productivity in agriculture is relatively low.

In fact, labour productivity and land productivity, as measured by grain yields, have had a slower growth rate during the early 1970s than the previous few years. Grain yields, in per capita terms, remained at about 300 kilogram during the early 1970s, with an average annual rate of growth of only 0.8 per cent.[15]   However, this rate of growth between 1963 and 1970 was 1.2 per cent (Orleans, 1975). Land productivity in terms of grain yield per hectare achieved a 2.5 per cent average annual rate of growth between 1971 and 1975, while the comparable figure for 1963 to 1970 was 3.6 per cent.[16]   In terms of output value, agricultural production was estimated to be growing at an average annual rate of about 4 per cent during 1965 to 1970 and at 3 per cent during 1971 to 1975 (National Foreign Assessment Centre, 1977, p.3). For the same period of time, the official Chinese figures for the average annual growth rate in industrial production was 11.7 per cent for 1966 to 1970 and 9.1 per cent for 1971 to 1975 (G. Liu, 1978, p.8). This means that both agricultural and industrial production have had a slower growth during the 1970s. Since agricultural outputs were still an important source of export earnings, this performance in agricultural production would affect the ability to finance the import of crucial technology, materials and machinery for China's pursuit of modernization.[17]

IMPACT OF MECHANIZATION ON THE PRODUCTION POSSIBILITIES IN AGRICULTURE

For the first three decades after 1949, China had relied on institutional changes to advance agricultural development. Direct public investment in the sector had not been significantly high. Apart from the increased use of chemical fertilizers since the mid-1960s, no modern inputs or technology have been adopted on a large scale. Farming technique remained basically labour-intensive and was mainly based on traditional technology. Up to the end of the Fourth Five-Year Plan, most of the efforts that were associated with the mechanization of agriculture had been geared towards the production of food grains. Hence, from the viewpoint of the rural collectives and indeed the Chinese government, the primary interest in the production effects from mechanization was centred on food grain production. Technically, mechanization could be a powerful means through which and by which additional chemical fertilizers, high-yielding improved seeds, irrigation and drainage, land improvements, expansion of cultivated land, plant protection, processing and storage, and diversification of agricultural production could be provided and applied more effectively. It is well established that, to obtain maximum yields from a new variety seed, more advanced agricultural technology is required for thorough land preparation and a regular water supply, and that human and animal power alone just could not reach the requisite technical standards (Marsden, 1973, p.3). In fact, notwithstanding other financial and organizational considerations, mechanized cultivation and harvesting are regarded as major determinants for the success of many high yielding seed varieties (Mudra, 1975, p.1).

In this context, the production effects of mechanization on labour productivity and land productivity are of the greatest interest. As far as land productivity is concerned, the effect is quite clear. Under optimal conditions with appropriate complementary inputs, the positive production advantages of mechanization are well established by agricultural engineers (Smerden, 1971, pp.53-4). Because of China's strategy to increase grain output through multiple cropping, the timeliness of certain operations thus demanded would certainly raise the effectiveness of using suitable machinery. Although the causal relationship will not be estimated here, the cross-sectional comparison in Table 1.1 does provide some indications and insights into the association between high land productivity and the level of modern inputs such as tractors and chemical fertilizers.[18] One implication of the comparison is that all those countries which have achieved significantly higher yields have also used and benefited from a much higher level of modern inputs than China.[19] The potential of achieving higher land productivity via increased use of agricultural machinery and chemical fertilizer has been demonstrated in the experience of these countries.[20] Of course, whether the primacy on grain output would limit the positive effects on land productivity is a separate question.

Table 1.1:   *International Comparison of Grain Yields and Level of Modern Inputs (1975)*

	(a)	(b)	(c)
Canada	2,051	14.8	28.4
USA	3,440	20.8	77.5
Japan	5,925	68	430.6
France	3,683	77.6	267.6
Netherlands	4,477	219	792
Hungary	3,849	12.2	261.7
Yugoslavia	4,183	26.5	92.5
USSR	1,101	8.2	49.2
China	1,933	1.4	44.6

(a) Grain Yield (kilogram/hectare);   (b) Number of Tractors (per 1,000 hectare of cultivated land);   (c) Chemical Fertilizers, Nutrient Weight, (metric tons per 1,000 hectare of cultivated land).

Source: FAO, Production Yearbook 1975, Tables 12, 13, 14, 124, 125, 126

In the long run, mechanization will displace labour from agricultural activities so that labour productivity in agricultural production in general must increase even if the same absolute amount of output is produced. On the more specific component of agriculture, such as the all-important grain production in China, the effects of mechanization need to be examined in more detail. Although the immediate aim of mechanization has clearly not been the substitution of labour, and although extra demand for labour may even be created in the short run (Perkins, et al., 1977-a, p.212; Ishikawa, 1977, p.95; D. Xiao, 1960), for those operations or activities that are mechanized, labour input would inevitably be reduced so that the labour productivity in those operations and activities will be improved. Whether there is a net gain in average productivity, measured by taking account of all inputs, cannot be determined a priori. It should be noted here that total employment of the labour force in the rural communes is the sum of agricultural and non-agricultural employment. Although the dividing line is not always so clear-cut, it is sufficient to note that non-agricultural employment in China's rural communes at that time generally included such tasks as simple manufacturing, processing, construction, repairing, transportation, mining, commerce and other tasks not directly linked to planting or other agricultural production. Displaced labour will occur when farming operations are mechanized, whether viewed in the short or long run. And this must increase average agricultural labour productivity (in terms of the remaining labour force or the skilled labour operating the machinery) even under the assumption that land productivity does not improve as a result of the introduction of new machinery.

Experiences in other developing countries indicate that in the initial phase of mechanization, labour displaced in mechanized operations could be gainfully employed in other activities such as planting new crops, livestock production, weeding, harvesting and threshing (Abercrombie, 1973, p.60, p.71; Barker, et al., 1973, p.106; Raj, 1973, p.24). In the case of China, where the rural collectives have regarded full employment of their members as a primary concern, the redeployment of the labour displaced should present no immediate political problems at the initial stage.

Indeed, from the experiences of those more advanced regions and collectives in China, there has been no shortage of alternative employment for the labour displaced from various activities connected with grain production which have been mechanized to various extents. Regions or collectives differ in their conditions and the actual alternatives available to each are not the same. In essence, alternative employment opportunities have fallen into the following categories: other labour-intensive operations directly associated with the grain production process; non-grain agricultural production; work in the collective-run enterprises; work in the factories or mines in the county-run local industry network; farmland improvement and irrigation projects. For instance, the collection, transportation and application of organic fertilizer, which is still the most important plant nutrient source in China, can take up to one-third of the total labour input of a rural collective (Yang and Wang, 1962; SWB, FE/W924/A1, April 13, 1977). Since these operations were not priorities in the selective mechanization that has

taken place, those outlets for the displaced labour were assured.[21]
It is sufficient to state here that, from the limited experience of the
few regions that have achieved some degree of mechanization, the
alternative employment opportunities have adequately absorbed the
displaced labour freed from the mechanized operations in grain
production.[22]   Hence, if the alternative employments do produce
positive marginal output and if the displaced labour does not lead to a
fall in the total output of those activities that are mechanized, then
the average labour productivity for the rural collective will increase.
As far as the experience in those advanced models is concerned, this
seems to be the case.

However, such labour displacement may present organizational
and employment problems if it takes place simultaneously in all rural
collectives. If the effect on labour displacement by the advanced
regions and collectives is any indication, then at least 60 per cent of
the total rural labour force can be expected to be saved merely as a
result of mechanization in a few key operations in grain production
(Xinzhou County Communist Party Committee, Hubei Province, 1974,
p.2, p.49; Bureau of Agricultural Machinery Administration,
Revolutionary Committee of Jinzhong Prefecture, Shanxi Province,
1974, p.2; Y. Chen, 1971; Renmin Chubanshe, 1972, p.62; Hubei
Renmin Chubanshe, 1975, pp.88-91 and 1976, p.13). Indeed, if basic
mechanization were to include non-grain production, the labour saved
would even be greater. As the then Vice-Premier Hua Guofeng
stated in the First Dazhai conference in 1975:

> When we achieve basic mechanization, i.e. 70 per cent of the
> main operations in agriculture, forestry, animal husbandry,
> fishery and subsidiary production are mechanized, it will be
> equivalent to a <u>doubling</u> of the nation's rural workforce
> calculating on the basis of cultivation, irrigation and drainage,
> and transport operations (Hua, 1975). (Emphasis added.)

Therefore, when both the scope and the extent of agricultural
mechanization are expanded, the question of arranging for the
redeployment of labour would certainly become a vital responsibility
for the Chinese government and not just an internal matter for the
rural collectives to solve alone. Judging from the available evidence,
that question did not seem to have received serious consideration in
1975 and it is not possible to speculate what measures if any might
have been planned for this eventuality. Coupled with the fact that
land productivity will be enhanced by the introduction of appropriate
mechanization, the potential for expanding agricultural production
should be quite significant. The experience in the advanced units in
China has clearly demonstrated that such an improvement in
production possibilities is indeed potentially feasible. On the other
hand, whether the success in these advanced units, mostly with
favourable natural conditions and many with special privileges, can
be repeated in the same manner all over the country is far from
certain. The point is that, with the less than satisfactory

performance in agricultural growth, the Chinese government in 1975 appeared to have favoured the advance of a programme of agricultural mechanization.

THE DEMAND FOR AGRICULTURAL MECHANIZATION

Apart from the possible gains in lifting agricultural productivity, the pursuit of agricultural mechanization could in fact satisfy many demands for 'socialist' development. The outline for mechanization made in 1975 has made this particularly clear. Hua Guofeng, in his Summary Report of the National Conference on Learning from Dazhai, stated that:

> The function of mechanizing agriculture is not confined to the raising of agricultural labour productivity significantly so that labour can be freed to engage in diversified production and to build prosperous socialist new-type villages. Agricultural mechanization has very important implications for utilizing the advantages of the bigness and publicness of the commune organization, and for the diminution of inequality between cities and villages, between industry and agriculture, and between mental and manual works (Hua, 1975).

The role of mechanization in the advancement of Chinese socialism is therefore definitely not insignificant. This role has evolved through a long process of changes and adaptation in the development of the agricultural sector. A set of conditions appears to have been created under which agricultural mechanization has become not only the preferred way of technical transformation but also a convenient vehicle to deliver this transformation, while at the same time serving to bring about socialist development.

Mechanization of agriculture on a national scale is qualitatively different from any other technical reforms made in the past. To start with, a large commitment of funds and resources is needed to acquire the relatively expensive agricultural machinery. Unlike other modern inputs such as chemical fertilizer, agricultural machines are major indivisible fixed assets which are expensive to run and to maintain. In addition, the effective use of such machines often presupposes certain technical and organizational conditions. For instance, the levelling of land and the construction of road paths are essential technical preconditions for the use of tractors. The optimal utilization of certain machinery may also involve a scale and pattern of operation which need not suit the existing ownership and management systems of the rural commune structure. Indeed, it is quite obvious that, for most production teams, it was beyond the reach of their ability to purchase and operate a full range of agricultural machines for their own exclusive use under the then existing rural development policy and priorities (in particular the emphasis on grain production).

Hence, even on an <u>a priori</u> ground, the pursuit of agricultural mechanization cannot be divorced from changes in the institutional and organizational structures of the economic system. Indeed, the objective of China's economic development is to achieve socialist modernization which had demanded a continuous process of change in the technical, institutional and organizational structures of the economic system in order to achieve stable and high growth in material production based on some perceived socialist pattern of production relations. It can be argued that, from a theoretical point of view, mechanization of agriculture satisfies the demands of socialist modernization.

On the one hand, mechanization could represent a crucial step in fundamentally transforming the production technology in agriculture into a modern one. And from the viewpoint of promoting socialization in the countryside, of enhancing equality between agriculture and industry and ultimately of achieving self-reliance in national development, agricultural mechanization has also been viewed as playing an instrumental role. As mechanization had to be financed by whatever available means other than foreign sources at that time when China has not embarked on an open-door policy, a substantial portion of the total income in the agricultural had to be saved. Therefore, as hinted by Hua Guofeng's statement, the upper levels of the commune organization (i.e. the commune and brigade) have to grow in relative economic strength in order to ensure that the savings are generated and utilized for such investment. Of course, the investment funds made by the rural collective as a whole need not represent a significant part of the total if government provides the necessary funds via policies on production, pricing, subsidies or grants. The significance is that a continuous high level of investment, which in itself is an important corollary of the socialization process, can be assured as a result of the move to mechanize agriculture. The strengthening of the economic power of upper levels of the commune system has clearly been regarded as an important step in furthering rural socialization. Starting with land reform, to the establishment of the commune system in 1958 and the subsequent modifications of the commune structure, this socialization process did not necessarily require a dramatic formal change in the commune ownership system, though in actual fact there appeared to be a trend that favoured such a change in the mid-1970s.

Therefore, the mechanization of agriculture was potentially a powerful force to help bring about changes in the relations of production that might have been considered desirable for China's socialist development. However, the way in which such changes are realized need not depend entirely on the immediate introduction of mechanization for China's agriculture. It is really the prevailing economic conditions, coupled with the commanding emphasis on the relative importance of various aspects of the idea of socialism, that have dictated the actual choice of means. Nevertheless, if the mechanization of agriculture is considered from both the context of technological and non-technical transformation of the economic system, then it clearly presents a plausible answer to the demands coming from both sides.

CONCLUSION

There is no doubt that if China is to succeed in her pursuit of rapid economic growth, the performance of agricultural production must be further improved in a significant way. On a priori grounds, both in terms of technical demands and the then desired form of socialist transformation, the mechanization of agriculture could potentially play a dual role, although it is a separate question whether rapid mechanization on a national scale at that time was economically feasible or justifiable.

For the introduction of a national programme of such importance, it would have been imperative that, not only operational programmes be planned but that the necessary preparations and the satisfaction of some preconditions be ensured. For instance, the availability and form of financial resources, rural labour employment and redeployment, production organization reforms, energy resources for agricultural machinery, attachments and spare parts, etc., must be adequately investigated and problems resolved. However, the 1975 decision to initiate the mechanization campaign appears not to be concerned with these aspects.

As will be studied, the reason seems to be that the Chinese leadership at the time was unable to come up with, or unable to agree upon, an overall economic development policy package for the next five to ten years. Instead, a piecemeal approach was adopted and agricultural mechanization was favoured as the way to modernize the rural sector because of its various attractions to the leadership.

In fact, as a result of the actual development in mechanization during the first few years of the Fourth Five-Year Plan period, the primary objective of mechanization in 1975 was really more concerned with bringing about further socialization in the countryside. In other words, the socialist demands for rural transformation appeared to have been the overriding consideration.

Hence, on the basis of the potential in changing the relations of production in the rural sector, agricultural mechanization was promoted as the course of agricultural development. In this regard agricultural mechanization's role in furthering the advance of socialism is reminiscent of some arguments put forward in the debate over the priority of collectivization versus mechanization during the mid-1950s. Indeed, what happened in agricultural development and mechanization policy formulation during the 1970s could not be divorced from the initiatives taken in the mid-1960s, and in a sense it was also a continuation of the process in rural transformation that was started in the 1950s. Therefore, in order to understand better the development process of agricultural mechanization during the Fourth Five-Year Plan period, it is necessary to investigate the experience and problems associated with this question during the first two decades of government under the Chinese Communist Party. In Chapter 2, a brief examination into the major issues of agricultural mechanization during the 1950s and 1960s will be made. It will provide some necessary perspectives against subsequent development in the 1970s.

NOTES

1.   Actually, many studies on Chinese agriculture have a part that tackles the question of agricultural mechanization in some way. However, their main concern is generally centred on estimates of tractors or other machinery and tools. The exception is Stavis' (1978) excellent study of the many facets of the politics of the agricultural mechanization issue in the 1950s and 1960s.

2.   The blackout on economic statistics has been relaxed since the later part of the 1970s, with the most notable example in the release of the 1979 State Budget in July 1979, the first time since 1961. However, the present relaxation is still selective, and so far no comprehensive information has been given to cover the development of the economy during the 1960s and the first half of the 1970s.

3.   Other studies have concentrated on one of the most remarkable developments in local industry, that is, the rapid expansion of chemical fertilizer production by local factories. See for example T.C. Liu, 1970; K. Chao, 1975.

4.   When the Cultural Revolution was launched, the aim of the movement was stated as:

> to revolutionize people's ideology and as a consequence to achieve greater, faster, better and more economical results in all fields of work. If the masses are fully aroused and proper arrangements are made, it is possible to carry on both the Cultural Revolution and production without one hampering the other, while guaranteeing high quality in all our work. The great Proletariat Cultural Revolution is a powerful motive force for the development of the social productive forces in our country. Any idea of counterposing the Great Cultural Revolution to the development of production is incorrect.

See, 'Decision of the Central Committee of the Chinese Communist Party Concerning the Great Proletariat Cultural Revolution', quoted in Joan Robinson, 1969, p.95. Of course, subsequently it has been shown that serious disruptions in industrial production did take place, but the basic objective of economic development appears not to have been completely abandoned.

5.   This problem is certainly not unique to China. As Kornai (1980) has argued in general a 'socialist' economy always has to resolve the dilemmas presented by the desire to implement some perceived socialist principles and by the need to improve efficiency in economic activities.

6. In simple terms, 'relations of production' means the form of ownership in the means of production, form of resource allocation mechanism and commodity exchanges, and the form of social organization. 'Productive forces' denotes the technological state of productivity and the material base of the economy.

7. For more detailed analysis on China's national goals and related issues, see for example, Y. Wu, 1965, Chapter 1 and Chapter 4; Eckstein, 1977, Chapter 2 and Chapter 5.

8. Gray actually argued that, 'it is the present writer's conviction, strengthened in the course of a succession of analyses undertaken since 1969, that these apparently non-economic statements are firmly based on economic experience (whether correctly interpreted or not is a different question) and have an unambiguous economic meaning', Gray, 1978, p.567.

9. For the second task, see the pioneering book by Montias (1976). Over the years, a number of dictionaries that concentrate on explaining Chinese official terms and slogans have been compiled and published. The contents are generally very brief and often do not distinguish the context and time they have been used. However, this is not to suggest that such reference aids are not useful but that they cannot be a substitute for detailed analysis of policy development. See, Doolin and Ridley, 1973; Broadbent, 1978.

10. Montias distinguished three types of ownership rights: 'ownership-disposition', 'ownership-utilization' and 'ownership-over-an-asset's-products'. According to this classification, the rural collectives in China nominally have all these rights but with varying degrees of restrictions. Montias, 1977, Chapter 9.

11. The document was first drafted in May 1961, the revised form was adopted in September 1962. The document was leaked and republished in Hong Kong by Union Research. Revised Draft Work Regulation for Rural People's Commune, June 1961.

12. This figure for budget revenue is not different from the estimates made by Western economists for the period of 1952-7. It was estimated that about 48 per cent of the state budget during 1956-7, net of foreign loan receipts was directly and indirectly borne by the peasants. See, Mah, 1961, p.45.

13. The term agricultural population was used in the Chinese press without precise definition. It seems to have included the population who live and work outside the cities, including those in the communes in the rural suburbs of major cities. For more detailed discussion of the problem, see Orleans, 1972, pp.59-63.

14. The estimates for the relative share of agricultural output were made with different assumptions and methods, and for different points in time. Perkins' estimate of 31.2 per cent was for the year 1971, Swamy's 39.6 per cent for 1972, and A. Eckstein's 20 per cent for 1974. See Perkins, 1975-c, p.117; Eckstein, 1977, p.229; Swamy, 1973-b, p.28. Although the weight of importance has been changing, grain production has been the most important item in agricultural

output. Most Western estimates of China's agricultural production relied on grain output for their derivation. See, for example, T.C. Liu and K.C. Yeh, 1965, pp.395-424; Askbrook Jr, 1975, pp.40-2; Swamy, 1973-a, p.19.

15. In the absence of relevant demographic data, agricultural productivity in terms of grain yield per capita serves to give some rough indication as to the possible situation of grain yield per unit of rural labour force. The estimates of grain yield per capita are calculated from two estimate series for total annual grain output and for population, respectively. Estimates for annual grain output (1949-5), excluding soybeans are from U.S. Department of Agriculture, 1976, p.62; estimates for population (1949-75) from Orleans, 1975, p.77.

16. The growth rates are calculated by using the same estimate series for grain output as in Note 15, while the estimates for cultivated acreage for the years 1966-75 come from N.R. Chen and W. Galenson, 1969, p.119. For the years 1966-75, a constant 110 million hectares was assumed. Although this last assumption may overstate the actual size of the cultivated acreage during the 1970s by a few per cent, the final result on the relative average annual growth rates would not be significantly affected.

17. The share of agriculture-related export commodities was estimated to be over 70 per cent of China's 1973 total exports (Perkins, 1975-b, p.11). Since China's trade policy was basically that of using exports for the sake of importing the necessary equipment and materials, the important role of agriculture in financing imports can thus be gauged. See also Eckstein, 1977, pp.259-60; N.R. Chen, 1975.

18. It must be noted that agricultural production involves highly varied activities even within a country. It would require a separate study to estimate a generalized production function or more disaggregate production functions on a commodity or territorial basis.

19. Of course, international comparison is further complicated by the fact that countries differ in their resource endowments, system of resource allocation, preferences, subsidies, size of cultivated land, the absolute amount of grain output and so on. It is felt that statistical regression analysis would not be particularly useful here. Furthermore, the selected point in time need not be the representative normal year for all countries.

20. The production effect of mechanization on raising per hectare yield has also been studied and affirmed on smaller scale production and experiments. See, for example, Zhu Daohua, et al., 1963; Audrey Donnithorne, 1967, p.114. However, there have been very few discussions on this subject in China since the mid-1960s.

21. For discussion on priorities of the selective nature of mechanization, see Chapter 4. The other categories of work opportunities will be discussed in more detail in later chapters.

22. A number of areas were claimed to have achieved remarkable progress in agricultural mechanization within a relatively short period of time during the 1970s. They included the Guangxi Autonomous Region, the suburbs of Shanghai, Xin Xiang Prefecture in

Henan Province, Yintai Prefecture in Shandong Province, Junhua County in Hebei Province, Xinzhou County in Hubei Province. Editorial Department of <u>Nanfang Ribao</u> (Southern Daily, Canton) (ed.), 1975, p.36. Under the new circumstances and freedom given to the peasants as a result of the economic reforms of the 1980s, the pattern and speed of agricultural development have been significantly affected. Mechanization is now being pursued mostly by those farming households which have 'prospered early' or are engaged in specialised contracts.

23. For discussion on the financial aspects of agricultural mechanization in practice, see Chapter 6 of this study. As for the industrial sector, where nearly all enterprises were state-owned, there was no question of deciding on the desirable rate of investment as all profits and depreciation funds were transferred to the state for revenue consolidation.

Chapter Two

AGRICULTURAL MECHANIZATION PRIOR TO THE FOURTH
FIVE-YEAR PLAN

In the context of policy emphasis relating to the mechanization of
China's agriculture, a number of separate periods between 1949 and
1970 can be identified. In the early 1950s, agricultural
mechanization was essentially an issue in the development of
socialism. Debates on the subject centred more on its implications
on the institutional and organizational structures of the economic
system than on any practical programmes to bring about
mechanization.

From 1957 to 1965, agricultural mechanization began to assume
more technological and practical relevance, that is, increasing
emphasis was placed on the question of what machines were needed
to mechanize which farming operations, and how machines were to be
produced and supplied. Within this time span, however, there were
the Great Leap Forward movement of 1958-9, and the economic
depression of 1959-61.

As the Cultural Revolution unfolded in full force in 1966, the
question of agricultural mechanization, like many others, became an
issue in the struggle of 'the two lines'. Although important
technological proposals and progress had taken place, the main
concern was on establishing the 'proper' production relations to
accommodate technical transformation in future.

As the major upheavals of the Cultural Revolution gradually
came to an end in 1969, the subject of mechanization entered an
experimental stage where both the technological and socialist aspects
were being tested out, probably with more policy emphasis on the
side of technical production. This experimentation continued into
1970 with relatively more definite objectives and plans, and carried
on into the Fourth Five-Year Plan period on a much larger scale.

The periodization outlined in this chapter was meant to provide
a broad perspective on this subject by highlighting the dominant
nature of pronounced policy emphasis and the accompanying debates
in the context of their relative significance in technological and
socialist transformation objectives. It is not to suggest that emphasis
on one necessarily eliminated efforts on the other, nor that the

two arenas of policy emphasis were completely independent. Neither does it suggest that the weight attached to the question of agricultural mechanization had been evenly distributed throughout the two decades.

In examining the span of these twenty years, the focus is on the rural collectives while leaving out the state farms. In terms of employment and output, state farms were not in the mainstream of agricultural development in China; they might play a greater role in future, but in this period it was the collective farms which commanded the attention of the policy makers. The analysis here will be concerned mainly with two major issues: policies towards the production of agricultural machines and implements; and policies towards their ownership and management.

These issues are of course not isolated from the overall strategy for economic development. The agricultural machinery product mix, for instance, could not be separated from the farming pattern imposed by the policy makers while at the same time it was also a part of the design for industrial structure. As for the question of machinery ownership and management, it has been closely related to the pattern of investment financing, the structure of rural collectives and to the more fundamental question of shaping the allocating mechanism for commodity exchanges. Such issues have dominated the policy development and actual performance in the mechanization of agriculture over these two decades. Indeed, they continued to be the main problem areas in the 1970s. Hence, the following study into the experience of the 1950s and the 1960s should provide the necessary perspective for subsequent investigation.

1949-1956: COLLECTIVIZATION VERSUS MECHANIZATION: PATHS TO 'SOCIALIST' AGRICULTURE

1953 was the year when the First Five-Year-Plan was supposed to commence. This Plan put top investment priority on industry so that a heavy industrial base could be built as soon as possible. It only envisaged that agricultural mechanization be experimented in a few individual cases and on a limited scale (First FYP for Development of the National Economy of the People's Republic of China in 1953-1957, 1956, p.118). Only state farms were planned to acquire 5,146 standard tractors (15 h.p.) by 1957. The one significant move, in terms of investment for mechanization, was the construction of China's first tractor factory in Luoyang City (Henan Province), built with Soviet assistance. The factory had a planned output capacity of 15,000 units of 54 h.p. tractors annually (equivalent to 54,000 standard tractors each year). Based on the Soviet experience, agricultural mechanization was then regarded as equivalent to tractorization.

At that time, the purchasing power of the peasants was very low. In a survey of 15,432 households from 23 provinces conducted in 1954, it was found that, on the average, the 'poor' peasants spent only 30 yuan (or 22 per cent of their total annual income) on non-consumptive expenditure, of which only 3.5 yuan was on agricultural implements. The 'middle' peasants, while spending an average of 80 yuan on non-consumptive expenditure (or 39 per cent of the average income), used only 7.6 yuan on agricultural implements (Su, 1965, p.22; Su 1976, pp. 37-8; Su (1976, p.48) stated that the 'poor' peasants accounted for 60-70 per cent of the rural population then).

While the campaign to organize mutual-aid teams was under way after the land reform had been completed, this form of organization did not offer a significantly greater scope for expanding productive investment from within. It was stipulated that:

> At present, the amount of reserve funds (for investment purposes) and public welfare funds should never be too large a percentage of the annual income of the mutual-aid teams or agricultural producers' co-operatives. Generally speaking, <u>one to five per cent</u> would be a comparatively reasonable amount; at a time of poor harvest, however, the accumulation of reserve funds may be discontinued (Central Committee of the CCP, 'Decisions on Mutual Aid and Co-operativization in Agricultural Production', February 15, 1953, in K.C. Chao, 1963, p. 63). (Parenthesis and emphasis added.)

This stipulation would have effectively put a ceiling on the amount that the mutual-aid team or co-operative could take away from their members, although the ceiling might have been well above the average peasant's rate of investment on agricultural tools as indicated by the survey mentioned earlier. In fact, the individual household was still very much the core of the production unit in 1953. The organization of a mutual-aid team was quite flexible, and members could join or disband without much difficulty. Thus, members in those teams could be considered basically as individual household units.

However, even at that early stage, opposition to a rapid move towards collectivization in agriculture was already evident. The underlying assumption of the arguments from the opposition were essentially twofold (The Mass Criticism Unit of Revolutionary Great Alliance Committee, Farm Machinery Management Bureau under the Eighth Ministry of Machine-Building, 'History of Struggle Between the Two Lines (On China's Farm Machinery Front)', <u>Nongye Jixie Jishu</u> (Agricultural Machinery Technique), No.9, 1968, in <u>SCMM</u>, No.633, November 4, 1968, p.8. Hereafter, this article will be referred to as <u>History of Struggle</u>). Firstly, the nationalization of industry and the adequate supply of tractors were argued to be the prerequisites for the nationalization of land and for collectivization. Secondly, it was argued that the nationalization of industry would not be completed immediately and that the capacity to produce tractors in sufficient amounts could only be established slowly.

Amidst the mediocre performance in grain production in the 1953 harvest, the movement to form co-operatives was slowed down and a number of them were dissolved in some provinces. However, the movement resumed its vigour at the end of 1953. In fact, the pace of the development turned out to be far more rapid than was expected in the initial plan. The limit of space here does not permit a full discussion on this upsurge in the collectivization movement.[1] However, it is sufficient to note that by the end of 1955, the percentage of households in elementary co-operatives had jumped to over 60 per cent (L. Liao, 1956, p.1).

Up to that stage, most of the co-operatives were of the 'elementary' form, which meant that members were still entitled to a land dividend based on the size of their land shares.[2] While there were no comprehensive figures on the weight of the land dividend in the total distributable income to members, a survey of 31,000 co-operatives of Hebei Province in 1954 indicated that land dividends actually claimed an equal share of distributable income to labour payment in 71 per cent of the cases.[3] Another sample survey in Fujian Province found that the land dividend actually accounted for an average of 30 per cent to 35 per cent of the co-operatives' total expenditures (Su, 1976, pp.76-7). Thus, it was quite clear that the perceived socialist transformation in the rural sector could not have been considered by its advocates to have successfully accomplished its main task when one of the most important factors of production, land, was still in private hands.

As the Chinese government continued to rely on institutional change to improve agricultural production, the co-operativization drive forged ahead. Hence, a move was made to eliminate this property income, also reflecting a desire to increase the investment fund available to the co-operative administration. Indeed, in April 1956 Mao proposed that 60 per cent to 70 per cent of the co-operative's total income could be distributed to its members, while 30 per cent to 40 per cent of the total income should be retained by the co-operative or be taxed by the state. (Mao, 1956-c, p.36).[4]

By June 1956, 91.1 per cent of all peasant households had joined co-operatives, with 63 per cent belonging to the co-operatives of the 'advanced' form in which land dividend had been abolished (Wo-guo nong-ye de she-hui zhu-yi gai-zao (The Socialist Transformation of Our Country's Agriculture), 1977, p.82). By the end of 1956, 96.3 per cent of peasant households were members of co-operatives, and members of the advanced form accounted for 87.8 per cent of all peasant households. This movement to the advanced-form co-operatives could be regarded as one of the most important steps in China's socialist transformation. This established the separation of individual income (apart from private plots) from personal owership of the means of production. A direct link between members' income and the economic performance of co-operatives was set up. Whether this link was enforced by an appropriate incentive system is another question. The development also signalled the start of the building of a formal organization for institutionalized savings and investments.

As will be discussed, these had important implications for the development of agriculture and for the pattern of income distribution.

It would be futile to speculate if expansion in production and investments would have been more effectively achieved had mechanization preceded collectivization. In retrospect, apart from the feasibility consideration, the debate in China over mechanization versus collectivization at that time seemed to be concerned principally with how a socialist agricultural economy was to be developed. As Chen Boda argued:

> If we have co-operativization in agriculture but no mechanization, can it be regarded as socialism? We will say: the problem is not whether it can be regarded as socialism or not, but what are the actual facts? In the rural economy of our country, if the advanced-form co-operatives are established, if all major means of production have been socialized, if the relations between members of co-operatives are based only on co-operation and mutual aid, and there is an absence of the relations of exploitation and being exploited, then what else can we have but socialism? (Chen, 1956, p.9).[5]

As a fait accompli, China's agricultural development had to proceed according to the framework of a collective rural economy.

1957-1959: NEW EXPERIMENT IN RURAL DEVELOPMENT

The bad weather of 1956 continued into the year 1957. The difficulties thus created had probably been the additional reason for the scaling down of investment construction planned for the year (Z. Deng, 1957; E. Zhou, 1957; X. Li, 1957; Bo, 1957). In contrast, the development of the co-operatives continued at a fast pace. By February 1957, over 90 per cent of the peasant households had become members of the advanced-form co-operatives. Because of the short length of time in existence, the lack of experience and the severity of the natural calamity, many problems and shortcomings were reported from the co-operatives. The consolidation of the co-operatives was said to be under threat (X. Deng, 1957, pp.13-21). Actually, this threat was not unrelated to the 'Hundred Flower' Campaign which was speedily aborted as the government thought that it started to get out of hand. The anti-rightist campaign which followed the 'Hundred Flower' launched its attack on the preoccupation of those peasants who promoted private undertakings at the expense of the collectives (Walker, 1965, pp.74-5).

It is sufficient to note here that the performance of agriculture then became one of the major concerns for the Chinese government (E. Zhou, 1957; X. Li, 1957-b, p.328). However, the government's solution was again to rely on utilizing the collective organization in the rural villages to increase yield per unit of area by labour-intensive methods. Under this policy, the organization and management of the rural co-operatives were to be modified and a revised programme for agricultural development was drafted. While the co-operatives were to be reorganized to rectify some earlier excesses and problems, moves were also under way to install <u>formal</u> provisions for the collective administration to raise accumulation funds from its members. It was thus hoped that, without large increases in government spending on agriculture – supporting investments, performance in agriculture could be improved. This policy was spelt out in a speech by Z. Deng in September 1957:

> The sources of investment fund for reproduction depend mainly on the self-reliance of the co-operatives and on the hard labouring of the members. In practice, the way to realize them is to increase gradually the share for public accumulation fund on the condition that members' income can have annual increase. Revision of the related regulations of the co-operative can be considered. Depending on the conditions of each locality and each co-operative, the constituted limit of 5 per cent to 8 per cent (share of accumulation fund in total co-operative income) <u>can</u> be exceeded. In years of good harvest, especially for areas growing economic crops, the share can be raised to over 12 per cent. At the same time, 10 per cent of members' work-days can be devoted to basic construction. Depending on individual cases, each locality can decide whether the work-days on basic construction should be paid or be voluntary. If they are paid, the work-point value should be relatively lower (Z. Deng, 1957-b, p.521). (Emphasis added.)

Indeed, this self-reliant approach to investment financing for rural development remained basically unchanged for the next twenty years.

In line with the rethinking on rural development, a <u>Revised Draft of National Programme for Agricultural Development 1956-1967</u> (hereafter referred to as the <u>Revised NPAD</u>) was published in October 1957 (Central Committee of the CCP, 1957-b). The programme was an affirmation to continue the semi-mechanization of agriculture via improved non-power-driven tools, stressing that animal-drawn implements would continue to play a major role for a long time in the future (<u>Revised NPAD</u>, 1957, pp.10-11).

Meanwhile, a movement towards decentralized administration was under way. According to E. Zhou, investigation into decentralization of administration had started in 1956 with a view to correct excess and weakness in tight central control (E. Zhou, 1957, p.93; X. Li, 1957-a, pp.142-3). In November 1957, a series of proclamations was brought out by the State Council on the new regulations concerning administration of industry, commerce and finance (State Council, 1957b, 1957-c, 1958-a; Editorial, <u>Renmin Ribao</u>, November 18, 1957; Editorial, <u>Caizheng</u> (Finance), <u>No.12</u>, 1957; Central Committee of the CCP and State Council, 1958-b,

1958-c, 1958-e; X. Li, 1958; Rong, 1958; Donnithorne, 1967, pp.151-7, 460-511; Perkins, 1966, 1968). As a result, levels of local government were to take a greater share of responsibility in planning and control of economic activities in their areas. Enterprises were given certain leeway in their operations; obligatory production and financial targets were reduced. Many central enterprises came under the control of local authorities, or subject to dual control by local authorities and central ministries.

Four months after the publication of the Revised NPAD and not far from the start of the Second Five-Year Plan, a 'programmatic' document entitled 'Opinions Concerning the Question of Farm Mechanization' was said to have been put forward by the Chengdu Conference convened by Mao (History of Struggle, p.12). The Conference (March 1958) was said to have made a number of proposals.[6]

Firstly, central and local industries were to be developed simultaneously, and the policy of gradual transition to semi-mechanization and mechanization through farm-tool reform was to be implemented. Secondly, the 'policy of the three emphases' in the spirit of 'relying on the mass' and 'self-reliance' was to be promoted. The thrust of this policy contained these elements: for the manufacture of agricultural machinery, the main emphasis was to be placed on local industries in general; in terms of products, the main emphasis was to be placed on small tools; in the purchase of agriculture machinery, it should rely mainly on the collective economy. Finally, farm-tool reform should be carried out in a manner consistent with local characteristics and not in a uniform manner.

All these policies were mostly consistent with those contained in the Revised NPAD in that a gradual approach to agricultural mechanization achieved through farm-tool reform was advocated. One important new development from the Chengdu Conference was the promotion of a broadly based local industry. Such a development was of course not independent of the commune movement and the strategy of the Great Leap Forward.

Prompted by the need to organize large numbers of peasants in numerous water conservancy projects since the winter of 1957, amalgamation of cooperatives had started to gain momentum by the spring of 1958 (Bureau of Water Conservation, Ministry of Agriculture, 1960). This move did in fact negate the earlier call to scale down the size of co-operatives. Communes were being formed.

The commune was to become not only an economic unit absorbing the functions of organizations such as the supply and marketing co-operatives, credit co-operatives, handicraft co-operatives, but also to become the lowest level of the government replacing the former village level government.[7] The formation of communes was rapid.[8] By the end of 1958, all the co-operatives had been reorganized into 26,578 communes, representing 99.1 per cent of the peasant households (Su, 1976, p.102).

With the formation of the communes and the decentralization move, the questions of ownership and production of agricultural machines emerged. As a result of the Chengdu Conference, tractors from the state stations were transferred to the communes (Zhongguo Nongbao (Chinese Agriculture Journal), No.5, 1958, p.8, cited by Donnithorne, 1967, p.117). As Table 2.1 indicates, the share of commune ownership of tractors had a marked increase in 1958. Not much is known about the exact nature of the transfer. On the one hand, there were reports that tractors and machines were simply 'transferred' or 'handed over' to the commune without specifying whether any payment had been involved (see, for example: History of Struggle; J. Cheng, 1969; 'Collective Strength of the People's Commune Is Mainstay of Mechanized Farming', 1968; S. Wang, 1968; 'Farm Mechanization Through Communes' 1968; H. Yang et al., 1968). On the other hand, some communes were reported to have bought the machines from the stations with their own funds. Hence, it is not clear how exactly the transfer of tractors was financed and how the various forms of transfer affected the classification of ownership and management of the tractors. As far as the state tractor stations were concerned, it should be noted that their name had been changed to be known as agricultural machinery stations (AMS) some time after 1959, presumably because of a widening of functions (K. Chao, 1970, pp.110-11).[9]

The Great Leap Forward movement was intended to push forward rapid industrialization through massive labour mobilization campaigns using the communes as the organizational instrument. Though the movement failed to achieve the desired results, some of the ideas of the 'walk-on-two-legs' approach survived. Despite the disastrous outcome of unsuccessful ventures such as the backyard furnaces, commune industries were to be further developed later as part of the local industry. The development of local industries was given some impetus by the decentralization move. Since 1957-8, medium and small-sized agricultural machinery plants had been put under provincial control (Donnithorne, 1967, p.119).[10] Amidst the general framework of farm-tool reform, Mao proposed in February 1959 that each commune should build a plant making agricultural implements (Z. Mao, 1959-b, p.274). He also proposed that each province should set up their own farm-tool research institute. Mao urged that commune plants could be built according to local conditions and that they should not be tried and abandoned in a hasty manner.

Before the disastrous crop failure of 1959 had been fully evident and realized, more important proposals concerning mechanization were made by Mao. In April, in a communication to Party Committees at the levels of province, prefecture, county, commune and brigade, Mao made the once familiar statement that 'the fundamental way out for agriculture lies in mechanization'. Furthermore, he outlined a rough but ambitious scheme to mechanize agriculture within a decade (Z. Mao, 1959-a, pp.292-4).

In this scheme, Mao envisaged that ten years would be needed to achieve agricultural mechanization. The scheme involved a three-stage process. The first stage, taking four years, would reach a 'minor solution' for agricultural mechanization. Thus, for 1959 and

Table 2.1:   *Tractor Production and Use of Tractor by Type of Ownership*

	(a) Tractors Produced (15 h.p. standard units)	(b) Tractors in Use (15 h.p. standard units)	(c) State Farms (%)	(d) Tractor Stations (T.S.) (%)	(e) Co-op or Communes (%)	(f) No. of T.S.
				Ownership Distribution		
1949		401	100	0	0	-
1950		1,286	90	2	8	1
1951		1,410	-	2	-	1
1952		2,006	87	2	11	1
1953		2,719	66	3	31	11
1954		5,061	55	15	30	89
1955		8,094	50	30	20	138
1956		19,367	37	51	12	326
1957		24,629	41	49	10	383
1958	957	45,330	37	24	39	-
1959	5,598	59,000	36	29	35	553
1960	24,800	79,000	36	-	-	-
1961	15,200	90,000	-	-	-	-
1962	14,800	103,400	-	-	-	-
1963	17,800	115,000	30	59	11	1482
1964	21,900	123,000	32	58	10	1488
1965	-	130,500	30	61	9	2263

-     sign indicates figure not available; and blank space indicates negligible quantity

Source: *Official figures cited by K. Chao, 1970, p.107, p.109; L.T.C. Kuo, 1976, p.51. Though citing different official sources, the figures presented by both writers are almost identical*

the next three years, the main emphasis was to be placed on improved farm implements and semi-mechanized tools. For the second stage, a 'medium solution' was to be reached within seven years, i.e. three years after the completion of the first stage. Within ten years, i.e. three years after achieving the second stage, a 'major solution' was to be reached.

However, this scheme was not accompanied by any specific plans and targets for actual implementation. In effect, the 'minor solution' was really a reaffirmation of support for the current farm-tool reform for which Mao proposed that all levels of local government, from the province and prefecture to the county, should take an active part. Hence, extending his proposal in February, Mao called for farm-tool research institutes to be established in every province, prefecture and county (Z. Mao, 1959-a, pp.292-4).

The significant feature about this scheme was the inclusion of chemical fertilizer in the concept of agricultural mechanization. Indeed, it turned out later that the progress in chemical fertilizer was faster and contributed greatly to the expansion in grain output during the late 1960s.

Meanwhile, some measures taken to rectify many excesses of the Great Leap Forward movement had already begun. One of them was to define the management responsibility for each level of the commune. By 1959 the production brigades took over from the commune and became the basic accounting units in the commune system. By mid-1959, there was open opposition to the Great Leap Forward from within the Party as evidenced by the dismissal of the most outspoken critic, Peng Dehuai, from his post as Defence Minister. In addition to the disruptions caused by mismanagement and poor planning, the bad weather had helped to bring about a severe downturn in agricultural and industrial production in 1959. As far as agricultural mechanization was concerned, the rough timetable suggested by Mao had to be postponed and the brief experiment with commune tractor ownership had to go along with other experiments of the Great Leap Forward.

1960-1965: SEARCHING FOR WAYS TO DEVELOP AGRICULTURE ON A PREFERENTIAL BASIS

By 1960, it was evident that the government had to start giving more material assistance to rescue the agricultural sector from a further downturn. The promotion of technical transformation of agriculture on purely productive considerations was to begin. The idea of 'agriculture as the foundation of the economy' was stressed (Second NPC Documents, 1960; F. Li, 1960, p.15). In this way, agricultural mechanization was no longer considered as the next logical stage after the formation of the commune but only one of the many technical measures to improve agricultural output. While the farm-tool reform via improved and semi-mechanized items was to be continued (F. Li, 1960, p.16; Editorial, Renmin Ribao, March 31, 1960), the mechanization of agriculture was only to be realized step by step, and from the initial stage of farm-tool reform to semimechanization and then to mechanization (C. Tan, 1960, pp.92-3). Indeed, this 'step-by-step' policy was to give a very important fresh meaning to the rough scheme for agricultural mechanization outlined earlier by Mao in April 1959.

According to the new explanations, 'minor solution' was interpreted to mean that only city outskirts, production centres for commodity grain, major industrial crops, and major non-staple food were to be mechanized in a 'preliminary' way. The rest of the rural villages should promote semi-mechanization and improved tools. Thus, the step-by-step policy had spatial implications along with its time dimension. This marked the beginning of the selective policy for favouring the key agricultural regions. In other words, agricultural mechanization would not be attempted as a mass movement. On the 'medium solution' in seven years, it was then explained as to mean that over half of the cultivated area was to have mechanization. As for the 'major solution' in ten years, there was to be the 'basic' realization of agricultural mechanization with extensive building of water conservancy works throughout the farmland with a considerable extent of electrification (Renmin Ribao, August 26, 1960; F. Li, 1960, p.16).

Meanwhile, the severe downturn in the economy continued and relations with the Soviet Union had deteriorated to the stage when all Soviet assistance was withdrawn suddenly in 1960. To deal with this economic crisis, a series of policies aimed at 'consolidation' and 'readjustment' for the economy was initiated.

In such a time of great difficulty when the average consumption level was brought to its lowest since 1949, there was really very little left for accumulation in the rural sector. As a result, the abandonment of mass movement in tool reform appeared to have been considered as a necessary part of the readjustment policy. Thus, local farm machinery plants were being closed. Between 1960 and 1963, it was reported that over half of the farm machinery plants in the country had been closed, and the number of workers in that industry was cut by two-thirds (History of Struggle, p.20). Most of the plants closed were local industry enterprises.

While the scaling down, or 'readjustment', of industrial production was continuing, the basic accounting unit in the commune system was further revised downward. It had already changed from the commune to the production brigade in 1959, and now the production teams were to replace the production brigades as the basic accounting unit in less than two years. As a result, the financial strength of the commune as a collective unit was weakened by the shifting down of the basic accounting unit. In view of this development, it was alleged that Liu Shaoji and his supporters decided that all stations should in general be restored to state ownership and run as State-owned tractor stations (N. Liao, 1968, pp. 5-6; History of Struggle, pp.22-3; Renmin Ribao, September 2, 1971). At a national agricultural work conference, it was proposed that the main form of operations for tractors should be reverted back to state ownership and state management (History of Struggle, p.18).

There appears to have been considerable confusion as to the actual procedures and process of transferring tractors back to the state stations ('Farm Mechanization Through Communes', 1968, p.16; 'Mao Zedong's Thought' Red Guard's Red Rebel Regiment, 1968, p.10; 'Overcome Resistance, Insist on Letting Communes Operate Machine', 1967, p.27). The main problem was again the compensation, or lack of it, to the rural collectives.

Actually, this change in the ownership and management for tractors was also the result of the shift in economic strategy to deal with the economic crisis of the time. In this regard, the transfer of tractors back to state control would allow the government to concentrate this limited resource, together with other modern inputs (such as chemical fertilizers, and the slack in electricity output due to reduced industrial production) to equip a few localities to achieve quicker increase in agricultural output. This was of course, in line with the then prevailing policy of applying 'economic methods' and rationalization in economic management.

By 1962, the readjustment policy had become the main task of the government. During the Second National People's Congress in April 1962, E. Zhou stressed that readjustment (or retrenchment) of capital construction must be continued (E. Zhou, 1962, p.59). These readjustment measures finally culminated in the announcement of the Communique of the 10th Plenary Session of the Eighth Central Committee of the Chinese Communist Party on September 24, 1962, and the formal approval of the revised draft for the 'Work Regulations for Rural People's Communes' (the 60 Articles). While admitting that mistakes were made in the past few years, the Communique reaffirmed that: 'The urgent task facing the people of our country at present is to carry through the general policy of developing the national economy with agriculture as the foundation and industry the leading factor' (Supplement, Renmin Shouce, 1962) (emphasis added). As for policy on the technical transformation of agriculture, the Communique stated that:

> it is necessary to mobilize and concentrate the strength of the whole Party and the whole nation in all possible ways to develop agricultural production and to strengthen the collective economy of the people's commune by way of assistance in materials, technology, finance, organization and leadership, and to realize the technical transformation of agriculture, stage by stage, and making suitable decisions and measures for each locality. (Emphasis added.) (Supplement, Remin Shouce, 1962).[11]

Stavis argued that the decision of the Communique to place priority on agriculture and that agriculture would go through a technical transformation was a watershed in the history of agricultural development in China (Stavis, 1975-a, p.96). However, it should be pointed out that this technical transformation was to be carried out 'stage by stage, and making suitable decisions and measures for each locality', that is, on a preferential basis. Hence, while the emphasis was thus shifted from social transformation to technical transformation in the agricultural sector, this technical transformation was only selective as there was no longer a mass movement to spread such a transformation all over the communes. Therefore, the whole approach to the production and distribution of major means of production, such as tractors, was also based on economic considerations.

Indeed, by the end of 1962, 88 per cent of the machinery and tractors operated by the communes were said to have been taken away from them (History of Struggle, pp.22-3). In order to formalize the transfer of tractors, a document entitled 'Opinions Concerning

Readjustment and Improvement of Tractor Stations' was said to have been adopted in November 1962 (N. Liao, 1968, p.5). Moreover, as the mass movement had been practically discontinued, most of the local agricultural machinery research organizations set up just a few years ago were also disbanded. Instead, a central research institute was set up under a directive from E. Zhou, amalgamating the agricultural machinery research departments in the First Maching Building Ministry and in the Ministry of Agriculture (Editorial Department of Nongye Jixie (Agricultural Machinery), 1978, p.60).

The many models of tractors, a result of importing from many countries and the lack of standardization in domestic production, had added to the problem of inadequate supply of spare parts and maintenance. During 1961 to 1964, investment in strengthening the production of spare parts and accessories for farm machinery was reported to have been doubled (K. Chao, 1970, p.119; New China News Agency, 1963; 'New Development in the Production of Agricultural Machinery', 1963, p.16).

Although there were claims that the supply of agricultural machinery had changed from dependence on imports to domestic manufacture, it was acknowledged that the repair and maintenance of tractors, irrigation and drainage equipment was a serious problem.[12] One of the key factors contributing to that poor performance was the policy which tied the technical reform in agriculture solely to the state industry's capacity 'to arm agriculture with modern equipment'.[13] Not only was the state industry unable to play such an active role at that time, there were other difficulties. One of them was a common micro-economic problem among socialist enterprises under the prevailing central mechanism for resource allocation, because the production of parts, components and the rendering of services for repair and technical upgrading were normally not success indicators of an enterprise. Therefore, they were generally neglected. And in a time when economic methods placed a demand on an enterprise's financial performance, the less profitable services would have to be glossed over.

1964 was a remarkable year: the general economy had basically recovered, oil began to flow in quantity from the Daqing oil fields, and there was Mao's call to learn from Dazhai and Daqing. In addition, there was a design reform campaign aimed at correcting the shortcomings of Chinese designers (Guangming Ribao, December 27, 1964; Dean, 1973). As for agriculture, apart from the experiment in trust organization for producing agricultural machinery, there were a number of important developments.

As early as 1963, after the convention of the National Work Conference on Agricultural Science and Technology in February,[14] preparations for the identification of agricultural zones for China began (Renmin Ribao, June 9, 1964). This involved marking off particular areas for growing specific crops according to comparative advantages and providing guidelines for how resources could be employed to make the most efficient use of the land in each zone. This reflected, of course, the application of economic methods of that time, which had demanded that flow of resources should not be organized according to administrative considerations and boundaries (Editorial, Renmin Ribao, March 23, 1963). And, in accordance with the policy adopted in the Tenth Plenary Section of the Eighth Central Committee of the Chinese Communist Party in 1962, 'high and stable yielding farmland' and 'model fields' (yang-ban-tian) were to be established on a nation-wide basis from 1964 (Editorial, Renmin-Ribao, March 31, 1964; Renmin Ribao, March 28, 1965; J. Yang, 1964). A highly concentrated resource package was delivered to those key regions to be developed into 'high and stable yielding farmland'. In addition to chemical fertilizers, electricity and irrigation equipment, agricultural machinery was also concentrated in those favoured regions. About 70 per cent of the counties which had established state AMS were situated in the key production regions (Renmin Ribao, October 29, 1964). Moreover, about one-quarter of the research manpower in agricultural science was assigned to those model fields on a permanent basis by 1965 (Z. Jiang, 1965).

However, it should be noted that, although national resources were to be concentrated in key regions for 'high and stable yielding farmland', the policy was that: 'to establish stable and high yielding farmland, the central task is to be directed at agricultural basic construction (water conservancy and land improvement projects) for which favourable conditions exist with the main resource, labour, being abundant' (Zhao and Zhu, 1964).

This policy underlined the continued dependence on a technology which was still basically labourintensive, even for the favoured regions. In addition, the policy permitted scope for the generation and utilization of more surplus from collectives in the key regions since they would be the more productive units and hence would produce a larger surplus. The stepping up of agricultural basic construction would thus be a powerful means towards this end while serving the technical requirements of providing better land conditions for applying other modern inputs such as chemical fertilizer.

State investment in agricultural machinery was recovering but was still at a low level in 1964, representing only less than one-quarter of the ámount for 1960 (see Table 2.2). As a comparison, it should be noted that, of the 203 above-norm construction projects[15] in the machine building industry in the 1960 Economic Plan, 55 were for agricultural machinery including the second stage of the Luoyang Tractor Works, the construction of the Tianjin Tractor Works and the Peking Agricultural Machinery Works (F. Li, 1960, p. 24).

As the services of agricultural machinery and other modern inputs were only concentrated in a few regions, those which received them might also benefit from a relatively higher amount of investment than previously possible. As for the collectives in general, the government again made it clear that for a long time to come the main emphasis would only be on semi-mechanization

(Renmin Ribao, October 15, 1964). In the meantime, however, the state AMS were to provide services of larger agricultural machinery to the key regions (Renmin Ribao, October 15, 1964).

Table 2.2:   *Investment in Capital Construction for the Agricultural Machinery Industry*

Year	Index
1960	100
1962	12
1963	16
1964	22

Source: History of Struggle, p.19

1966-1970: REVIVAL OF 'MASS MOVEMENT' AND 'SELF RELIANCE'

By the end of 1965, overtures to the Cultural Revolution were already in sight. One of the prominent Chinese economists Sun Yefang (Director of Economic Research, Academy of Science) was under increasing attack in the Chinese media for his advocacy for using profit as the enterprise performance indicator and for his general support for using economic methods in all economic matters and his alleged disregard for their implications in the realm of production relations, or 'class struggle'. While it is not the purpose of this study to analyse fully the causes, process and effects of the Cultural Revolution, it will examine the changes in policies relating to agricultural mechanization to highlight some of the features of the Cultural Revolution.

In a letter written on March 12, 1966, Mao made a series of suggestions and proposals for the mechanization of agriculture.[16] Once again, Mao proposed to carry out a three-step 10-year plan to mechanize agriculture similar to the one he proposed in April 1959 when he envisaged 'minor', 'medium' and 'major' solutions. However, this time Mao's proposals were more definite on the framework under which the plan was to be implemented, and indeed they set the pattern under which experiments with agricultural mechanization in the next decade were to be conducted. The main points from Mao's letter were:

(1)   The Central Planning Group, the regional bureaus and the provincial government were to draw up tentative plans covering five, seven and ten years for their regions.

(2)   The mechanization of agriculture should be carried out by the provinces mainly through self-reliance. The

central government could only provide some assistance in materials but all these were to be paid by local funds.

(3) In line with the self-reliant principle, basic materials (iron and steel), machine tools and agricultural machinery were to be placed under state control and management. For local manufacturing, if output far exceeded the state targets (by 100 per cent or more) they should be allowed to buy 30 per cent to 50 per cent of the over-fulfilled portion for local use.

(4) On the relations between the central and provincial government under this scheme, Mao said that he did not favour concentrating everything in the hands of the central authorities by imposing rigid controls. Hence, he proposed that:

A. 'For agricultural mechanization, produce more items for agriculture, forestry, animal husbandry, side-lines and fishery, with the right for the localities to manufacture some of the machinery. This right means the right to share in the above-target portion where the portion is sufficiently large, but not otherwise' (Mao, 1966-b).[17]

B. 'The accumulation of the state itself must not be too high. There are three reasons. Firstly, there are still some people without sufficient food and clothing. Secondly, we must spread our reserves for preparations against war and calamities. Thirdly, we must let the localities accumulate funds for investment purposes. Thus, agricultural mechanization must be combined with those aspects so that the mass can be mobilized for realizing the plan in a faster but stable manner'. (Mao, 1966-b).[18] (Emphasis added)

It was clear that the proposals in Mao's letter ran contrary to the then prevailing policy on limited and selective mechanization through state management and trust organization. It was alleged that in the few months preceding the writing of this letter and the few weeks which followed, there was intense contention over the issue (China Institute of Research in Agricultural Mechanization,Capital Worker's Congress, East Is Red Commune, 1967, pp.24-8). However, with the political force of the Cultural Revolution and purges of political opponents, Mao's proposals got through and practically set the framework for the development approach to agricultural mechanization over the next decade. In July 1966, the Central Committee of the Chinese Communist Party convened the 'On-Site Conference on Agricultural Mechanization' in Hubei Province in order to discuss the 'question of gradually realizing the planning (sic) of agricultural mechanization' (N. Liao, 1968, p.6).

This meeting was later (after 1976) referred to as the First National Conference on Agricultural Mechanization (Editorial Department of Nongye Jixie, 1978, p. 24).

Although no details of the Conference were released then, the Conference was said to have reached two resolutions:

(1)   'Agricultural mechanization must firmly adhere to the policy of mainly relying on the efforts of the collective economy, and on relying on local industries to manufacture farm machines and tools'.

(2)   Tentative plans and measures should be made for the basic realization of agricultural mechanization by 1980.

Semi-mechanization was reaffirmed as the main link to basic mechanization. The policy of 'three main emphases' proclaimed a few years ago was modified and stressed again (Renmin Ribao, October 18, 1966): first, the development of agricultural mechanization should rely mainly on the collective economy. Secondly, the development of agricultural machinery industry should mainly come from local industries. Thirdly, the main emphasis for development of agricultural machinery should be placed on small items. In terms of allowing local authorities to manufacture agricultural machinery, the development was rapid. It was reported that the administration of manufacture of more than 800 varieties of agricultural machines had been transferred to local provincial authorities after 1966 (Great Criticism and Repudiation Group of the First Machine Building Ministry, 1977), and 1966 was hailed as the fastest growing year for the agricultural machinery industry since 1949.[19] In 1966, all the semimechanized tools (for water lifting, processing of agricultural and sideline produce, transportation, plant protection and cultivation), attachments to agricultural machinery, and power-driven machinery with less than 20 horse-power, were said to be 'dependent' on local industries for their manufacturing. Furthermore, it was reported that the value of output by local agricultural machinery industries accounted for two-thirds of the total output value of the country's agricultural machinery industry (Renmin Ribao, October 18, 1966).

In contrast to the speed in transferring manufacture right to the local authorities (mainly at the provincial level), the agricultural machinery of the state AMS (Agriculture Machinery Stations) was only being 'sent down' to the collectives gradually. Existing evidence is scarce and no generalization can be made on how such transfer had been carried out.

Perhaps more significant than the transfer of tractors from the state AMS was the fact that collectives had started to purchase tractors and other machinery. In this regard, the new arrangements established for the collectives to finance such purchases were to have a far-reaching effect for the next ten years or so. In an article written by the Red Guards during the Cultural Revolution, the essence of the new arrangement was described in the following passage:

> For the purpose of buying machines, quite a number of communes and teams have enlarged their accumulated public funds or mobilized their members to make investments. Say the commune members: '<u>less</u> distribution (for personal income) is made now so that we may step up output in the future in aid of national construction' (S. Wang, 1968, p.12). (Emphasis added.)

In fact, it was reported that the 'communist winds' and arbitrary transfer of collective and private properties without compensation were widespread during 1967 to 1969 when Lin Biao and his supporters were said to have tried to nullify the rules set out in the <u>60 Articles</u> (Department of Economics, Peking Univesity, 1975, p.145).

After some years of experimentation, a new system of agricultural machinery management was beginning to emerge. By 1968, some communes had set up a 'management system of unified leadership, management by grades, and operating machines at three levels' ('Farm Mechanization Through Communes', 1968; see Chapter 5 for further details). The system worked in the following way:

(1)   The commune would operate tractor stations, big electric irrigation stations and substations.

(2)   The production brigade (or groups of production teams) would operate electric irrigation stations and processing machines for farm and subsidiary production.

(3)   The production team would operate plant protection, shelling, threshing machines and semi-mechanized transportation apparatus.

The rationale for such an arrangement seemed to be based on a desire to harmonize machinery management (and ownership) and production needs. Thus, when the investment outlay is greater and the area affected larger, the responsibility and control then rest with the upper levels in the commune system. When the farming operations are smaller and more specialized, they become the responsibility of the production teams.

Although the system was by no means universal yet, indeed many collectives could not even afford to have any machinery and many were not able to get supply, this was nevertheless a very important first step. This is because it set out a new pattern, intentional or otherwise, by which others had to follow mechanically and formally in the years to come. Mechanization then depended very much on the collective economic strength of the commune or brigade levels. Furthermore, the process of agricultural mechanization need no longer be gradual and uniform, i.e. from farm-tool reform to semi-mechanization and to basic mechanization, along a time span on a nation-wide basis. With this selfreliant approach, no uniform progress across the country could thus be expected, semi-mechanization and mechanization would in theory be pursued at the same time by different collectives all over the country. However, it should be noted that the rural collectives (whether commune, brigade or team) could not attempt to achieve agricultural mechanization on their own. As noted in Mao's letter (March 1966), it was really the local governments (province and county), and in a less obvious way the central government which ultimately determined how the new process of agricultural mechanization would be (unevenly) distributed among collectives.

After 1969, a number of conferences dealing with various aspects of agricultural mechanization were reported (Y. Zhao, 1973, p.302). They called for the rapid establishment of farm-tool repair and manufacture plants at the county level. Some government support for such a call seemed to follow in a short while (R. Tan, 1969, p.60). A series of conferences on the subject, convened at the provincial level were subsequently held (Zhonggong Nianbao (Communist China Year Book), 1969, Section 2, p.163). Since the state supplied only the machine tools in support of this exercise, this necessitated the development of local industries and mines to produce a part of the required materials. The county was henceforth placed for the first time as the administrative unit responsible for carrying out semi-mechanization and mechanization. There were also indications that each province was about to build for itself a relatively comprehensive industrial system which would supply the necessary equipment to develop agricultural machinery plants, electricity generation plants and fertilizer plants in the prefectures and counties ('Hunan Province Machinery Industries Conference', 1969, p.163). In addition, the county-run local industry was to help build, in a systematic way, agricultural machinery repair and manufacture substations in the communes and brigades.[20]

In spite of the apparent success in boosting chemical fertilizer output from local industry, there were many problems and obstacles facing the further development of local industry as a whole. Between 1965 and 1970 it has been estimated that an average of over 100 new chemical fertilizer plants were established annually by the local authorities, compared with only 10 per year between 1958 and 1964 (Perkins et al., 1977-a, p.94). Output by local chemical fertilizer plants accounted for about 40 per cent of the total national output in gross weight in 1970 (Sigurdson, 1975, p.48). Paradoxically, one problem for the local industries was that they were required to serve agricultural production. This objective was of course the reason for their coming into existence.

Products made by local industries in support of agriculture were generally sold at a low price controlled by the state, while unit cost of materials (e.g. steel) for the small-scale operation might be four times as high as the national standard prices (Berger, 1975).[21] Furthermore, the prices of chemical fertilizer and other locally produced industrial products had been consistently reduced (Qi, 1970). It should be noted that most of the local industry undertakings were financed by the local government, while the communerun enterprises were actually financed by their members' income. Therefore it is not difficult to find a reluctance to incur such a low return (in many cases, loss, especially in the initial stage) for their investment. In fact, with several consecutive years of good harvest, some enterprise management began to think that prices of industrial products to be used in agricultural production should no longer be sold at a low (or negative) profit. With a renewed emphasis on increasing production and personal income following the Ninth National Congress of the Chinese Communist Party, local industry thus encountered yet another pressure. An additional reason for the lack of enthusiasm in promoting local industry to support agriculture was that giving support to key construction projects, rather than to agriculture-supporting local projects, was normally rewarded with easier access to funds, equipment and factory supplies.

In early 1970, a renewed criticism campaign was launched against Sun Yefang. The main attack was again on his advocacy of relying on economic methods and 'putting profit in command'. His critics argued that if economic plans were based solely on the profit criterion, it would be impossible to develop those industries which turned out finished products with low exchange value and low (or negative) profit margin but which performed an important function in supporting agricultural production.[22] Thus, it was clear that local industry development was to proceed in spite of some degree of reluctance on the part of some of the parties concerned.

The role of the county in carrying out technical transformation in agriculture was reaffirmed in 1970 (Writing Group of Henan Provincial Revolutionary Committee, 1970). In addition, a mass movement was also to be revived. At the same time, an equally significant development in agricultural mechanization was taking place at a higher level of the government. Since the 'National Working Conference on the Establishment of Farm-Tool Repair and Manufacture Plants' was held in July 1969, there were signs of the gradual emergence of provincial comprehensive industrial systems. In June 1970, an article in Hongqi urged provinces to establish, under national planning, 'small and comprehensive' (xiao er quan) industrial systems.[23] The promoting of the provincial industrial system was certainly not independent of the campaign to help further develop local industry to serve agriculture.

By June 1970, stronger leadership over countryrun industries was urged (Qi, 1970). In July 1970, the 'National On-Spot Meeting to Exchange Experience on Transplanting of Paddy Fields' warned that progress in this area had been unsatisfactory, and established the county as an operational unit in the mechanization of transplanting and field operations. The conference also resolved that this mechanization process was to be realized 'stage by stage' and 'batch by batch'.[24] Thus a gradual (in terms of stages) and preferential (in terms of geographical area) approach of mechanization was again promoted. It could be considered as a variation on the earlier policy of concentrating resources on a few selected target areas to obtain maximum results, only this time the exercise would not be co-ordinated by the central government (which still retained a dominant influence) but by the local provincial and county administration.

On September 6, 1970, the Second Plenary Session of the Ninth Central Committee of the Chinese Communist Party adopted a revised draft of the Constitution of the People's Republic of China.[25] The discussion on various aspects of economic policies prior to the convention of the Second Plenary Session could be viewed as working sessions for the formulation of the coming Five-Year Plan. At about the same time as the Session was meeting, there was an important conference on agriculture in progress. The name and the details of the conference were not publicized then. Only a few years afterwards did the event come to be known as the 1970 Northern Agricultural Conference (Revolutionary Committee of Fenglai County, Shandong Province, 1976, p.9). However, the objectives set out by the Conference were reported in the Chinese press which was renewing a mass campaign to learn from Dazhai. There were two main points from the Conference which had great significance for China's rural development in the following five years:

(1) The county government (Party Committee and Revolutionary Committee) should be the key in transforming the countryside through learning from Dazhai.

(2) Plans should be made to increase activities in agricultural basic construction for transforming the land. (Editorial, Renmin Ribao, September 23, 1970; Y. Chen, et al., 1975)

The campaign to engage rural collectives in labour-intensive construction projects, unlike those during the Great Leap Forward, was to be planned and co-ordinated. They were to serve not only water conservancy, but were also linked to the building of small hydroelectric stations as well as preparing for the use of agricultural machines such as pumps and tractors (R. Lu, 1971, p.73; Revolutionary Committee of Fenglai County, 1975, pp.20-2; Gan, 1976, p.9). The construction activities were to be completed in three to five years. Therefore, in terms of technological change for agricultural production, it meant that the labour-intensive approach was to continue playing the main role.

Thus, just before the Fourth Five-Year Plan was about to commence, a number of important developments concerning agricultural mechanization were taking shape. One saw the emergence of the provincial industrial systems with their networks of local industry in support of agriculture, although it was very much subject to the control of the central government. As stated in Mao's 1966 letter, the essential materials for these undertakings were still controlled by the state.[26] At the same time, the rural collectives were asked to transform their economy through a self-reliant mass movement based on labour-intensive projects.

A mixed approach to economic management appeared to have emerged. On the one hand, the central government had allowed individual provinces to develop their own industrial capability. Though this local development was by no means completely free from the direct and indirect influence of the central government, it was still a far cry from the short-lived idea of establishing national trusts based on specialization of production. On the other hand, the provinces were expected to direct their resources in a way which would maximize production growth. In other words, whereas a relatively greater degree of decentralization of administration was operating on the national level, the provincial (and county) governments were to take up a more centralized role within their territories in order to apply stricter economic controls for faster material growth. Under the prevailing conditions, economic rationality was apparently given an increased emphasis at the local level. Whether this self-reliant approach for provincial development, coupled with the limited application of economic rationality on a regional basis would have produced the desired economic and political results is difficult to ascertain. However, this situation did indicate one significant thing, i.e. the majority of the rural collectives could anticipate developing their economy mainly with their own resources through a basically labour-intensive technology. For those collectives or areas receiving priority treatment, they could expect an increase in the level of modern inputs to improve their production. The implication was that the central government at that time was not prepared to, or was unable to, commit and divert resources to modernize agricultural production on a larger scale.

CONCLUSION

In the search for a socialist way to develop agriculture in China, the question of agricultural mechanization had from the start assumed a significance beyond pure production technique. It had always been associated with the way socialist transformation in the rural sector was to proceed. After the formation of co-operatives and communes, however, considerations over the actual feasibility and methods for mechanizing China's agriculture began to receive more serious attention. In general, the focus was on the pattern of ownership and management of tractors, and on the organizational set-up for the manufacturing of these machines.

During the period of economic readjustment up to the mid-1960s, agricultural mechanization lost its previous theoretical status as the succeeding stage after the completion of collectivization. Though there was no lack of debates on the role of agricultural mechanization, and indeed new initiatives had been made (e.g. national trust), it was relegated to being only one of the elements for modernizing China's agriculture.

With the coming of the Cultural Revolution, issues over the socialist aspect for agricultural development resumed their dominance. Agricultural mechanization, as a long term development objective, re-emerged as a policy issue in the search for alternative paths to develop China's socialist agriculture. By the end of the 1960s, some preliminary systems for the management and production of agricultural machinery began to appear. At the same time, a mass movement for agricultural development based on local self-reliance was being launched. The mass movement was not directly related to the realization of agricultural mechanization but was firmly linked to the massive farmland construction projects with labour as the main input. Development in agricultural mechanization, which nonetheless was entering a new phase, was to be a task for the selected few (collectives or areas).

The essence of the whole process of rural development from the formation of co-operatives and communes to the labour mobilization programme proposed by the 1970 Northern Agricultural Conference, was based on a common strategy. The strategy was to use institutional and organizational changes aimed to produce improvements in agricultural output so that a minimum amount of state investment would be needed. Though assistance to the rural sector had increased after the failure of the Great Leap Forward, it was still relatively small. The strategy was an attempt to improve production mainly by self-financed projects within the rural production units, most of which could only afford to expand labour input and hold back growth in personal consumption under the then prevailing policies. Thus, this in effect also provided an extractive mechanism to generate and to increase the share of investment in the total income of the rural collectives. To ensure the effectiveness of the strategy, and to satisfy various perceived ideological commitments, continuous transformation in the institutional framework of the rural production unit was carried out. Hence, in practice, agricultural development was reliant on a more or less continuous process of increasing rural socialization, with or without formal changes in property relations. With the possible exception of the few years during the readjustment period of the early 1960s, this strategy had been an integral part of the dominant ideological and economic thinking. Indeed, what happened during the early 1970s owed very much to this momentum of socialist development. As will be discussed in the following chapters, this approach appears to have been basically followed but had been encountering increasing difficulties in reconciling the demand for growth with certain objectives and desires to advance socialism. As a result, the Chinese government sought, in 1975, to install formally agricultural mechanization as the next stage for agricultural development which was thus intended to continue the long process of socialist transformation.

NOTES

1. For analysis on this subject, see, for example: Walker, 1966, pp.1-43; Breth, 1974; L. Liao, 'An Explanatory Note on the Draft of the National Programme for Agricultural Development 1956-1967', in Draft of the National Programme for Agricultural Development 1956-1967 (hereafter referred to as the Draft of NPAD), 1956, p.26.

2. Central Committee (Sixth Enlarged Plenum), Chinese Communist Party, 'Resolution on Agricultural Co-operativization' (October 11, 1955) in Chao Kuo-chun, 1963, pp.88-94; State Council, 'Draft Model Regulations for the Agricultural Producers' Cooperatives' (November 10, 1955) in Chao Kuo-Chun, 1963, pp.95-102.

3. Su, 1976, pp.76-7. The survey found that only in 17 per cent of cases were labour payments greater than land dividends.

4. The part retained by co-operatives or the state included agricultural tax, surtax, accumulation fund, welfare fund and management costs. This was in line with the argument Mao made in the same month in which he argued that an 'appropriate' level of investment in the co-operatives should be maintained and that the burden of the peasants be reduced. See, Mao, 1956-b1, pp.40-59.

5. This publication was from a speech made by Chen during the Second Plenary Session of the Second National People's Political Consultative Conference held on February 2, 1956.

6. History of Struggle, p.12; The Mass Criticism Unit of the First Ministry of Machine Building, 1977. The two sources differed on two points concerning the 'policy of three emphases'. In the History of Struggle, it stated that emphasis should be placed on small-sized machines but in the Hongqi article, it included medium sized machines as well. Another discrepancy was that the History of Struggle omitted the aspect of financing the purchase of machinery but the Hongqi article included this.

7. For studies into the formation and development of the commune, see, for example: Lippit, 1977; Strong, 1964; Gurley, 1975; Birrell, 1970; A. Tang, 1968; Z. Tao, 1964; L. Liao, 1963.

8. At the beginning of 1958, there were 740,000 advanced co-operatives. In August 1958 when the Chinese Communist Party issued its first major policy statement on the establishment of the commune, there were already communes of various forms and sizes with membership accounting for 30.4 per cent of the total peasant households. See, Central Committee of the CCP, 1958-f; Su, 1976, p.102.

9. It should be noted that after 1958, the provincial government was responsible for the state tractor stations. See Ishikawa, 1975, p.446.

10. The term local industry is used here in a loose sense associated with the level of administration rather than using the choice of production technique as the criterion. Later discussion on local industry in this study, however, will tend towards including only

those industries at or below the county level, but each case will be treated separately.

11. Supplement, Renmin Shouce, 1962. It is interesting to note that Stavis (1975) quoted Current Background's translation (No.691, p.4) which merely reads as 'realized the technical transformation of agriculture, stage by stage in a manner suited to local conditions'. The translation lost the connotation in the original text which may imply that, due to the concentration of resources, some localities would not be given assistance at all.

12. Chang, 1963. It was also reported that petroleum production reached basic self-sufficiency in 1963. Renmin Ribao, December 26, 1963.

13. This policy was of course just a derivative of the more general economic policy of that period, i.e. placing the central government as the initiator which must concentrate resources on areas where highest returns in the shortest time could be achieved. As for the derived policy for agriculture, see, for example, W. Wang, 1963, p.28.

14. Renmin Ribao, February 23, 1963 and April 6, 1963. The Conference was held between February 8 and the end of March 1963.

15. The 'above-norm' investment referred to a standard amount of investment. The 'norm' varies with different industries; it was 10 million yuan for the iron and steel industry for the First Five Year Plan. See, N.R. Chen, 1967, p.24.

16. There are now two slightly different versions of this letter. The first version was published by the Red Guards during the Cultrural Revolution for internal circulation. The second version was officially published only recently in the Party journal, Hongqi (Red Flag). The two versions differed in their title as well as a few points in Mao's proposal. The text this author used was from the Red Guard publication but when there were substantial differences or lack of clarity in the Red Guard version, the Hongqi version was compared. See, Mao Zedong, 'An Instruction Letter on the Question of Agricultural Mechanization' in Mao Zedong Sixiang Wansui (II) (Long Live the Thoughts of Mao Zedong), pp.632-3; Mao Zedong, 'A Letter on the Question of Agricultural Mechanization', Hongqi, No.1, 1978. An English translation of the Hongqi version can be found in Peking Review, No.52, December 26, 1977.

17. Ibid. The Hongqi version was: 'To mechanize agriculture and increase output in agriculture, forestry, animal husbandry, side-lines and fishery, it is necessary to win for the localities some right to the machinery they make. Here some right means that right to share in the above-target portion where that portion is sufficiently large, but not otherwise'. Here, the differences really reflect the recent emphasis put on achieving diversified rural economy and in downplaying the role of local manufacturing by the Hongqi version.

18. The two versions are identical here.

19. Renmin Ribao, October 18, 1966. Of course, the production of the factories which were being constructed in the past few years would have accounted for the major share of increase.

20. R. Tan, 1969. This was the start of a development for the commune and brigade industry which would play a greater part in the mechanization effort in future. See Chapters 4 and 5 for details.

21. The broader issue of static versus dynamic efficiency of such small-scale local industries will not be discussed here due to limit of space. For the theoretical and empirical aspects of the concept of efficiency and its relation with small-scale local industry, see, for example: Riskin, 1969; Ishikawa, 1973; Stewart, 1973; Dean, 1972, 1973; Perkins (ed.), 1973; Sigurdson, 1975.

22. Writing Group of Jilin Provincial Revolutionary Committee, 1970; The Revolutionary Workers' Criticism and Repudiation Group of Peking Knitting General Factory, 1970; Writing Group of the Revolutionary Criticism and Repudiation Group of the Ministry of Textiles, 1970; The Revolutionary Criticism and Repudiation Group of the Daqing Oilfield Workers, 1970.

23. Writing Group of the Heilongjiang Provincial Revolutionary Committee, 1970. It is interesting to note that exactly the same terms, 'small and comprehensive', had been used to criticise those enterprises with a high degree of verticle integration during the early 1960s.

24. *Zhonggong Nianbao* (Communist China Yearbook), 1971, Section 11, p.131. A meeting for the same objective was previously held in 1969.

25. This Session was believed to represent the start of an open split between Mao and Lin. The revised draft of the constitution was not officially published. See 'Text of the 1970 Draft of the Revised Constitution of the People's Republic of China', 1971, pp.100-6.

26. For instance, provincial governments were still dependent on the allocation of machine tools from the state to equip their local industries. See R. Lu, 'Speech on the Yunnan Province Agricultural Work Conference', *Zhonggong Nianbao*, 1971, p.73. For discussion on China's material allocation system, see Chapter 5 of this study.

Chapter Three

POLICIES ON AGRICULTURAL DEVELOPMENT AND AGRIC-
ULTURAL MECHANIZATION IN THE FOURTH FIVE-YEAR PLAN
PERIOD: AN OVERVIEW

China entered the Fourth Five-Year Plan period with a certain
degree of uncertainty as to the general development approach to be
followed in the initial year. Although preparations for the
formulation of the Fourth Five-Year Plan should have been
completed by the end of 1970, and indeed the convention of the
Fourth National People's Congress was scheduled to take place early
in 1971 (when the Plan would have been discussed and nominally
approved) (Joint Editorial, Renmin Ribao, Jiefangjun Ribao, Hongqi,
January 1, 1971), the political struggle and leadership change
(symbolized by the Lin Biao incident) delayed the Congress for four
years.[1]

Despite the apparent absence of a comprehensive economic
plan adopted at the beginning of the period, the basic developmental
policy for agriculture had more or less been decided by the 1970
Northern Agricultural Conference. Indeed, the development of
agriculture was to continue on a technology which, with some
selective use of modern inputs, would remain essentially
labour-intensive and dependent on the effective manipulation of
institutional and organizational arrangements. While there were
some modifications in strategy during the period, this basic approach
had been maintained.

DEVELOPMENTS IN ECONOMIC AND AGRICULTURAL POLICIES

In spite of the absence of major policy initiatives during the early
months of 1971, the 1970 Northern Agricultural Conference appears
to have set out the domain of tasks to be done. By the end of 1970,
one saw the campaign on the revival of the application of certain
economic methods within localities. Amid the rebuilding of the Party
and government, adherence to the established rules of economic
transactions was urged via the promotion of 'realizing the Party's
rural economic policies'. This lasted through to 1971. The move in
1971 to correct the excess of 'leftist' policies was really first started

in a smaller way in 1970 when calls were made to distinguish between 'work point in command' and the socialist principle of 'remuneration according to labour'. As a direct result of the 1970 Northern Agricultural Conference, the role of the county in the campaign to learn from Dazhai was firmly established. Thus, in 1971, counties started to make plans for the Dazhai campaign even though the rectification and rebuilding of the Party, the real management machinery, were still going on. In general, hardly any remarkable new policy development occurred in the first half of the year.

It was only towards the end of 1971 that major policy initiatives were being taken to set new plans and guidelines for future development. This gathered momentum in 1972 when new policies on economic development and management were being formed and promoted in increasing numbers. Most of them were basically designed to correct and reverse some of the practices which had developed since the Cultural Revolution. The gist of this series of new policies was the increased emphasis on more effective controls of resource allocation and distribution of income <u>through</u> improved planning, regulations and plan management. Thus, more concentration of economic controls was seen to be needed, but that did not necessarily mean that all decision-making power was to be centralized. Rather, it meant that certain freedom given to local units in the past few years was to be scrutinized and that plans and management organizations were to be tightened up within and across localities. Indeed, 1972 must be viewed as another turning point in the development of the Chinese economy, because it marked the beginning of the formation of a new policy mix which clearly marked a departure from the one adopted from 1966 to early 1971.

However, this break with the recent past was neither complete nor instant, and in fact the economy was only about to become firmly committed to a possible new course in the last year of the period (i.e. 1975). Riskin argued that, after 1972, unified central plans had replaced 'the stage of great local autonomy in industrialization' (Riskin, 1978, p.90). However, this restructuring of policy mix had in practice been a long and often compromised process. Notwithstanding the uneven pattern of implementation in different localities and enterprises, the movement had been subject to several setbacks. The most important resistance to the movement seemed to come from the campaign to criticize Lin Biao and Confucius during early 1974. This campaign, and a number of issues in economic policy and management, had been used for the purpose of promoting contention among factions of the leaders. This setback in 1974 was clearly demonstrated by the complete disappearance of the campaign promoting the Party's rural economic policies during that time. However, this interruption did not last long. The convention of the Fourth National People's Congress in January 1975 and the First National Conference on Learning from Dazhai in September appeared to have restored the momentum at least until the second downfall of Deng Xiaoping in 1976. In fact, the new course of policy mix was being pushed forward with more determination, although it did turn out to be short-lived as well.

The motive behind the move in 1972 was a desire to achieve faster growth in the economy, and the adopted strategy was considered to be the most effective way of achieving it under the prevailing conditions. Those conditions certainly did not exist before that time. They included the international recognition of the government and its implications for trade and technology transfer, the gradual settling down of purges and disruptions after the Cultural Revolution and a reorganized Party and government. The pursuit of faster growth was also placed under the apparent uncompromised stand on maintaining the role of central command in resource allocation. The swing back to the use of rules and regulations and indeed more centralized control of the economy was evident after 1972. Riskin (1978, pp.88-90) argues that the move back to more centralized control was due to the technical limitations of local autonomy and to the resultant socio-economic factors which were counting against 'self-reliance'. These factors were thought to be causing undesirable inequality within the community. In fact, this development towards more centralized management of the economy was directed in part at maximizing the share of investment in national income with a view to achieving faster material output growth. It should be noted that this development has a greater effect on the industrial sector than on the agricultural sector which, as will be studied, has already been placed under various formal and informal constraints for its pattern of income and expenditures. As far as the rural sector was concerned, more centralized controls exercised by the local governments were considered as necessary to permit the channelling of resources to selected areas to obtain greater and faster results in output growth.

THE PRIMACY OF GRAIN PRODUCTION

Taking grain as 'the key link' in agricultural production development and promoting self-sufficiency in grain in a national as well as local context has been consistently maintained as the cornerstone of agricultural policy. One of the main exemplary virtues of the Dazhai model was that it achieved grain self-sufficiency in spite of adverse natural conditions (Wen and Liang, 1977; Steidlmayer, 1976; Gurley, 1975; Maxwell, 1975). The imposition of grain primacy not only has implications for the input-output matrix in production but also has far-reaching consequences for investments and the pattern of rural development. By its very nature, the primacy placed on grain output would impose constraints on the output mix of the collectives. This in turn would affect the derived demand for inputs and the incomes of the collectives and their members. During this period, this policy had often been translated into practice by promoting multiple cropping of grains and extension of grain acreage (Renmin Ribao, December 16, 1974; X. An, 1976, pp.83-5; Reporting Team Stationed

51

in Dazhai, 1977, p.177). In addition, it had even pushed localities and collectives to transform dry lands into paddy-rice fields (Renmin Ribao, February 23, 1973; Jiang, and Shu, 1975, p.90).

The primacy of grain was effectively enforced because of the political pressure exerted on the rural cadres via the constant campaigns to learn from Dazhai and to urge peasants to achieve or surpass the targets set by the Revised NPAD (Timmer, 1976, p.65; Editorial Team of Xin yu-gong yi-shan ji, 1977; Shen, 1976, p.7; Fung, 1974, pp.41-55). The primacy of grain production did not only dictate the pattern of resource allocation in the rural economy, it also affected the rate of investment, the level of indirect taxation of the peasants and the property rights of the rural collectives. Sales of grain produced by the rural collectives could only be made to state marketing organizations.[2] Such sales, plus the agricultural tax paid in grain (or its equivalents), were important extractive measures to channel surplus from the rural collectives which might or might not benefit directly from the use of such surplus by the government. The production of grain, which was sold at state-determined prices, was generally not a profitable activity for most collectives. Therefore, the Party machinery had to be used to maintain incentive, either by enhancing 'political consciousness' or by simply applying pressure. It was not unusual to equate 'rural capitalism' with failure to comply with the assigned grain production plans (Jiang and Shu, 1975, pp.83-4). Indeed, 'free planting' was equivalent to a 'capitalist way of management' and that unwillingness to grow grain was part of 'revisionist policies' (You and Tian, 1976, pp.15-16). Although respecting the rights of the production teams had been promoted constantly as part of the Party's rural economic policy, the right to make production decisions was a qualified one. For rights were recognized only on the conditions of accepting the guidance of state plans. This can really be regarded as a common and typical manifestation of how plans and control gained priority over ownership rights. This was so because no cadres or Party members would have survived long if accusations of being 'capitalist' or 'revisionist' were levelled against them during the period.

DEVELOPMENT OF POLICIES ON AGRICULTURAL MECHANIZATION

Following the 1970 Northern Agricultural Conference, the role of the county as the centre for carrying out agricultural transformations has been firmly established. Thus, along with the continued expansion of output from county-level fertilizer plants, efforts by the county to produce agricultural machinery also gained increased attention. The percentage of counties which claimed to have established factories to make agricultural machinery and equipment increased from 80 per cent in 1970 to 90 per cent in 1971 ('China's Farm Machinery Industry Grows by Leaps and Bounds', 1970, p.19; Renmin Ribao, October 1, 1971).

The 1971 National Conference on Agricultural Mechanization

In September 1971, a national conference on agricultural mechanization (hereafter referred to as the 1971 Mechanization Conference) was held.[3] The objectives for agricultural mechanization had actually been predetermined before the convention of the conference. The proclaimed objective of agricultural mechanization was to ensure stable and high yields in agricultural production against drought and flooding (Renmin Ribao, September 2, 1971). The envisaged process of agricultural mechanization was that it should start 'from small to big (machinery)', and that the level of mechanization could only be raised gradually, and efforts should be based on local conditions. There was no ambitious programme to be rushed through, and mechanization was basically viewed as one of the many measures to improve production.

What the 1971 Mechanization Conference reaffirmed were the ideas of 'self-reliance' and 'walking-on-two-legs'. Hence, the policy stand which emerged after the 1966 On-Site Meeting on Agricultural Mechanization was reiterated. There were three major features (Writing Group of the First Ministry of Machine-Building, 1971). First, the policy on the 'three main emphases' was to be continued, i.e., main emphasis should be placed on small and medium machinery; agricultural machinery should be produced mainly by local industries; the purchase of agricultural machinery should mainly be done by the collectives so that ownership and management were to be 'integrated' and the peasants' initiatives for agricultural mechanization could be raised. Second, both modern and indigenous technology were to be promoted and employed. Third, with a mass movement in farm-tool reform, both semimechanization and mechanization were to be simultaneously pursued.

One important aspect of the new development from the Conference was the greater role placed on planning by local governments (province, prefecture, county and commune) in drawing up annual plans, three-year, five-year and even ten-year plans for agricultural mechanization for each province, county, commune and brigade (Renmin Ribao, September 29, 1974; SWB, FE/W654/A11, January 4, 1972; SWB, FE/W659/A15, February 9, 1972; Renmin Ribao, February 18, July 9, 1975; Xinzhou County Communist Party Committee, 1974, p.83; Bureau of Agricultural Mechanization, Volume I, 1976, pp.10-11). Within the local administration, the increased power of the county and commune appears to have given rise to an impetus in some areas to move to higher levels of rural socialization. Thus, for instance, as a result of the 1971 Mechanization Conference, some communes in Shandong Province began to use brigades as the unit for unified management in order to accommodate 'the coming large-scale, mechanized production'.[4] This tendency of using a higher level in the collectives as an administrative unit without shifting up the basic level of ownership was an attempt to find some acceptable organizational arrangements that would facilitate this kind of modernization without having to make a formal decision to change the institutional structure.[5]

After the 1971 Mechanization Conference, the mechanization of agriculture as an objective was incorporated in the campaign to learn from Dazhai in some counties (Hubei Renmin Chubanshe, 1975, p.43). However, while the pursuit of agricultural mechanization was thus raised closer to the stage of action on a wider scale, it was clear that the 1971 Mechanization Conference had done no more than reaffirm a broadly defined long-term objective and try to tackle some existing problems. Many of the problems were in themselves products of the overall economic approach from which policies and measures related to agricultural mechanization were derived.

Consolidation from 1972 to 1974

After the conclusion of the 1971 Mechanization Conference, there was no further significant decision or move on the future course of agricultural mechanization. One plausible explanation was to be found in the extreme difficulty posed by the severe drought in 1972, when the mass campaign had to be drastically cut back and resources directed to well-sinking and equipping these wells with mechanical power.[6] It should be noted that these mechanically powered wells were mainly provided and managed by the government, not by the collectives.[7] Instead of arguing for more machinery to be used for agricultural basic construction projects, it was stressed that the existing equipment could and should be better utilized in these projects (Renmin Ribao, March 16, 1972; SWB, FE/3877/B11/2, January 1, 1972).

By 1973, attention to agricultural mechanization increased somewhat and the focus was on resolving a number of operational problems which could be identified clearly. On the surface, the obvious problem was the utilization, or rather under-utilization, of agricultural machinery. Apart from the restriction resulting indirectly from the primacy of grain production, the problem of utilization was mainly a result of failure in providing adequate repair and maintenance services. The latter depended on the availability of repair facilities, accessories and spare parts as well as the necessary technical personnel. Besides the shortage of auxiliary equipment and spare parts, effective utilization of agricultural machines could not be achieved or maintained if peasants themselves were seeking temporary non-farm employment to boost income at difficult times (Renmin Ribao, September 19, 1971, August 6, 1972, September 21, 1972, March 11, 1973, May 12, 1973; SWB, FE/W686/A10-11, August 16, 1972; Hubei Renmin Chubanshe, 1975, p.44). It is sufficient to note here that if the primacy of grain production had not dictated the use of farmland, the diversified nature of production would have prevented adverse seasonal factors affecting all farm activities at one time.

In 1973, one saw the first major attempt by the Chinese government to overhaul and to consolidate the efforts in agricultural mechanization, focusing on the problem of utilization and repair.

There was, at the same time, an attempt to formulate specific targets for the future of agricultural mechanization. A rather bold but vague plan was revealed in an internal document to army officers calling for efforts to be made to increase the level of mechanization from 27 per cent in April 1973 to 40.50 per cent by 1975 (Propaganda Division, Political Department, Kunming Military Region, 1974, p.195). However, it was also argued that agricultural mechanization had to be a gradual process. Therefore, when there were shortages in materials, technology and machinery, one should not depend on agricultural machinery alone to raise productivity (Renmin Ribao, August 15, 1973). The emphasis, it was argued, should still be placed on farm-tool reform.

In dealing with the problem of utilization and repair, the solution put forward was rather simplistic: to improve the availability of accessories and spare parts (Renmin Ribao, May 12, August 15, September 25, November 12, 1973; SWB, FE/W741/A10, September 12, 1973). Two approaches were suggested to tackle the problem.

First, it was argued that since 96 per cent of the counties had already established factories for repair and manufacture of agricultural machinery, they could and should put the main emphasis on repair at the present stage. In addition, these factories should start to produce and repair accessories or second-hand spare parts so as to lessen their dependence on state supply of essential materials. The actual arrangement made was not known, and it could not be established how this campaign, without tackling the root causes of the problem, would be effective and workable.

The second approach was to improve availability of accessories and spare parts through better planning by the state's ministries and by the various industry departments in the localities, but principally by the First Ministry of Machine-Building (SWB, FE/W725/A9, May 23, 1973; SWB, FE/W731/A3, July 4, 1973).

The desire to strengthen planning was one of the practical sides of the policy of applying economic criteria for management to obtain better results. There was already evidence by late 1973 that provinces were told to devote their resources to equipping only a selected number of counties by stages (SWB, FE/W758/A2-4, January 16, 1974). It was also claimed later (in 1978) that in 1973, all machine-building industries, including the agricultural machinery industry, were to adopt the principle of specialization and collaboration in production (Z. Zhou, 1978, p.45).

No major initiative on agricultural mechanization was made during 1974, with the campaign to criticize Lin Biao and Confucius going on throughout the early part of the year, and with Zhou Enlai being ill. One of the major tasks regarding agricultural mechanization during that time was to build up some sort of management system for agricultural machinery, to be backed by an adequate supply of inputs and spare parts as well as trained operators (Renmin Ribao, April 8, 1974). It should be noted that there were, again, severely adverse weather conditions affecting many areas at the time. This emphasis on management, planning and the

policy of concentrating resources seemed to dominate through to
early 1975.

The Emergence of Agricultural Mechanization as a Major Policy Instrument for Agricultural Development in 1975

When the belated convention of the Fourth National People's
Congress eventually took place in early 1975, there was talk of the
coming of a 'new leap forward' in agriculture. The main concern in
agricultural mechanization seemed to be shifting slowly to encompass
a much wider spectrum of economic considerations. Not only was
agricultural mechanization to be organized and integrated with
agricultural basic construction projects for the attainment of grain
yield targets of the Revised NPAD, it was also to serve the 'alliance
of workers and peasants' (Renmin Ribao, January 7, 1975; SWB,
FE/W763/A3-4, February 20, 1974; Department of Water
Conservancy, 1976, p.106).

Industrial enterprises were urged to carry out reforms and
innovations to utilize the existing production capacity, because this
approach was considered to be the most effective, the least
expensive and the fastest way to develop production (Renmin Ribao,
August 30, 1975). In this context, a limited form of specialization
(within the local boundaries) in production of agricultural machinery
was being promoted during the year.[8] Localities were urged to
increase their capability in producing complete sets of agricultural
machinery. The successful convention of the Fourth National
People's Congress should have resulted in reviewing and setting new
objectives and policies for the development of the economic system,
though only the broad goal of the four modernizations was known
outside the Congress. Those developments were, however, the
prelude to a new stage for policies on agricultural mechanization. As
far as agriculture was concerned, a new stage was set when the First
National Conference on Learning from Dazhai in Agriculture (The
First Dazhai Conference) decided on a package of aims and policies.

In his opening address to the First Dazhai Conference in
September, Chen Yonggui outlined the objectives of the meeting
(Renmin Ribao, September 16, 1975). For the first time, agricultural
mechanization was to be adopted as the practical means to transform
and modernize agriculture. Indications were that a disguised and
modified version of the early 1960s programme to equip a hundred
counties with modern inputs was again contemplated at the time.[9]

The declared objectives of agricultural mechanization from the
First Dazhai Conference were much more ambitious than those of the
1971 Mechanization Conference.[10] There were three broad
objectives for agricultural mechanization outlined in the 1975 First
Dazhai Conference (Hua, 1975):

(1) It should be directed at raising labour productivity in
agriculture so that more time can be made available to
develop a diversified economy and to build prosperous
'socialist new-type' villages.[11]

(2)   It should facilitate the full utilization of the advantages of the 'bigness and publicness' (yi-da-er-gong) of the commune system which must assume the full role of an integrated unit combining industry, agriculture, commerce, education and the military.

(3)   Through the mechanization of agriculture, the 'three big differences' (differences between industry and agriculture, urban and rural sectors, mental and manual labour) were to be lessened.

Though these objectives were not completely new, there should be no doubt that the new initiatives involved much more than technological measures to improve production. From the stated objectives alone, it was clear that agricultural mechanization was to be used also as an instrument to achieve social and economic objectives other than those directly related to agricultural production.

The basic strategy of the First Dazhai Conference was that agricultural mechanization should be attained within a short period of time via selfreliance of the localities, and that it should be done by batch and by stage, but not all over the country at once. In contrast to the past, the way that agricultural mechanization was to be implemented was outlined in relatively detailed and specific terms. The major policies on the way mechanization should be implemented are noted below.

First, the Party's leadership over agricultural mechanization was to be strengthened through both the state sector and the collective organizations. A hierarchical management system was to be established at the provincial, prefecture and county levels. Agricultural machinery management centres were also to be set up at the commune level, and 'three-in-one' management stations at the brigade level. In this way, there would be a complete system of management organization ('Make Resolution to Achieve Within Five Years', Renmin Ribao, October 12, 1975). In practice, leadership would then be strengthened to bring works on agricultural machinery under centralized management (Chiang, 1975).

Secondly, the prefecture and county governments were urged to continue with their endeavour to develop their system of 'five-small' industries and the provincial governments were to expand their agricultural machinery industry (Hua, 1975). The five-small industries included fertilizer, cement, agricultural machinery, energy (coal and hydropower), and iron and steel. In this way, increased supply of modern inputs was to be made available to the rural collectives.

Thirdly, the promotion of the Dazhai campaign was to be spearheaded by the establishment of models. However, the 'mechanical' transplanting of experiences and practices from models to other rural collectives was to be discouraged. The preferred approach was to extend the experience gained from models to one-third of the collectives in the locality first, and then gradually apply it to the rest (Renmin Ribao, December 27, 1975). Indeed,

57

provinces were actually given the exact number, or quota, of how many counties were to become Dazhai type models by the state (Editorial Department of <u>Nanfan Ribao</u> (ed.), 1975).

Fourthly, it was decided that rural suburbs of large and medium-size cities should be among the first to realize agricultural mechanization. They were to make a success in mechanized and semimechanized pig farms, poultry farms, dairy farms, fisheries and production bases for vegetables.

While semi-mechanization and mechanization were to be promoted simultaneously, the main focus was clearly on mechanization. A series of policy guidelines on the production of agricultural machinery was pronounced. The most important element that emerged was the promotion of specialization. It was stressed that agricultural machinery production should incorporate in its output characteristics that distinguished conditions between the south and the north, and between mountainous regions and plains. Specialization of production in factories was also promoted so that each factory was to produce only one component for final assembly in one specialized assembling plant. Although this specialization objective was really promoted under a regional or local context,[12] it represented a significant move towards the rationalization of the industry.

Although it was meant to become one of the major steps in the modernization drive, the mechanization of agriculture was only conceived in a rather limited framework. Despite the ambitious objectives and the revised approach to production of machines, no comprehensive consideration appears to have been given to the derived resource demands and to the implications for such problems as financing (at the micro and macro level), management, incentives and commodity exchange arrangements. While only a selected batch of counties in each province were to achieve basic mechanization at a time, the effects on the economic system would still be felt by almost all enterprises and rural collectives. However, at the time of the Dazhai Conference, the main concern was to institute the quest for agricultural mechanization into a continuous campaign to learn from Dazhai. The overall feasibility and the required adjustments in general did not seem to have been carefully examined and discussed. Such an approach was perhaps not all that surprising because mechanization was really being installed as the next stage of socialization transformation, the completion of which was intended to be able to get around all these questions and still be able to bring about sustained economic development.

CONCLUSION

For most of the time during the period under investigation, the issue of agricultural mechanization has basically been secondary to other pursuits such as farmland improvement projects. It was only at the First Dazhai Conference of 1975 when mechanization started to be promoted as an operational objective. So far as any efforts on mechanization that have been exerted during the period, they were mainly concerned with improving the technological viability for accommodating a limited degree of mechanization in selected regions. The development of policies towards agricultural mechanization followed closely the process of changes in the overall rural development strategy. At the same time, it was clear that the development of rural policy was in turn determined by the prevailing emphasis and orientation of the general economic approach for national development. While the latter was moving towards increased application of economic criteria within the various constraints and demands of perceived principles of socialist development, this move has not been a straightforward and smooth one. Indeed, as the campaign to criticize Lin Biao and Confucius has shown, the lack of consensus over an acceptable way to develop a socialist economy has caused significant reorientation in the course of policy formation. Being a derivative of the strategy for economic development, agricultural mechanization policy therefore embodied the characteristics as well as the many problems associated with the changes in the general strategy.

NOTES

1.   For discussion on this development, see the text of a 'big-character poster' written by three ex-Red Guards in 1973-4. They were later arrested by the authorities and were only cleared of charges in 1979. 'Le Iche's Poster', in Hsuan (ed.), 1976.

2.   There were two price schemes for the sales of grain. There was one for sales within the compulsory delivery quota and another one, at a slightly higher level, for sales over the compulsory quota. However, both prices, while being gradually lifted, have been low in relation to production cost.

3.   It was not until the end of 1974 when this Conference was first publicly mentioned in the Chinese press as the 1971 National Conference on Agricultural Mechanization. Since 1977, however, this Conference was given the name 'The Second National Conference on Agricultural Mechanization', obviously referring to the 1966 Meeting as the first national conference. See, Renmin Ribao, August 5, 1975; Xinzhou County Communist Party Committee, Hubei Province, 1974, p.82.

4.   Editorial Team of Xin yu-gong yi-shan ji, 1977, p.84. See Chapter 5 for more detailed analysis of the management system in the communes.

5.   On the tendency of using the higher level as an administrative unit, see, for example, Renmin Ribao, August 5, 1975; Zinzhou County Communist Party Committee, 1974, p.83; see also Chapter 5.

6.   Bureau of Agricultural Machinery Administration, Revolutionary Committee of Jinzhong Prefecture, Shanxi Province (ed.), 1974, p.6. Of course, the building of mechanical wells was an important aspect in the pursuit of agricultural mechanization. However, the effort was mainly restricted to northern China.

7. See Chapter 5.

8. <u>Renmin Ribao</u>, August 30, 1975. This form was similar to that adopted by Guangxi Autonomous Region in 1972.

9. This time, the design was not so clear, furthermore, the method of implementation was also different. For the inferences upon which this hypothesis was based, see the following section of this chapter.

10. Just in 1974, the objective of mechanization was still 'to achieve stable and high yields irrespective of drought and water logging', which was the same as the one pronounced in 1971. <u>SWB</u>, FE/W798/A17, October 23, 1974.

11. These 'socialist new-type' villages only started to appear in larger numbers during the 1970s. A typical example was the village of Dazhai Brigade where peasants lived in apartments all located right in the main administrative and commercial centre of the brigade. These apartments were really houses built next to each other, each having its own facilities, such as water taps, electricity, and kitchen. From the author's observations, not all 'socialist new-type' villages were alike. Some may have 'private' gardens (or 'private plots') allocated to their houses. For more details see, for example, Shanghai Renmin Chubanshe (ed.), 1974.

12. Indeed, provinces were urged to build up a province-wide network of the agricultural machinery industry within their territories. However, there was no evidence to suggest that a national trust manufacturing concern as promoted during the mid 1960s had been revived. For a report on these provincial networks, see for example, Hubei Renmin Chubanshe, 1977, Volume 3, pp.19-20.

Chapter Four

TRENDS IN THE PRODUCTION OF AGRICULTURAL MACHINERY

In contrast to the ambitious goal to advance agricultural mechanization as contemplated by the First Dazhai Conference in 1975, for most of the time during the Fourth Five-Year Plan period, it was a process of experimentation and continuous adjustments in search of acceptable ways to incorporate the production, supply, distribution, utilization and management of agricultural machinery in the general pursuit of rural development. Although the 1971 Mechanization Conference did put forward proposals to formulate long-term plans, available evidence does not indicate that any serious move had been made on an extensive scale as a result.

During the Fourth Five-Year Plan there were some notable developments in the production of some agricultural machines, but the overall performance had been modest considering the potential requirements for the mechanization of farming operations to achieve better yields under the then existing conditions. This could be attributed to a number of factors. On the one hand, it was a result of the policy emphasis on agricultural output mix, the priorities thus given the manufacture of different agricultural machines and accessories, and the progress in the actual process of producing these goods. On the other hand, the outcome was also governed by the system of resource allocation, the management organization of machines and the financial conditions that affected the utilization and provision of agricultural machinery. The first set of factors will be the subject of study in this chapter.

PRIORITIES FOR MECHANIZING AGRICULTURAL OPERATIONS

Since each rural collective was a separate economic entity and because the price mechanism was not being consciously used to determine the allocation of resources, the priorities for mechanizing various agricultural operations would have to be determined by some form of plans or directives from various planning authorities. The chosen priorities will determine directly the machinery output mix for agricultural mechanization, which, in turn, will affect the production organization and the technology used to produce and provide the finished products.

In China's case, the production organization and technology were predetermined as part of the desirable 'production relations' for the economic system. In fact, the desired form of 'production relations' can be regarded as the basis, and the objective, upon which the priorities for mechanization were to be realized. In the final analysis, priorities were derived from the objectives for economic development set by the demands of the economic system. As discussed earlier, policies on agricultural mechanization prior to the First Dazhai Conference were basically derivatives of the general economic and agricultural policies.

The emphasis on increasing grain-output self-sufficiency was probably the most important factor affecting the choice of priorities in determining the mechanization of agricultural operations. However, because of the diversity in Chinese agricultural production, priorities for mechanization of operations must be seen from a regional viewpoint. Furthermore, agricultural mechanization, however defined, was not the central theme for transforming Chinese agriculture during the period. Thus, it was generally those collectives or localities which were in a more favourable position (due to superior natural endowments or special privileges) that needed to consider the question of priorities. Because of their exemplary function and their ubiquitous nature, and since agricultural mechanization was in an experimental stage in the period, the priorities in those collectives could serve to illustrate the overall tendency in a nationwide context. The fact that production of agricultural machinery was directly determined by administrative plans also helped to identify the priorities.

Given that increasing grain output had been a primary objective and that increasing the multiple cropping index had been adopted as a desirable way to achieve the task of producing more grains,[1] the question of deciding on mechanization priorities had to centre around the demands which thus arose. In this context, the overriding concern was to determine what operations were to be mechanized so that the multiple cropping index could be lifted and increased grain output could be sustained. For instance, mechanizing some operations in the peak season would eliminate a labour bottleneck to allow for an increase in the multiple cropping index, while mechanization of irrigation would be vital to the effective use of chemical fertilizer to ensure good harvest.

Evidence from a number of reported cases seems to suggest that irrigation and drainage, preliminary processing of grains and certain operations for land preparation were generally among the first to be mechanized.[2] It should be noted that, while agricultural mechanization was to begin in this sequence in fairly advanced collectives and localities, the use of chemical fertilizer was already well established in all cases.

The operations which were also likely to be mechanized first tended to be the bottleneck operations for introducing new varieties of crops and for new cropping systems (Ishikawa, 1977, p.98). Of course, the elimination of labour bottlenecks was really meant to serve the aim of further grain output increases, although it was clear that the displacement of labour from the rural sector had never been the intention.

In a broader context, it was claimed that, to ensure stable and high yields, each agricultural region in China had in fact followed its own set of priorities for mechanization.[3] Thus, the plains in the north-east had put priority on tractors and harvesters; in the North China Plains, pump wells, mechanized irrigation and drainage were emphasised; in the southern paddy-growing regions, priority was on wet-land machinery and rice transplanters (Renmin Ribao, October 12, 1975).

For the most part of the period, the priorities in mechanization were not determined in a systematic programme but were often dictated by the particular needs in various places and at different points of time to alleviate obstacles in developing grain output and to ease natural calamities. Even in the model brigade, Dazhai, it was admitted that priorities were not at all clear at the beginning and that it was only after a number of years (since 1971) that they gradually sorted out the form of mechanization they required (Bureau of Agricultural Machinery Administration, 1975, p.19). Therefore, in practice, not all mechanized operations were those which should have received priority, nor were all priority operations being mechanized. For example, the use of tractors for transportation is a typical case of the first category, while that of paddy field machinery belongs to the second category.[4]

A significant feature of the policy of the First Dazhai Conference in 1975 was to broaden the scope of agricultural mechanization to include not just grain production but also forestry, animal husbandry, sideline production and fishery (Department of Economics, Peking University, 1975, p.240; Zheng-zhi jing-ji-xue jiang-hua: she-hui-zhu-yi bu-fen (Talks on Political Economy: Socialism), 1976, p.128). Agricultural mechanization was thus given a more definitive policy content, which was to include the use of machinery for cultivation, farmland construction projects, irrigation and drainage, plant protection, transportation, harvesting, processing of agricultural and sideline products, forestry, fishery, and animal husbandry (Renmin Ribao, October 12, 1975). Seventy per cent of the work done in these production activities was to be mechanized so as to achieve 'basic mechanization' although the measurement of that percentage was not given precise meaning.

The extension of the scope for mechanization set by the Conference could not really be explained by the requirement to satisfy agricultural production alone; it was born out of the new design for transforming the Chinese economy. The development and assignment of mechanization priorities should be viewed and explained in the context of policy development towards the modernization of the economy during the period. It is sufficient to note here that the absence of a set of specific guidelines meant that the priorities for mechanizing operations were often determined by a complexity of factors many of which were not necessarily related to pure economic considerations. The investigation of the proclaimed priorities for mechanization is a necessary but not sufficient condition for analysing and understanding the process and trends involved in the production of agricultural machinery. An examination of the extent and manner in which these objectives and priorities were translated into reality is also required, and this will be done in the following sections.

ESTIMATION OF AGRICULTURAL MACHINERY OUTPUTS

With the statistic black-out still in force during the period, there were only fragmentary output claims on the production of agricultural machines. Unfortunately, the recent flood of official statistics does not extend adequately to cover those 'dark' years. Nevertheless, it is still possible to reconstruct, however incomplete and tentative, a series of estimates which will give some indication of the emerging trends. That these claims were made was in itself a significant fact, because they often showed the production trends of those machines for which priorities were placed and realized. Though those claims were far from comprehensive and did not include all the priority machines, they provided the basis of analysis of the overall development.

In Table 4.1 and Table 4.2, estimates of annual output for tractors are presented. The output figures in Table 4.1 are for conventional four-wheel and crawler tractors, normally over 12 h.p. Table 4.2 contains estimates for hand-held tractors, or walking tractors, usually two-wheeled and under 12 h.p.[5]

Table 4.1:   Conventional   Tractors   in   China   1971–1975
(in 15 h.p. – standard units)

Year	Annual Production	(Index)
1971	89,568	(100)
1972	98,525	(110)
1973	140,700	(157)
1974	135,780	(151)
1975	164,150	(180)

Source & Notes: See Appendix A

The rate of growth in the production of hand tractors was clearly much faster and steadier than that of the conventional tractors. Overall, there was a remarkable increase in the production of conventional as well as hand tractors in 1973. That was not inconsistent with the increased efforts directed towards agricultural mechanization after the 1971 Mechanization Conference.

Table 4.2:   *Hand Tractors in China 1971–1975*

Year	Annual Production (units)	Index of Annual Production	
1965		100	
1971	31,250	625	100
1972			
1973	60,000	3200	512
1974	180,000	3600	576
1975	250,000	5000	800

Source & Notes: See Appendix A

1974 was the year when tractor production, both hand-held and conventional types, had the lowest rate of growth during the entire Fourth Five-Year Plan period. In fact, according to the estimates in the tables, the production of conventional tractors actually fell by about 4 per cent in 1974, while the production of hand tractors achieved a 13 per cent increase in 1974 compared with an average annual growth rate of 68 per cent during the whole period. This slow-down might have been caused partly by the consolidation and improvement measures as well as being the result of the readjustment policy of shifting more emphasis to repair services in 1973. In addition, there was the campaign to criticize Lin Biao and Confucius in 1974, and it was later reported that there were widespread disruptions and stoppages in many major state tractor factories (Renmin Ribao, November 15, 1977).

By 1975, tractor production recovered and in fact showed an increase. The successful convention of the Fourth National People's Congress early in 1975 might have been one of the factors that led to a revived growth in tractor production. That was because agricultural mechanization had been assigned a more central role and the disruptions in the previous year had ceased. Furthermore, it might have been due to the completion of some major tractor factories commissioned at the beginning of the Fourth Five-Year Plan.[6]

It is interesting to note that the estimated number of conventional tractors in use as of 1975 was 613,350 standard units, or just about equal to the total output between 1971 and 1975.[7] Unfortunately, there was no information on the service life, durability and annual working hours of the machines. Thus, it is not possible to estimate the pattern of depreciation, rate of breakdown and replacement. Hence, estimation of the number of tractors in active service for the other four years cannot be made with accuracy and any claim should best be regarded as tentative.

However, in spite of the absence of comprehensive quantitative data, it is instructive to examine a number of hypotheses that may explain that outcome. First, it may be due to the fact that tractors produced prior to 1971 had all ended their serviceable life and that the stock of tractors in the 1970s was mostly currently produced.

The second hypothesis is that it was only in 1975, for which an estimate was made, that such a low level of serviceable tractors was observed and the levels had not been the same for the past four years. Thirdly, due to continuous negligence, poor quality of products, lack of spare parts, attachments and repair services, the serviceable life of tractors was extremely short and the breakdown rate was high. Since only one estimate for tractors in use could be made for 1975, it is really not possible to know how this figure might have changed over the past years. The lack of the necessary information makes it very difficult to decide on the rejection or acceptance of the alternative explanations. However, for reasons to be studied in the next section of the chapter, it seems most likely that the third explanation should not be rejected.

The recently released official data for 1977 and 1978 also support this hypothesis. An increase of 14,200 standard units was recorded in 1978 over 1977 in the production of conventional tractors, but the increase in the number in use increased by 90,000 standard units.[8] A similar situation is even more dramatically illustrated by the case of hand tractors. In 1978, production of hand tractors increased only by 3,700 units whereas the stock of tractors in use jumped by 280,000 units.[9] The much publicised campaign (late 1976) to strengthen tractor management, training, quality control in production, improvement of availability of spare parts, attachments and repair services seems to be the only plausible explanation for that expanded stock of serviceable tractors if the official claims are to be accepted. The implicit assumption of the argument is that it was because of the absence of those factors which had been responsible for a relatively low level of tractors in use.

Perhaps an even more important parameter to be considered is the farm acreage worked by tractors. Rather than just looking at the number of tractors that were available or claimed to be in use, tractorized acreage would indicate better how extensively and effectively the tractors were used. Information on this subject is scarce and the definition of tractorized regions has often been vague. In general, the term ji-geng-mian-ji (machine-cultivated acreage) was used to designate the area on which tractors regularly worked, and in terms of practical usage, it usually means the acreage ploughed by the tractors. With the little information that is available, a series of estimates for tractorized acreage (ji-geng-mian-ji) is provided in Table 4.3. Although there was no information on 1972 and 1973, it is reasonable to assume that tractorized acreage for those two years would be under 20 million hectares.

An important implication that can be drawn from this estimate series is that, despite the rapid growth in tractor production during the period, there has been no corresponding expansion in the tractorized acreage by any significant degree. This outcome was no accident. That means either that the additional tractors were not

Table 4.3:   Tractorized Acreage (<u>Ji-geng-mian-ji</u>) (in million
              hectares)

1960	6
1965	10
1971	15-20
1972	
1973	
1974	20
1975	20
1976	20

Source: See Appendix A

intended to be used for expanding the tractorized acreage, or that the machines were being employed in such a way that expansion was not possible. As will be discussed in the following chapters, both factors appeared to have been responsible when considered in the context of policies on the management and financing of agricultural mechanization.

Apart from tractors, there were a number of equally if not more important agricultural inputs for which production estimation can be made. Basically, these inputs were connected with the use and generation of energy and the conservancy of water resources in the rural sector.

Table 4.4 presents estimates of rural electricity consumption, and related data on small hyroelectric stations.[10]   According to the estimated results, the consumption of electricity in the rural sector rose by 40 per cent in five years while the number of small hydroelectric stations increased by 70 per cent. Thus, the increase in the number of small hydroelectric stations has not led to an equivalent increase in rural electricity consumption. A number of facts need to be noted.

First of all, the geographical distribution of water resources in China is not even. While the southern part of the country is endowed with 75 per cent of total water resources and only 38 per cent of farmland, the northern plains have 52 per cent of farmland but only 7 per cent of the total surface water (Kang Chao, 1970, pp.120-1). The distribution of small hydroelectric stations was also uneven. Actually, about 25 per cent of the counties were reported to be mainly reliant on about 70,000 stations for electricity supply in 1977.[11]   It is conceivable that newly-added stations were being installed with smaller generating capacity so that they would account for a smaller share in the source of electricity supply to the rural sector. The stations were getting to be of smaller capacity because of technical constraints posed by water resources and more importantly the nature of financing for such stations. One plausible reason for the discrepancy of growth rates between electricity consumption and the building of small hydroelectric stations was that these stations were not fully utilized due to factors such as drought, mismanagement, and repair problems.

Though there is only one estimate (for the year 1975) on the actual output generated by these small hydroelectric stations, its implied share in the total supply of rural electricity is actually supported by evidence in individual provinces. In Table 4.4, from figures in column (I) and column (IV), the electricity output from small hydroelectric stations can be calculated to have contributed 30 per cent of the total electricity consumption of the rural sector in 1975. This percentage is indirectly verified by evidence in two provinces where potential hydroelectric power is high and which have built the largest number of small stations.[12]

Table 4.4:   *China's Rural Electricity*

	(I)	(II)	(III)	(IV)
1971	10,850	35,000	(16% of total hydroelectric generating capacity in	
1972		35,000	China)	
1973	13,760	50,000		
1974		50,000	1.9 million kW	
1975	14,400	60,000	1.9 million kW	4,310 million kW

(I)   Rural electricity consumption (million kWh.);
(II)   Number of small hydroelectric stations;
(III) Total generating capacity of small hydroelectric stations;
(IV)   Output from small hydroelectric stations

Source: See Appendix A

Therefore, the implication is that about 70 per cent of the electricity supply to the rural sector must have come from sources other than those supplied by small hydroelectric stations. The alternative sources of supply would have to come from the national network and power grid connected to larger and medium hydroelectric stations and thermal electricity generation plants. That means the supply of rural electricity depended heavily on the availability and growth of electric power from state enterprises, which in turn hinged on the conditions of hydroelectricity potential, availability of coal and fuel, and other economic and financial considerations.[13] It is a well-known fact that electricity supply, even for major state industrial enterprises in major cities, continued to be a serious problem for many years.[14]

By 1975 it was reported that about 70 per cent of the communes and half of the brigades in varying degree, 'were supplied with electricity' (Renmin Ribao, August 30, September 4, 1975, June 13, 1976; SWB, FE/W845/A20-21, September 24, 1975). However, in actual fact, it only means that electricity was available to the various economic undertakings by the commune and brigade administrations but not to all the member units (i.e. the production teams). Furthermore, the availability of electricity to different localities was unevenly distributed.[15]

Table 4.5:   Availability of Electricity Supply at Different Levels of the Commune in Selected Provinces (in percentages) (1974/75)

	Commune	Brigade	Team	House-hold
Fujiang Province	100	50		
Hunan Province	90	96	70	
Shandong Province	63	25		
Jilin Province	89	73		
She County, Anhui Province	80			
Chuanan County, Anhui Province	100	69	44	43
Hui County, Henan Province		96		

Source: See Appendix A

In Table 4.5, some scattered local data on the availability of electricity supply are given. The table shows that the incidence of supply increases with the level of administration in the commune system. As far as the communes and brigades are concerned, electricity was mostly used to run their collective industries engaged in processing, repairing and other non-farm production and activities. Since the production teams engaged mainly in farm production, electricity would be used for irrigation, drainage, processing, etc. It should be noted that, because of the limited number of samples, the data in Table 4.5 cannot be readily generalized to apply to the rest of the country. Furthermore, almost all the cases in the table were advanced models in terms of progress in agricultural mechanization and the figures might therefore overstate the true extent of availability.

In Table 4.6, estimates for the mechanical power available for irrigation and drainage are presented. The figures represent the power available from electrical and internal combustion engines in the countryside. If the estimates of rural electricity generation capacity (column III Table 4.4) are correct, then it can reasonably be concluded that the power used for irrigation and drainage during the period would have come mainly from national power grid or non-electric sources such as internal combustion engines using petroleum products.[16] With the subsidized price of petroleum products for rural use and the multiple purpose of diesel engines, it is most likely that these engines were a major source of power for most rural collectives' irrigation. Information on the annual production of internal combustion engines is not readily available. It is only possible to construct an index of estimated production, as presented in Table 4.8. It should be noted that these engines were used not only for irrigation and drainage but also to power many other agricultural machines such as processing equipment, plant protection machines, hand tractors or even used to generate electricity (Bureau of Agriculture and Forestry, 1975, pp.512-60; Y. Zhang, et al., 1976).

Without data on the final uses of the engines, it is not possible to estimate how many of them were being used for irrigation and drainage. However, when the estimates contained in Table 4.6 and Table 4.8 are compared, the production of internal combustion engines is found to have achieved an average annual growth rate of about 45 per cent but that the power capacity of irrigation and drainage equipment only started to increase after 1973. If this outcome is compared to the increasing number of mechanical wells during the period (Table 4.7) an interesting picture emerges.

First, the growth of production in internal combustion engines did not contribute to a corresponding expansion in the power capacity of irrigation and drainage equipment between 1971 and 1973, in spite of the fact that these engines were probably the main power source. This would mean that, apart from replacing worn-out machines, the

Table 4.6:   *Power Capacity of Mechanical Irrigation and Drainage Equipment (in million h.p.)*

1971	20
1972	20
1973	20
1974	30
1975	40
1976	50

Source: See Appendix A

engines would have been used for other purposes (such as building hand tractors). In fact, Table 4.2 shows that hand tractor production was increasing at an average annual growth rate of 79 per cent in the same period, (1971-4). On the longer term basis, between 1966 and 1976, hand tractor production was reported to have achieved an annual average growth rate of 46.4 per cent (Renmin Ribao, December 24, 1977). However, without adequate information, it is not possible to establish exactly the relation between hand tractor and internal combustion engine production.

Table 4.7:   *Number of Irrigation Wells Designed to be Powered by Electricity or by Internal Combustion Engines, and the Area Irrigated by these Wells*

Year	Number of wells sunk	Cumulative total number of wells	Area irrigated by wells (million ha)
1965		100,000	
1971		690,000	
1972	210,000	900,000	
1973	300,000	1,200,000	6.6
1974	100,000	1,300,000	7.3
1975	400,000	1,700,000	10.7

Source: See Appendix A

Table 4.8:   *Production Index for Internal Combustion Engines*

1965	1971	1972	1973	1974
100	420	525	800	1300
	100	125	190	310

Source: See Appendix A

A comparison of the estimates contained in Table 4.7 and Table 4.8 indicates that the doubling in the number of mechanical wells was not accompanied by any substantial increase in the power capacity for irrigation and drainage between 1971 and 1973. The implication would be that these wells, designed for use with power by electricity or engines, were not fully equipped with these facilities at the time when they were built. This was in fact indirectly confirmed by official claims that, between 1973 and 1975, the number of wells that had been equipped with power surpassed the total of the past 24 years.[17]

However, it is not clear by how much the increase in power capacity for irrigation and drainage since 1974 had gone into equipping the wells. Nevertheless, the acreage brought under mechanical irrigation by those wells did jump from 6.6 million hectares in 1973 to 10.7 million hectares in 1975 (Table 4.7). Unfortunately, there is no available information to ascertain the effect of these mechanical wells on the overall expansion of irrigated acreage.

From Table 4.7, if the estimate in the third column is divided by the figure in the second column, we derive an estimate series of the average acreage irrigated by each mechanical well. The results show that each well, on average, irrigated 5.5 hectares in 1973, 5.6 hectares in 1974 and 5.9 hectares in 1975. This reflects in part the effects of better availability of attachments and power source, and in part a rationalization of location and better management. However, the claimed results are still short of the official target for an average of 6.7 hectares per well.[18] It is interesting to note that 80 per cent of the mechanical wells were reported to be located in the North China Plains and that the area irrigated by mechanical wells accounted for 50 per cent of the total irrigated acreage in North China in 1972 (Renmin Ribao, May 26, 1972).

Table 4.9:   *Estimates of Area with Irrigation and Drainage System (in million hectares)*

Year	Irrigated Farmland	Effective Irrigated Area by Dams	Area with Drainage Facilities (or with Controlled Waterlogging)	Farmland Protected against Drought and Flooding
1971	40.4			
1972	42			
1973	43.6			
1974	45.2		(16.6)	33
1975	46.8			33
1976	48.4			33
1977	50	21	15.3	33

Source: See Appendix A

In Table 4.9, estimation of the area of farmland with drainage and irrigation is presented. During the whole Fourth Five-Year Plan period, total area of farmland under irrigation increased by 16 per cent only. The total irrigated acreage claimed to have been achieved in 1975 was just about 78 per cent of the target set by the Revised NPAD.[19] In a later economic plan, a target of 63.3 million hectares of irrigated farmland was set for 1985.[20] Thus, the new target was actually not so different from the one set earlier by the Revised

NPAD. However, the Revised NPAD had warned that even if the target were achieved, it would only enable prevention of ordinary floods and drought (Tan Chenlin, 1960, p.89). What is more significant, in this regard, is the area of farmland protected against drought and flooding, or those fields with 'high and stable' yields. In Table 4.9, high and stable farmland is estimated to be 33 million hectares. A later target was to have 53.3 million hectares of such high and stable-yield farmland by 1985 (Commentator of Hongqi, 1978, p.32).

Table 4.10:   *Available Mechanical Power Per Unit of Farmland*

	1971	1972	1973	1974	1975
Horsepower from tractors per hectare of tractorized farmland					0.7
Horsepower from irrigation and drainage equipment per hectare of irrigated farmland	0.495	0.476	0.459	0.664	0.855
Horsepower from tractors per hectare of cultivated land					0.14
Horsepower from irrigation and drainage equipment per hectare of cultivated land	0.2	0.2	0.2	0.3	0.4
Total horsepower from tractor, irrigation and drainage equipment per hectare of cultivated land					0.54

Source: See Appendix A

Based on various estimates on tractor stock, acreages and power capacities contained in the preceding tables, an interesting indication of per hectare results can be constructed. In Table 4.10, estimated availability of power input from tractors and irrigation-drainage equipment was calculated from previous tables. Great care must be taken in the interpretation of these calculated figures. They represent the average power capacity for each unit of farmland, but the amount of power actually applied in the field in each year cannot be ascertained. The figures in Table 4.10 serve as an indication of the maximum power capacity available for such uses; a number of factors could render that maximum unattainable. For instance, factors such as shortage of fuel and electricity, machinery breakdown, lack of spare parts and attachments, mismanagement and the diverting of use of machinery from agricultural production.

In a study that attempted to relate crop yield per hectare to power input per hectare in 23 developing countries and regions, Giles found a statistical correlation between total power input and yield, with separate trends for the developed and for the developing countries.[21] From Giles' results, it was found that a total power input of 0.5 h.p. per hectare seemed to be the threshold for increasing grain yield above 2.5 tons per hectare (Giles, 1975, pp.16-7).

Perkins and others estimated that 0.4 h.p./ha (excluding irrigation) was actually used for field operations in China during 1973.[22] From Table 4.10, the estimate indicates that 0.54 h.p. was available from mechanical sources (including irrigation and drainage equipment) for each hectare of cultivated land in China. Excluding power from irrigation and drainage equipment, the estimate from Table 4.10 was 0.14 h.p. per hectare.

Without additional information, the share of mechanical power in the total power input into the farmland cannot be estimated. And without knowing this share, total power input (animal, mechanical and human) cannot be established. Based on information from three regions which excluded China, Giles estimated the percentage distribution of the three kinds of agricultural power inputs.[23] If China had the same distribution pattern of the three sources of agricultural power as in the Asian region, then it could be derived from the estimates in Table 4.10 that there was 0.608 h.p. per cultivated ha in 1975. This figure (0.608 h.p./ha, excluding irrigation and drainage) would place China in a position well above most developing countries in terms of agricultural power input. Indeed, per hectare grain yield in 1975 did amount to just over 2.5 ton/ha so that this may be consistent with the statistical relationship between yield and power input found by Giles. It should, however, be noted that these estimates represent national averages. Notwithstanding the difficulties encountered in international comparisons of this kind, for a country such as China with diversified agricultural production, national averages do not tell much about regional disparities.

In China, mechanical power for agriculture had been far from evenly distributed among localities and collectives. Thus, it would be desirable to ascertain the relationship between grain yield in tractorized areas and the total power input they received.

Unfortunately, there has been virtually no information on which an investigation of this kind can be based. In the early 1960s, there were individual studies, usually from records and accounts of the state farms, of the various output and financial effects of using agricultural machinery, but there seem to have been no systematic studies of this nature being carried out or being published since the Cultural Revolution.

If an assumption was made that in tractorized regions mechanical power accounted for 50 per cent of total power input, then a total power input of 1.4 h.p. would have been applied in each tractorized hectare in 1975.[24] In this regard, it would be instructive to take this estimated national average for total power input availability and compare it with the actual requirements as occurred in individual localities which had reached a relatively high degree of mechanization and high level of grain yield.

Table 4.11 presents estimates of the requirements of power input into the farmland and the corresponding grain yields based on available information from a number of advanced collectives and localities. It should be noted, as is clear from the figures in Table 4.11, that this set of cross-sectional data was not complete and represented only the high end of the distribution. Although the samples are probably too biased and too small to be conclusive, they nevertheless indicate that a wide range of grain yields was associated with a similar level of power input. This would mean that some localities, or collectives might have been using more power than had been necessary to achieve a certain level of grain output. If the data in Table 4.11 had been more comprehensive, a comparison with the yield-power relationship in other countries would have been revealing.

In summary, from the available information upon which estimate series for various national averages have been constructed, a number of observations can be made. First of all, tractor production, both conventional and hand-held, has in general been increasing during the five years, with the number of hand tractors growing at a much faster rate.[25] However, that growth in output was probably not sufficient to meet the requirements for basic mechanization whether measured in terms of the number of machines actually needed or in terms of the required horse-power per unit of farmland. The growth of tractor production was accompanied by an increase in the number of model designs and by a growing number of local brand names and designs. Nevertheless, while tractor production had been expanding there was no significant expansion of tractorized farmland.

Perhaps a more notable progress was to be found in the expansion of power capacity for irrigation and drainage, and in the increase in mechanical wells. The rates of growth in these areas actually exceeded growth in conventional tractor production (because hand tractor output was measured in physical units, not standard units, no meaningful comparison can be made). However, again, the significant growth had not been accompanied by an equivalent expansion in the irrigated acreage, although, in this case, it is

Table 4.11:   *Power Input Requirements and Corresponding Grain Yields in Individual Collectives*

Provinces in Which Collectives are Located	(A)	(B)*	(C)
Hebei	2.14	4.28	5.36
Hubei	1.63	3.26	6.54
Shanxi	7.1	14.2	8.25
Anhui	1.64	3.28	9.65
Hunan	2.54	5.08	10.1
Jiangsu (Wuxi County)	4.16	8.32	11
Hubei	4.1	8.2	12
Shanghai	5	10	13.85
Shanghai	4.87	9.73	13.95

(A)   Available Mechanical Power (h.p. per hectare of cultivated land);
(B)   Total Power Input (Manual, Animal and Mechanical) (h.p. per hectare of cultivated land);
(C)   Grain Yield (metric ton per hectare).
*   Total power input is calculated on the assumption that available mechanical power actually accounted for 50% of total power input.

Source: See Appendix A

difficult to draw any inferences due to the lack of relevant information and the tentative nature of the estimates. Since the area nominally under irrigation was already quite large in the beginning of the period (Table 4.9), a further increase would only show a moderate growth rate. In addition, the change in irrigated acreage did not really indicate the qualitative aspects of such change. For instance, the increased capacity may have improved efficiency many times without expanding total irrigated acreage. In any case, the rapid development in the production of tractors and in the supply of irrigation and drainage equipment did reflect the important priorities they have been assigned for transforming Chinese agriculture during the period.

Rural electricity supply was mainly limited to the higher levels of the collectives (i.e. commune and brigade levels), and its use was mainly for purpose of collective production and not personal consumption. So far as electricity was available, the supply seems to have depended heavily on the national networks. In spite of the fast development in building small hydroelectric stations in rural areas during the period, this dependence had not changed.

The whole pattern and progress in the material production of various agricultural machinery would have reflected the priorities of mechanization in practice, but it also gave some indication of the institutional and organizational process through which production had been initiated and realized. The latter will be the subject of investigation in later chapters.

THE SUPPLY OF ATTACHMENTS AND REPAIR SERVICES

During the 1961-5 period, the problem of inadequate repair and maintenance services was basically a matter of failure on the part of the state industry to produce sufficient quantities of spare parts. This problem continued into the 1970s. While the use of agricultural machinery was limited only to a small number of places and to a few machines in the 1960s, the problem in the 1970s had become more complex.

In the 1970s, many more machines were scattered all over the country, although distribution was still uneven. Furthermore, production of machinery spare parts and attachments was no longer the sole responsibility of central enterprises. Numerous local enterprises were producing locally adapted models relying mainly on local resources and finance. Since there was little effort made in the direction of standardization of machine parts and components, inter-changeability was not common. All these factors contributed to the inadequate supply of attachments and spare parts and thus to lowering the utilization of machines. In this section, the developments and problems of producing attachments and spare parts, and of providing repair services for agricultural machines are examined.

Production of Attachments and Spare Parts for Agricultural Machines

In spite of the increasing attention paid to the improvement in utilization through increased supply of attachments and parts, especially since 1973, the actual progress had been slow because of constraints imposed by the system of allocation of materials, finance and management. As far as the growth rate was concerned, production of spare parts lagged far behind that of agricultural machinery.

Between 1970 and 1978, production of the main items of agricultural machinery was planned to have a 19 per cent average annual growth rate (Renmin Ribao, July 28, 1978). The target was reported to have been over-fulfilled in all those years. On the other hand, spare parts for repair and maintenance were planned to have a 10 per cent average annual growth rate, but the target had never been reached in any year.[26]

The shortage of attachments for agricultural machinery had also been causing problems of poor utilization. Indeed, it was reported that if attachments were properly and adequately fitted, the effective irrigated acreage in China could be raised by 30 per cent without additional machinery (Renmin Ribao, July 28, 1978). With the pursuit of local self-sufficiency, local governments were preoccupied with the task of setting up basic industries from which most material inputs could then be made available to produce the most urgently required agricultural machinery. As will be discussed in the following section, often it was the suddenly and urgently needed machinery which promoted real response in production (within the ability and constraints of local production). The larger enterprises were normally engaged in making machines and machine tools for the smaller enterprises while the smaller enterprises were supposed to concentrate on the provision of repair and maintenance services. Thus, the production of suitable attachments and spare parts was usually left out of the priority list.

The lack of adequate attachments affected operations of machinery of all kinds. Almost half of the mechanical pump wells in Hebei Province were out of action because of the lack of attachments and accessories. Table 4.12 gives some indication of the problem based on data of Hebei Province. As indicated earlier in Tables 4.6 to 4.9, irrigated acreage did lag behind the increase in available equipment. Certainly, the lack of attachments would not have helped to improve the situation.

Table 4.12: *Utilization of Mechanical Pump Wells in Hebei Province*

Area	Number of Pump Wells Sunk (Year)	Operating Pump Wells Completed with Attachments (Year)
Hebei Province	150,000 (1973)	90,000 (1973)
Tangshan Prefecture	25,000 (1973)	14,400 (1973)
Heng Shui Prefecture	14,000 (1973)	10,000 (1973)
Shijiazhuang Prefecture	42,600 (1975)	29,000 (1975)

Source: Renmin Ribao, November 2, 1973, January 13, 1975

The lack of adequate attachments was also causing problems in the effective utilization of tractors. As a result, many tractors could only perform a small proportion of the designed operations.[27] The extremely slow growth in tractorized acreage also attests to this problem. It was estimated that a minimum of eight attachments to each tractor would be required for the economic utilization of the machine (Z. Lu, 1978, p. 37). However, there was only an average of 2.6 attachments to each tractor as of 1977 (Editorial Department of Nongye Jixie (Agricultural Machinery) (ed.), 1978, p.103). The distribution of attachments among collectives which owned tractors was also uneven.[28]

Khan argued that the availability of spare parts in the rural areas was not a serious problem as many agricultural machines were produced at the local level and he further argued that communication was fairly developed in the rural areas (Khan, 1976, p.22). However, it was probably because of the fact that most spare aparts and attachments were to be produced locally that problems arose. It was not because local industry was not in a position to find out what was needed, and not because there were greater difficulties in transporting the locally produced goods to the final users. It was because of production input problems, financial arrangements as well as technical factors that had prevented satisfactory progress in the supply of sufficient spare parts and attachments. There were cases where county factories were reluctant to make attachments even when pressured (SWB, FE/W701/A5, November 29, 1972). Most local factories found it unprofitable to make spare parts and attachments because of the small batch and the large varieties involved (Renmin Ribao, November 13, 1972, November 13, 1975; Hubei Renmin Chubanshe, 1975, p.82; Xie, 1976, pp.19-22). In addition, the technical requirements would normally preclude many countyrun enterprises from production of a large number of attachments. Furthermore, it had always been more difficult to obtain finance and materials for production of attachments and parts (SWB, FE/W723/A6, May 9, 1973).

The attempt in 1973 to strengthen the supply of spare parts and attachments relied mainly on the First Ministry of Machine-Building to ensure better material balance in the production plans. However, that would not be sufficient because there should also be a corresponding increase in investment for productive capacity for that purpose. In the 'success' case of Shandong Province, where a desirable ratio of attachments to machinery was said to have been achieved, 58 per cent of the investment on small agricultural machinery was earmarked for the manufacturing of attachments and spare parts (Renmin Ribao, February 26, 1973). With all the drawbacks associated with producing attachments and spare parts, it would be most unlikely that other local government and its enterprises would devote such a high share in the investment for attachment and spare part production.

Finally, it should be noted that hand tools were still widely used in many places even where the degree of mechanization was quite high. However, with the expectations of the advantages (some were misconceived) from using machinery, the production of hand tools had at times been neglected so that occasional shortages did occur

(Renmin Ribao, June 16, October 7, 1975; X. Xue, 1977, pp.18-23). In theory, most of the hand tools could be manufactured by simple equipment in the county factories and commune workshops. But the real problem was the neglect of designs and research efforts devoted to the improvement of existing models and to the making of new ones to suit the local conditions and the ever changing patterns of farming.

The Provision of Repair and Maintenance Services

In spite of the intensified promotion during the 1971 Mechanization Conference (Renmin Ribao, August 18, 19, 21, 24, 30, September 1, 2, 1971), progress in establishing a repair and maintenance delivery system among the rural collectives was not remarkable. The rate of breakdown in agricultural machine operation was running at a high level of 30 to 40 per cent (Zhan, 1979-b, p.9).

During the period of the Fourth Five-Year Plan, two systems for providing repair and maintenance services had been used. The first system, dominant during the first two years, involved industrial enterprises in extending and organizing repair and maintenance services to rural collectives. The second system involved the building of repair and manufacture networks with participation by the county as well as its communes and the brigades. The two systems seem to have co-existed since the beginning of the period, with the second system gradually becoming the more dominant form.

The first system basically required county factories connected with the manufacturing of agricultural machinery and implements to devote part of their resources and manpower to provide repair and maintenance services for the communes. Agricultural machinery factories were also expected to provide such services at the factories when machinery was brought in from the communes for servicing. However, the unique feature of the system was that these factories had to actively extend and deliver these services to where the machinery was used, i.e. to the communes, brigades and teams. They were to organize mobile service teams touring the rural collectives and performing repair and maintenance services (Renmin Ribao, February 19, 23, 26, April 5, July 22, August 24, 1971; September 25, 1972; August 26, 1973). Existing evidence suggests that this system was mainly used at the times and in those places where rural collective agricultural machinery enterprises were still in the initial stage of development or were still to be established.

There were certain obvious problems for the system of the mobile service teams to be widely adopted. First of all, the quality and regularity of the services provided could not be guaranteed. Major repair and overhaul would still have to be performed back in the factories. Furthermore, there was no guarantee that the mobile service team would be staying in those places where services were most urgently needed since there appeared to be no effective co-ordination among all the participating enterprises or organizations and the whole exercise seemed to be ad hoc in nature. From the point of view of the enterprises or units which provided such mobile service teams, there were few material benefits to be gained from such operations. On the contrary, they had to divert their valuable resources and technical manpower, with the additional cost of travelling, while their revenue from supplying the services would be low because of the low price they could charge.

The second system for the provision of repair and maintenance services required the setting up of permanent repair facilities within the communes by the communes. It was a system of repair and manufacture with the division of work according to the level of administration. In general, it was known as the agricultural machinery repair and manufacture network. The network usually had three levels, although in some places it had a four-level organization (with the direct participation of the prefecture-level administration). In essence, this three-level system attempted to strike a workable balance for division of work between the county, the commune and the brigade in the effective provision of repair and maintenance services. With the rapid establishment of repair and manufacture enterprises in most counties and the economic policy favouring unified management to utilize resources, the county was placed at the centre of the network. While over 90 per cent of the counties were claimed to have established repair and manufacture network systems, there is no indication as to the percentage of communes and brigades that joined these schemes.

The counties were to provide not only the more complex repair and maintenance services, but also to produce equipment and parts for the commune and brigade level workshops. Thus, the success of the network depended largely on the efforts and initiatives made by the county level. However, unlike the first system of mobile service teams, the financial burden of acquiring repair facilities at the commune and brigade workshops would be borne by the rural collectives themselves. Figure 4.1 presents a schematic outline of the functional organization of the three-level repair and manufacture network. The management and control aspects of the network will be analysed in the next chapter.

Such a network, based on a division of work according to the level of administration, necessitated the supply of machine tools and repair equipment to the permanent collective workshops if the functional role of each level could be carried out effectively. In fact, apart from satisfying the objective of utilizing local resources and attaining self-financing, one raison d'etre for the setting up of these networks was to provide on-the-spot repair and maintenance service with minimum delays. It should be noted that land transport to and in the rural sector remained inadequate.[29] Thus, locally and readily available services were a necessary condition for the success of any agricultural mechanization effort. In order to achieve that, it was thought that commune- and brigade-run workshops had to be equipped with certain equipment and machine tools.

The equipment and machine tools installed in the workshops were determined by the assigned function for the different levels of the workshops. In general, the commune workshops were to perform medium repairs, while the brigade performed only minor repairs.[30] However, there might be exceptions. For instance, in Wuxi County, a very rich region, the commune workshops were expected to perform major repairs while the brigade attended to medium repairs (Peking Review, August 19, 1977, pp.34-5).

Figure 4.1:   *Functional Organization of the Three-Level Repair and Manufacture Network for Agricultural Machinery*

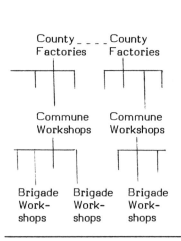

Major repair and overhaul. Production of accessories and attachments. Training of technical personnel for commune and brigade workshops.

Medium repair. Production of small tools and implements. Repair of small and medium machinery and tools. Training for brigades.

Regular check up and maintenance. Repair or manufacture of small agricultural equipment and hand tools.

Source: See Appendix A

The operational guideline for the network was that while both repair and manufacture were to be promoted, the emphasis should be placed on repair (F. Lin, 1976, pp.69-70). The target for the network was to reach a stage when major repair could be done within one's county, medium repair within one's commune and minor repair within one's brigade (Renmin Ribao, September 9, 1971; Jiang and She, 1975, p.87; Z. Ji, 1977, p.73). In some counties, it was claimed that tractors could be repaired with locally made parts such as crank shafts, gears and bearings (SWB, FE/W794/A15, September 25, 1974).

While the network concept was being promoted and extended after 1972, the practice of sending mobile service teams by the county- or urban-based enterprises continued. This happened even in those areas where the network system seems to have been well established (Renmin Ribao, April 19, 1974; November 13, 1975; SWB, FE/W766/A1, March 13, 1974; Bureau of Agricultural Machinery Administration, 1975, p.18). The continued practice of sending mobile teams could be regarded as a complementary measure to the development of the three-level network. Those teams were actually an important vehicle in the domestic technological transfer process (see, for example, Sigurdson, 1972, 1973, 1977). The collective workshops' services were often ineffective due to lack of adequate facilities and insufficient parts. Thus, some production teams were not even willing to take their machinery to the collective workshops for repair but insisted on having their machinery repaired by the county factories (Renmin Ribao, February 2, 1972). The truth was that the network system had not developed to a stage where all required services could be satisfied from within the network.

As late as 1977, only 40 per cent of all the county agricultural machinery enterprises were reported to be capable of providing major repair and overhaul services for agricultural machinery (Editorial Department of Nongye Jixie (Agricultural Machinery) (ed.), 1978, p.105). In other words, it implied that more than half of the existing county agricultural machinery enterprises could not even carry out their assigned task of providing major repair services (see Figure 4.1). Furthermorewhile industrial enterprises for repair and manufacturing of agricultural machinery could be found in 96 per cent of the counties, regardless of their effectiveness, the number of communes and brigades which had actually set up industrial enterprises of any kind was much smaller and the geographical distribution of these rural collective enterprises was not even.

As of 1975, 90 per cent of the communes and 60 per cent of the brigades were reported to have established enterprises, including those dealing with agricultural machinery repairs, totalling 800,000.[31] Of this total, 120,000 were concentrated in Hunan Province (Editorial Department of Nanfang Ribao (ed.), 1975, p.88). It is interesting to compare these percentages with the estimates of electricity availability to communes and brigades contained in Table 4.5. The two sets of figures suggest that availability of electricity to the rural collectives may have been a determinant of the success in setting up the repair network.

Thus, what determined the supply of rural electricity might also have a significant impact on the functioning of the network which was one of the most important aspects of the agricultural mechanization process during the period. Of course, this is not to suggest that electricity supply alone was sufficient to explain the pattern of agricultural mechanization. What is implied is that the management organization and control over resource flow in the rural sector, such as those over the availability of electricity, certainly played a vital role in shaping the direction and pace of agricultural mechanization.

Whether it was the system of mobile service teams, or the three-level network (and its variation), the county was the centre which had to bear the responsibility and initiative in putting these systems into reality and making them effective. In many ways, the two systems were complementary to each other, particularly at a stage when neither of them could meet the demand on its own.

In summary, while in terms of organization and institution, the repair and manufacture of agricultural machinery was gradually being brought into more established form, the complementary production of attachments and spare parts was not making sufficient progress. This, together with a failure to develop an acceptable management system for the use of agricultural machines (to be discussed in Chapter 5) had led to the sub-optimum utilization of agricultural machinery. The problem of providing adequate attachments and repair services was certainly also a reflection of the effect of general production policy on the development of agricultural machinery industry.

THE PURSUIT OF SELF-RELIANCE IN AGRICULTURAL MACHINERY PRODUCTION

Since the mid-1960s, the objective of developing comprehensive industrial systems at the provincial level has gradually been pushed forward along with some changes in the material allocation system, financial arrangements and plan administration. Mao in 1966 started to advocate the building up of provincial capacity in making their own agricultural machinery. The idea had been adopted and was affirmed by the 1971 Mechanization Conference.

During the Fourth Five-Year Plan period, the concept of self-reliance as applied in the sphere of agricultural machinery production was to establish a varying degree of self-sufficiency in the ability to produce agricultural machines by the different levels of local government, i.e., the province, prefecture and county. This section will investigate the forms and developments in the pursuit of local self-reliance during the period.

Development of Self-Reliance in Local Production

To a large extent, the success of the network system for provision of attachments and repair services was dependent on the ability of the county to have a ready supply of the necessary machine tools and production inputs. This in turn often hinged on the degree of success of the province or county in building up its own basic industries. In order to understand better the local production set-up, it is worthwhile to examine first the practical meaning of self-reliance for the various levels of local government.

At the county level, self-sufficiency generally meant that the county government was able to produce a number of machine tools, drilling machines, planers, electric welding machines, etc. for the commune and brigade-run agricultural machinery workshops (Renmin Ribao, January 31, 1971). In other words, self-sufficiency was the necessary condition for setting up the three-level network system of repair and manufacture. In turn, such a level of self-sufficiency in the counties depended on the progress made in developing their five-small industries.

At the prefecture level, self-sufficiency seemed to centre on essential materials, such as steel products, which most individual counties would have found it impossible to make on their own. For this purpose, a 'small steel complex' (xiao-gang-lian) would be established in the prefecture to produce a part of the steel requirement for making agricultural machinery.[32] Therefore, self-sufficiency would mean that factories within the prefecture should be able to manufacture agricultural machinery with some locally-produced essential materials.

At the provincial level, self-sufficiency meant an ability to produce a relatively full range of agricultural machinery (SWB, FE/W711/A/10, February 14, 1973; SWB, FE/W752/A9, November 28, 1973; SWB, FE/W803/A13, November 17, 1974; Bureau of Agricultural Machinery Administration, 1975, p.43; Renmin Ribao, August 1, 1978). Furthermore, in producing such machinery and other modern agricultural inputs (such as chemical fertilizers, cement and insecticide), the province would have to be able to supply self-produced materials (such as coal, iron ore, etc.) and machine tools (Renmin Ribao, January 7, 1971; SWB, FE/3887/B11/3, January 13, 1972; SWB, FE/W749/A9, November 7, 1973). Of course, all that was supposed to be done according to the local conditions, i.e., taking due account of local resource availability and local demand. In general, most provinces would still attempt to establish a certain heavy industrial capacity, including an ability to produce major agricultural machinery such as internal combustion engines and tractors though the more complex such as carburettors, fuel injection equipment, electrical and hydraulic components would normally be produced at selected centralized plants.[33]

Within the provincial system, there gradually emerged some pattern of division of work by levels of government for the manufacture of agricultural machinery. This was carried out according to a loose network for division of work between the central and local government. It should be pointed out here that this division of work between central and local governments was not a complete one and that it was mainly concerned with production arrangements while the broader central control mechanism of all enterprises via wage fund and production targets did not change.

Thus, in principle and in practice, more complex machines with greater horsepower were generally built by factories directly funded and controlled by the state, simpler machines with smaller horsepower were produced by enterprises run by localities. For instance, production of tractors over 30 h.p. and hand tractors of 12 h.p. and over was normally financed and managed directly by the state. Indeed, most of the larger and more complex tractors continued to be produced by a handful of state enterprises which were scattered in various parts of the country. They included, for example, the tractor plants of Luoyang, Shanghai Fengshou, Jiangxi, Tianjin, Zhangchun, Shandong, Liuzhou and Anshan (Renmin Ribao, November 15, 1977).

At the same time, a much larger number of local enterprises largely run by the province, prefecture, county and commune were making a wide variety of agricultural machinery and accessories. Figure 4.2 illustrates in a general schematic representation the ways a tractor could be manufactured, or really assembled, by factories under direction and organization by various levels of local

Figure 4.2:   *Alternative Organizational Arrangements for the Production of Tractors*

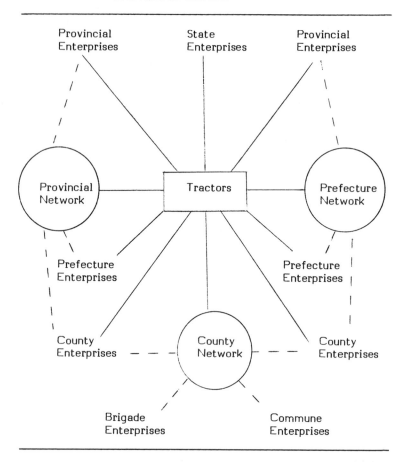

government and planning authorities. Such a scheme would also be applicable to the production of many other machines such as water pumps or engines. The diagram indicates a broad static framework, but it does not show, for example, the relative importance in terms of output quantity for each alternative arrangement at a certain point of time and over time. Nevertheless, within the provincial system, a relatively stable working relationship, with some kind of work division, seems to have been established. Some provinces had progressed at such a pace that, by the end of the Fourth Five-Year Plan period, they were able to produce complete sets of farm machines and implements, complete sets of equipment and tools for making walking tractors, diesel engines, equipment sets for equipping small chemical fertilizer plants and electricity generation.[35]

By 1975, all provincial level governments were reported to have built their own heavy and light industries, varying in the degree of development, and to have achieved a higher degree of selfsufficiency in industrial products and manufactured consumer goods (SWB, FE/W821/A12, April 9, 1975). In 1971, there were only 20 provisional level governments which were claimed to be able to manufacture hand tractors and small power engines (SWB, FE/W654/A2, January 5, 1972; Renmin Ribao, October 1, 1971; Peking Review, No.1, January 7, 1972, p.17). By 1975, not only all the provincial level governments were said to be producing hand tractors, but 24 of them could also make big tractors (SWB, FE/W885/A1, July 7, 1976). However, it is not clear how many tractors, big or small, were actually produced by each province.

It is appropriate to consider here the question of the increasingly enhanced role played during this period. It was reported that, since 1971, some provincial governments had started to let their prefecture governments take over the administration of a number of industrial enterprises previously controlled directly by the provinces (Renmin Ribao, January 7, 1971). An underlying economic reason for the emergence of the prefecture as an administrative unit to assume the responsibility of making major agricultural machinery (hand tractors, diesel engines) seems to rest on the desire to utilize better the productive capacity of the county factories and on consideration of scale economies. The purported scale economies, however, appear not to have been substantiated by systematic investigation by the Chinese government.

One important issue needs to be considered here. Although conditions might vary in different places, it was not known nor was it carefully examined by the Chinese government whether the provinces (or indeed the central government), rather than the prefecture, would have been better suited to gain any economies of scale in the production of various machines. Although the prefecture level was starting to gain some prominence in the manufacturing of agricultural machinery, this did not seem to have undermined the importance of the county. For most of the cases, the real responsibility and execution still rested with the counties. The prefecture could be viewed as an intermediary for the province and county, acting as an additional administrative organ which co-ordinated and set rules for practical local selfsufficiency. The use of the prefecture as a unit to organize agricultural machinery production was nevertheless still at the initial stage.

In fact, even in a province where this kind of development seems to have made substantial progress, there were still many counties which continued to make agricultural machinery (e.g. hand tractors) with their own facilities and resources (Hubei Renmin Chubanshe, 1975, p.96). For instance, counties such as Wuxi in Anhui Province, Xinhui in Guangdong Province, Zunhua in Hebei Province continued to develop their own production capacity for diesel engines and tractors (Peking Review, August 19, 1977, pp.34-5; Xie, 1976, p.27; SWB, FE/W726/A8, May 30, 1973). Indeed, during this period the county was supposed to develop the 'five-small industries', one of which being agricultural machinery. Therefore, it was not unusual to find counties setting up agricultural machinery plants of their own, especially when they had built up basic industries such as steel, coal and chemical fertilizer production (Jiang and Shu, 1975, p.87).

Apart from power-driven machinery, the main items of production from the county factories were supposed to be medium and small hand tools to meet the increased demand as farming became more intensive and diversified due to development of agricultural production following increased mechanization (Xie, 1976, p.88). The importance attached to semi-mechanized and hand tools had been stressed all along.[36] With the majority of localities still dependent on non-power driven tools and implements, the fastest way to provide these rather specialized items would often come from the local county factories. For example, the production of urgently needed ditchers could be made by county factories quickly and at a fraction of the price that would have been charged by the central enterprises.[37] In another case, ditchers were produced at short notice whereas production by the central enterprises was said to need three years. In yet another case, because of the urgency of fighting drought, iron water pipes under trial production by the county factories were turned into mass production even though the production cost could not yet be brought down and loss had to be incurred (Bureau of Agricultural Machinery Administration, 1975, pp.634). The primacy placed on grain production therefore ensured that the county factories had to meet the demands associated with such an objective even at the risk of loss and quality control.

In summary, while there was some kind of work division between central and local enterprises, each province had gradually moved to establish an agricultural manufacturing capability with varying degrees of success. Within the provincial manufacturing system, the county was the basic unit of operation. Though progress was uneven, the county could in general provide a portion of the small agricultural machines and tools for use within its territories. The county also participated in a province- or prefecture-wide network of machinery production. The county produced simple equipment and machine tools for the agricultural machinery workshops at the communes and brigades. In terms of co-ordination and organization, evidence suggests that the prefecture governments began to play a greater role in the local production network.

The Collaborative Production Schemes

While the pursuit of local self-sufficiency in the production of agricultural machines and tools was no doubt a primary objective, the arrangements of production organization to achieve this could take different forms. There were basically two types of formal production arrangement within the local context. There were the large enterprises with a high degree of vertical integration, a legacy from the Soviet models of the 1950s. However, over the years during the Fourth Five-Year Plan period, a new form of production arrangement for agricultural machinery emerged and it had been tried in a number of localities and at different levels of the local government. It was generally known as 'collaborative production' (xie-zuo-sheng-chan), or sometimes referred to as 'socialist collaborative production'. Since this new development was an important experiment in the modernization process and is at present being adopted in a greatly modified form and in more extensive scale as part of enterprise reforms, it would be worthwhile to examine this new development more closely.

In essence, the collaborative production scheme resembles loosely a horizontally- integrated system of factories. Such schemes were usually conducted and co-ordinated by the province, prefecture or county government in a local regional context. The local government, such as the county administration, would organize existing industrial enterprises into some formal association, which was likened to a huge assembly line, so that each enterprise would turn out components to be assembled in a 'head' factory. However, neither the management, finance, manpower nor the overall supply and marketing activities of the individual enterprises would be affected by this kind of participation.

Early in 1971, the idea of a collaborative scheme was promoted at the provincial level in a number of industries which included light industries, machinery industries and mining equipment industries (Renmin Ribao, January 2, March 31, June 2, 1971), with the most notable example in China's largest industrial centre Shanghai City. The aim of the socialist collaborative production scheme was to establish production capacity for certain urgently needed machinery within a short time (Renmin Ribao, January 14, 1971; SWB, FE/W781/A11, June 26, 1974). Although the practices in each case differed, the collaborative production schemes during the period possessed some common characteristics.

First, at whatever the level where the collaborative scheme was operated and controlled, once the scheme was established, it could be certain that materials, labour and the necessary finance for the participating enterprises, especially those chosen as the 'key factories' would be guaranteed, i.e. they would receive priority in obtaining their supplies (Hubei Renmin Chubanshe, 1976, pp.18-9; Xie, 1976, pp.33-4; SWB, FE/W814/A14-5, February 19, 1975). However, the channelling of resources for this purpose was only done within the jurisdiction and control capability over the resource flow that rested with the coordinating level of the local government. In practice, such production schemes would involve as much co-ordination at the controlling level of the government organization as among the participating enterprises.

As an illustration, consider the attempt by Jianli County (Hubei Province) in setting up a county-wide collaborative production scheme. In establishing a collaborative scheme for the production of boat-type tractors in the county, enterprises under the following organizations of the county government were to be involved: the office of agriculture and the office of industry of the revolutionary committee; the planning commission of the county; the agricultural-machinery bureau; the bureau of supply and marketing co-operative; the bureau of industry; the bureau of resources and materials; and the bureau of transport (Hubei Renmin Chubanshe, 1976, pp.18-9). In other cases, a special task force might be set up by the co-ordinating government to take over the coordinating work under the supervision of the initiating government.

Secondly, a collaborative production scheme often necessitated complex arrangements for the flow of physical and financial resources. Since a coordinated scheme often involved factories under controls of different ministries or departments,[38] some formal arrangements had to be made between ministries and enterprises regarding the processing of inputs and movement of semi-finished goods. Normally, the co-ordination and control were placed under the ministry that was responsible for the enterprise, or 'head factory', which assembled the final product. For other participating factories, they were required to leave the management of production, supply and marketing for the parts and components which they made for the scheme to the coordinating ministry or unit (J. Wu, 1978, pp.25-31). However, this applied only to the production of components for the scheme; the participating factories would still be under the control of their original ministries so that the structure of management organization in each enterprise hardly changed.

It appears that the local administration which initiated collaborative production schemes had little freedom to change the price of the finished products which had to be sold at the level set by the state. However, it was necessary and possible to manipulate the internal transfer prices of components and parts produced by the participating factories for the assembly factory. There existed some broad guidelines for the fixing of an internal transfer price structure. The principle was that these transfer prices should provide adequate 'incentives' to all enterprises participating in the scheme, they should enhance better utilization of the factories' capacities and they should improve the standard of management and should lower costs. Lowering costs, however, was ambiguous because it was not stated which parties should lower costs and how.

Changzhou City started to operate a collaborative scheme for hand tractor production early in 1975 (F. Tan, 1975). In Changzhou's scheme, the internal transfer prices of diesel engines, gears, shock absorbers and three other major components were allowed to be reduced by 10-20 per cent below the state prices. To accommodate the price reduction, the profit targets for those factories producing the components were adjusted so that, it was claimed, the larger volume of output due to the participation in the scheme would still generate an overall increase in the absolute amount of realized profit in the affected factories (Lin and Liu, 1978, pp.51-2; J. Wu, 1978).

Based on available information, the pricing arrangement adopted by Changzhou seems to be the only clear-cut policy then in existence. For instance, for the collaborative schemes in Yunnan and in Liaoning Provinces, while production contracts were used to fix the supply of components to the 'head' factory, no specific pricing arrangement had been installed except for the vague understanding that the transferring of commodities should be done according to the principle of equal value of exchange (Renmin Ribao, June 14, 1973; July 30, 1974).

Thirdly, many of the collaborative schemes that have been attempted seem to be of a temporary and ad hoc nature. The participating factories normally would not specialize completely and permanently in producing the assigned component for the scheme (except in the case of the final assembly plant). Many schemes were actually set up because there was a sudden or urgent need to produce agricultural machines such as irrigation and drainage equipment (Renmin Ribao, May 2, 1974), high-pressure sprayers (Hubei Renmin Chubanshe, 1975, pp.60-1), winnowers, water pumps, water pipes, electric motors (Liaoning Renmin Chubanshe (ed.), 1973, p,9), husking machines, crushers (Hubei Renmin Chubanshe, 1975, p.86), and diesel engines (SWB, FE/W809/A13, January 15, 1975). When the urgency subsided, the scheme would be discontinued. In fact, different urgent needs might be dealt with at different points of time, and some localities might have to meet a different urgent need each year. This type of operation is certainly not unfamiliar to students of non-market economies in which the 'storming' technique might be applied when deficiency or sudden upset in supply or demand occurs in material balance planning.

Apart from the possible gain in scale economies, the original reason behind the establishment of such schemes was to utilize the existing capacity in the participating factories to turn out products which would otherwise be impossible without new investment or new plants. Idle capacity in the participating factories could of course change easily. Thus, stable relations in such collaboration were not guaranteed. The temporary nature of such schemes also prevented the participating factories from becoming more specialized in their production.

This modest attempt to use co-ordinated schemes for production during the period did encounter some technical obstacles which had to be resolved before further development was possible. First of all, an appropriate and workable control and management system had to be installed to organize effectively the many enterprises under different ministries. This task was complicated by the need to work out an acceptable price structure for the internal transfer of intermediate inputs.

If transfer prices were set at too low a level, the participating enterprises would find it difficult to generate sufficient revenue to achieve the profit target. On the other hand, if the transfer prices were not lowered (compared to the state prices), particularly in cases where many stages of intermediate inputs were involved, the additional tax and profit thus charged at each stage by the participating factories would mean a very high aggregate cost for all the components and therefore make the operation of the assembly plant financially uneconomical. Indeed, the aggregate of all intermediate input prices might well have exceeded the price of the finished product which was fixed by the state and could not be altered by the co-ordinated scheme.

The scale of operation might pose another problem. When the varieties and number of components were large and the production run for each was small for each participating factory, there would be little incentive for the factory to produce them. This was especially so when there was the risk of having to produce them at a reduced profit or even a loss because of lowered transfer prices. Thus, some factories considered the participation in such schemes as a burden (Renmin Ribao, January 21, 1971). Because of this, reluctance to continue involvement which caused delays in production or even withdrawal from participation in the scheme could result in serious disruptions.[39] That was probably why 'socialist' collaboration was promoted so that the interest of the state was emphasized.

Another issue was the lack of specific regulations governing the financial arrangements associated with the supply or transfer of manufacturing equipment between participating enterprises. This problem was particularly significant in regard to transfers of production facilities from government enterprises to commune or brigade enterprises which were becoming more common participants in such schemes (J. Wu, 1978, p.29). Indeed, collaborative schemes would undermine the overall planning control over resource flow if there were no systematic and uniform rules or procedures to follow. Since it often involved a transfer of products as well as production equipment between enterprises under separate planning authorities, gaps in meeting demand could easily arise. Worse still, some enterprises had abused the scheme by engaging in unauthorized expansion or diversification of output and entering into 'self-serving' collaboration with one another.[40]

In summary, while the collaborative scheme could potentially be an effective way to utilize existing productive capacity to bring about faster growth in agricultural machinery output within the context of local self-reliance, there were many unresolved problems. As the network system was being promoted as a practical way to advance agricultural mechanization, the success in making collaborative schemes work would have been a positive complementary force.

CONCLUSION

While there had been notable growth in the aggregate outputs in some agricultural machines, the overall development in terms of mechanizing agricultural production was not remarkable. There were large gaps between the output growth of machines and accessories and there was a serious problem in achieving effective utilization of agricultural machines. Progress in employing machines for field operations and water conservancy works appears to have proceeded relatively faster in the north than in the paddy fields of the south.

The establishment of local manufacturing capacity for agricultural machinery, basically at the provincial level, appears to have been achieved though the development has not been evenly distributed. The whole agricultural machinery industry, whether it is in the national or local context, has not been very successful in delivering a comprehensive range of products including appropriate attachments and spare parts in sufficient quantities.

Despite the fact that local manufacturing of agricultural machinery was promoted as an integral part in the pursuit of self-reliance, much of the development remained dependent on the plans and actions of the central government. For instance, major items such as larger tractors, axles, machine tools and energy sources for the machines were dependent on state supplies.

Under the general objective of applying more economic methods to production and construction activities, measures were taken in an attempt to incorporate increased economic rationality which would at the same time promote self-reliance in production. As a result, the concept of division of work and specialization for scale economies was tried in a limited form. Thus, a certain degree of division of work between local regions such as the prefectures, and within the local framework, also began to emerge in the realm of agricultural machinery production.

The collaborative production schemes were organized as a specific means to enhance selfreliance in production while attempting to satisfy the criterion of economic calculations. These schemes were expected to be set up without any significant increase in investment and were aimed at utilizing the existing slack capacity to obtain economies of scale in production. In practice, such schemes can really be regarded as a kind of 'model' building exercise in which resources were concentrated to guarantee speed and results and which were often used to meet some sudden and urgent needs in agricultural production. Indeed, the uneven distribution of progress among collectives and localities in their rural development might suggest that model building could have in practice been carried out on a national and regional scale. And such an exercise would certainly not be incompatible with the spirit of more unified control and applying economic methods for maximum effect.

Hence, during this period, though progress in mechanization was not spectacular nor was it meant to be, there appeared to have been no apparent urgent need to engage in an immediate national programme with mass campaigns (which was initiated by the First Dazhai Conference) to raise the speed of agricultural mechanization. There was certainly rapid development in the establishment of local repair and manufacture network systems involving the rural collectives in a direct way. However, the mass movement during the period was clearly centred on the farmland improvement projects which could be regarded as a pre-condition for the gainful introduction of agricultural machinery on a larger scale provided the projects were designed and constructed properly.

The local network system was a vital element in the efforts towards agricultural mechanization during the period but seems to have failed in carrying out its designated functions. It might be argued that the resources devoted to setting up a rather ineffective network system could have been better employed in other more profitable activities and that alternative ways to perform the functions of the network system might thus be better paid for. However, the cost and benefit of the exercise probably need not be determined in simple terms. As part of the relations of production which was then perceived to enhance the desired objective of self-reliance and to diminish the disparities between rural and urban conditions, the role of such systems could not be discounted and seen only in terms of agricultural machinery utilization. In addition, the benefit from the technology and skill acquired from participation by the rural collectives would need to be considered.

The pattern and trends in the physical flows of agricultural machinery and repair services were examined in the context of development in production in this chapter. However, under China's economic system, these patterns and trends were also a product of the financial system as well as the organizational and institutional structures that governed the production and flow of goods in the economy. Thus, having discussed a facet of the mechanization process in the context of machinery outputs, the other aspects of the process are examined in the following chapters.

NOTES

1. See B. Stavis, 1978-b, p.636. Stavis found that complex patterns involving multiple cropping and intercropping were widely practised, but that there were very few tests to prove that the two quick crops yield more than one slow big one. Stavis saw that only as a general weakness in research methods which failed to have systematic field experiments to prove the validity of this practice. This, in fact, involved more than just research method, as it reflected the general approach to economic development at that time.

2. See, for example, Bureau of Agricultural Mechanization, Ministry of Agriculture and Forestry (ed.), 1976, Volume 1, p.50; Xinzhou County Communist Party Committee, Hubei Province, 1974, p.2. Observers of Chinese agriculture had also worked out some desirable sequences of mechanization for the various farming operations. Khan's scheme: (1) land development, irrigation, (2) food and fodder processing, (3) transportation, (4) threshing, (5) land preparation, (6) paddy transplanting, (7) harvesting. Timmer's scheme: (1) processing basic food grain, (2) land preparation, (3) mechanical transplanting, (4) harvesting. See Khan, 1976, p.18; Perkins et. al., 1977-a, p.118; Timmer, 1976, pp.55-9.

3.   Renmin Ribao, October 12, 1975. However, it should be noted again that, after the Cultural Revolution, the concept of using agricultural regions for differentiated development was not favoured.

4.   For more details see the following chapters.

5.   Jian-ming nong-ye ji-xie-hua ci-dian (Concise Dictionary of Agricultural Mechanization), 1977, p.454. In general, tractors were classified as large, medium or small-size according to the h.p. of the engine. Those over 50 h.p. were termed large tractors, with 20-50 h.p. medium tractors and under 20 h.p. small tractors (p.377).

6.   For instance, the Hunan Tractor Works construction began in 1971 and it was completed and started to produce in 1975. SWB, FE/W860/A14, January 14, 1976.

7.   It was claimed that the number of tractors in use in 1975 was 4.7 times that of 1965. Since the Chinese media normally used the term tractors to mean conventional tractors and generally refer to hand tractors separately, this reported increase would thus apply to conventional tractors. From Table 2.1, the number of tractors in use in 1965 was estimated to be 130,500 standard units. Thus, the estimate for 1975 can be derived. See, SWB, FE/W885/A1, July 7, 1976; K. Chao, 1970, p.109. If the recently released figures for 1977 and 1978 are correct, then the claim for 1975 might have been exaggerated. For the figures on 1977 and 1978, see note 8.

8.   The official figures for annual production were 99,300 and 113,500 standard units for 1977 and 1978 respectively. The numbers of conventional tractors in use for each of the two years were 467,000 and 557,000 standard units. State Statistics Bureau, 'Report on the results of the 1978 National Economic Plan (June 26, 1979)', Renmin Ribao, June 28, 1979. During the year, there had been only a small number of machines imported. See China Business Review, 1978, 1979, passim.

9.   Ibid. Annual outputs for 1977 and 1978 were 320,500 and 324,200 units respectively. The numbers of units in use for the two years were 1,090,000 and 1,270,000.

10.   In general, small hydroelectric stations are defined by a generating capacity of less than 6,000 kw, while a medium hydroelectric station has a capacity of less than 50,000 kw. SWB, FE/W881/A7, June 9, 1976; Perkins, et. al., 1977-a, p.107.

11.   Renmin Ribao, December 27, 1977. This means that a great majority of the small hydroelectric stations were concentrated in a quarter of the total number of counties.

12.   They were the Guangdong and Fujiang Provinces in South China. For Guangdong, the percentage was 30 per cent while it was 40 per cent for Fujiang. SWB, FE/W845/A20-21, September 24, 1975; SWB, FE/W849/A9-10, October 22, 1975.

13.   In other words, the optimism expressed by some observers over China's electrification of the countryside via small hydroelectric plants needs to be qualified. See, for example, Norton Ginsberg, 1977, p.360.

14.   For instance, the author was told by the cadres of Wuhan Steel Works, one of China's biggest iron and steel complexes, that steel output could be increased by over 40 per cent if

sufficient supply of electricity were available. Mr Yang, Office of the Revolutionary Committee of Wuhan Steel Works, interview on December 27, 1977.

15. Renmin Ribao, June 13, 1976. Indeed, only about 130 counties were equipped with generating capacity of 10,000 kw in their medium hydroelectric stations.

16. Since the units of measurement in the tables were different, they need to be standardized for comparison. The conversion rate is 1 h.p. = 0.736 kW. See, N.R. Chen, 1969, p.45.

17. Renmin Ribao, June 16, 1976. It should be pointed out that, in another official statement, it was reported that the number of wells equipped with power between 1974 and 1977 was equal to the total of the past 24 years, 1949 to 1973. In both cases, however, the increase was actually from 1974 onwards. Zhong Guo Duiwai Maoyi (China's Foreign Trades), No.2, 1977, p.6.

18. Department of Water Conservancy (ed.), 1976, p.106. However, the quality of the claimed 5.9 hectares per well in 1975 is not clear. For instance, the number of days which the wells operated each year is not known.

19. The target of the Revised NPAD was 60 million hectares. C. Tan, 1960, p.89.

20. Commentator of Hongqi, 1978, p.32. It should be noted that this target of 63.3 million hectares for 1985 was a downward adjustment of a target set earlier in the same year. In February 1978 the target was to achieve 66 million hectares by 1980. See for example, Peking Review, No.8, February 24, 1978, p.10.

21. Giles, 1975, pp.16-7. Giles expressed power input as the horsepower utilized per hectare in field operation through three power sources: human, animal and mechanical.

22. Perkins et al., 1977-a, p.135. However, it is not known from what information and method the estimate was obtained.

23. Giles, 1975, p.20. Giles found the following pattern for the distribution of agricultural power:

Region	Percentage of available power per hectare			
	Total h.p./ha	Human	Animal	Mechanical
Asia (excluding China)	0.22	26%	51%	23%
Africa	0.10	35%	7%	58%
Latin America	0.25	9%	20%	71%

24. Calculated from the estimate in Table 4.10. From personal observations in China, the assumption of 50 per cent may have been overestimated because in many collectives which were claimed to have achieved basic mechanization, manual work was still predominant. The reason is that, at this stage of mechanization, as

argued earlier, the sole purpose was not to replace labour but to increase land productivity.

25. See Tables 4.1 and 4.2. It was also claimed that, between 1966 and 1976, conventional tractor output achieved an average annual growth rate of 20.3 per cent, while hand tractor output achieved 46.4 per cent. However, the precise meaning of outputs was not given. Renmin Ribao, December 24, 1977.

26. Renmin Ribao, July 28, 1978. The quality of output was also said to be poor.

27. Renmin Ribao, November 13, 1972, January 7, 1975; SWB, FE/W710/A5, November 29, 1975; Xinzhou County Communist Party Committee, Hubei Province, 1974, p.52; Bureau of Agricultural Mechanization, Ministry of Agriculture and Forestry (ed.), 1976, Volume 1, p.11).

28. Xinzhou County Communist Party Committee, Hubei Province, 1974, p.86. Some collectives might have up to 20 attachments to each tractor while some might have less than 2.5. It appears that the advanced units or models generally have a greater number of attachments.

29. It was reported that only 77 per cent of all the communes in China were accessible by motor vehicles in 1974 (83 per cent in 1976), and that only 50 per cent of brigades were joined by highways. Again, accessibility was only limited to the seats of the communes and brigades administration. SWB, FE/W759/A15, January 23, 1974; SWB, FE/W893/A11, September 1, 1976.

30. See Figure 4.1. It may be necessary to define what the different classes of repair (i.e., major, medium and minor) mean so as to understand better the implications for the setting up of the network. For major repair, it means that, at fixed intervals, thorough and complete repair of the machine be made so that all technical specifications and economic targets for the machine can be reached. For example, in the case of tractors, major repair means that the engine plus most of the components of the chassis are to be taken apart, checked, repaired and replaced with new parts when required. When all parts were reassembled, testing and adjustments are to follow. As for medium repair, it involves mainly the repairing of a machine's parts and components which are subject to faster wear and tear. The objective is to enable the machine to achieve normal functioning between two major repair services. Again, using tractors as an example, medium repair requires a complete disassembling of the engine and its thorough checking and adjustment, then repair and replacement of damaged components with testing afterwards. In addition, there is checking and adjustment of the transmission system, the rear axle and the moving parts; partial disassembling and replacement of damaged parts if necessary. Minor repair really only involves some regular check-up and repair of small and simple machinery items and hand tools. Jian-ming nong-ye ji-xie-hua ci-dian (Concise Dictionary of Agricultural Mechanization), p.3.

31. Editorial Department of Nanfang Ribao (ed.), 1975, p.88. There is no breakdown on how many were repair workshops for agricultural machinery.

32. For example, Changwei Prefecture in Shandong Province. Renmin Ribao, September 20, 1975; Hubei Renmin Chubanshe, 1977, Volume 3, p.47.

33. Perkins (ed.), 1977-a, p.143. In fact, during a visit to China in 1977-8, the author was told that the Luoyang Axle Plant supplied more than half of the country's need for construction of tractors and other vehicles.

34. Renmin Ribao, June 23, 1979. Perkins and others observed that large four-wheel tractors of over 20 h.p. size and the larger four- and six- cylinder diesel and gasoline engines were produced by national or provincial factories; and that small one - or two-cylinder diesel and gasoline engines, smaller four-wheel riding tractors of less than 20 h.p. power tillers were produced at country- or city-managed plants. Perkins (ed.), 1977-a, p.143.

35. For instance, Jiangsu, Shandong and Zhejiang Provinces were all reported to have achieved this. SWB, FE/W798/A16, October 23, 1974; SWB, FE/W871/A8, March 31, 1976.

36. See Renmin Ribao, September 17, 1971; Renmin Chubanshe (ed.), 1972.

37. Renmin Ribao, May 25, 1973, July 27, 1973. However, the county factories obviously did not go through thorough trial testing before mass production.

38. For instance, in Guangxi Autonomous Region, 70 enterprises belonging to 7 different ministries and departments participated in the collaborative schemes for producing tractors. SWB, FE/W854/A14, November 26, 1975.

39. Therefore, in Changzhou, there were rules laid down to prevent sudden withdrawal of participation by individual enterprises. Wu Jiapei, 1978, p.29.

40. Renmin Ribao, 1977, 1978, passim. For details on the material allocation system used in the period, see Chapter 5.

Chapter Five

CONTROL AND MANAGEMENT OF AGRICULTURAL MECHANIZATION

The pursuit of modernization in China involved more than just solving the problems of what to produce and how much to produce. It posed a series of equally important questions on how the whole production process should be structured. Whereas resource endowments and technical requirements played an important role in shaping the pattern and pace of the modernization process, the objectives concerning how production should be organized, to which production units and by what mechanism and criteria inputs and finished goods were to flow also played a significant part in determining the pattern and outcome of the process.

After 1966, these objectives had become so predominant that they had often set the boundary in which technological and material production were to take place. Though there was increasing policy emphasis being placed on applying economic methods after 1972-3, it was not equivalent to a diminishing of the role of central planning in resource allocation. Physical plans still played the major role in determining the flows of inputs and finished goods, with the price mechanism for commodity exchange playing a subdued function. In general, the form of organizational, institutional and control structures was an integral part of China's economic policies and measures during this period.

As far as agricultural mechanization was concerned, the technical aspects of production had been very much linked, indeed often subordinated, to the desirable forms concerning the controls over resource flows, the management of agricultural machinery and the financing and ownership patterns in the process itself. Thus, the means, or the control mechanism, were often inseparable from the ends which incorporated more than pure economic objectives.

In broad terms, the control mechanism can be conveniently identified by its basic elements: direct and indirect policy measures. Direct control measures involved the transferring and distribution of resources and goods via physical and financial planning with the use of targets, allocations, compulsory sales and so on. Indirect control measures included actions such as manipulation and restriction of market exchange for commodities, and rules and regulations on various production activities.

The purpose of this chapter is to analyse the general mechanism of resource allocation that was relevant to the supply and production of agricultural machinery, and the management system under which the experiment in agricultural mechanization was carried out during the period 1971-5. However, because of limits of space, a comprehensive study of the control and planning mechanism of China's economic system is not attempted here.

CONTROL MECHANISM FOR THE FLOW OF INPUTS AND GOODS FOR AGRICULTURAL MECHANIZATION

The pattern in the flow of inputs for the production of agricultural machinery and the flow of the finished goods cannot be separated from the objective of building a relatively independent industrial system in each province. The flow of inputs and outputs in China generally had to go through a number of vertical and horizontal channels which were administered and controlled by various separate government agencies. The whole process of making and supplying major agricultural machinery was a highly controlled operation. How those controlled channels functioned will be the subject of investigation in this section.

First, the general features in the material allocation system of the economy will be examined. This will be followed by a study of the way agricultural machines were actually allocated and supplied to the end users. It should be noted that the analysis in this section is general in nature, for the mechanism can be applied to sectors of the economy other than agricultural machinery.

Control Over Flows of Material Inputs

In order to understand the forces determining the production of agricultural machinery, it is necessary to investigate the supply system of material resources and goods in general as the system has been a critical factor in affecting the pattern and outcome of production. The main focus of this investigation is on the actual channels and framework for the flows of material resources underChina's economic system. For the purpose of this study, it will examine how the supply system worked in relation to making agricultural machinery available. The discussion here is mainly concerned with what the Chinese planners called the material allocation system and with its development.

Based on Soviet procedures, material allocation has been a critical device in China's economic planning system. In this way, the use of the material balance table to determine material allocation had been a principal instrument. Allocation plans were formulated on the basis of balance between resources and final needs achieved through the compilation of the table (S.Zhou, 1955, pp.30-3; see also Eckstein, 1978, Chapter 4; Y. Wu, 1965).

During the First Five-Year Plan, the distribution of materials was placed in a strictly centralized vertical command framework. The first major reform of the system of economic planning and management came in 1957 and 1958. Increased power and expanded responsibilities were given to the provincial governments. As for the supply system, a number of significant changes were pronounced. Under the principle of unified planning and decentralized administration, new regulations were enacted (Central Committee of the CCP and the State Council, 1958-d).

First, after fulfilling the state plan's targeted transfer of essential raw and processed materials, equipment and consumption goods, the provincial government was allowed to allocate materials within its region; except for a small number of items for which approval from the state had to be obtained for local use, a portion of the above-target output for some essential commodities could be kept by the local government for its own distribution. The portion would be determined by an 'appropriate' sharing ratio.

Secondly, under unified national planning, the system of material transfer and allocation would be mainly administered by the provinces and be mainly balanced within the provinces (Central Committee of the CCP and the State Council, 1959, p.100).

Thirdly, having fulfilled the assigned targets for production, key construction projects, new fixed capital investment and materials to be transferred for use in other areas, the provinces, municipalities and autonomous regions were allowed to distribute and make adjustments in the use of the materials allocated by the state.

Thus, in addition to vertical controls through central ministries, local governments, namely the provincial-level governments, were given the task of co-ordinating and planning the production and supply arrangements of enterprises within their territories. This reform was accompanied, among other things, by a reduction in the number of commodities under unified central distribution (see Table 5.1), and by devolving control of industrial enterprises to provincial government.[1] By the end of 1958, only about 13 per cent of the previously centrally controlled enterprises continued to be so, and the number of commodities under direct central distribution was reduced by 75 per cent (J. He, 1979, p.39). However, of the enterprises devolved to the provincial government, many were actually placed under dual rule, i.e., they were controlled jointly by the central and provincial governments.

The importance of this development was that horizontal 'blocks' based on the administrative region (i.e. province) were superimposed onto the existing material allocation system which was basically a vertical command system based on sectoral division. Within these 'blocks', the provincial government was to take up increasing control of the intra-provincial distribution of commodities by adopting a scaled-down version of the vertical command distribution system. The provincial economic plans and material distribution schemes included not only enterprises under local or joint control, but also those enterprises with continuing direct central administration.

101

In brief, the national economic plan, then, was to be drawn up by integrating the ministries' plans and the provincial governments' plans. However, it was clear that the reform was not meant to give complete autonomy to local government. Lardy argued that,

> in spite of increased provincial authority in economic planning, particularly in manpower and commodity distribution, there has been substantial continuing central government control of basic resource-allocation decisions, particularly planning of production, commodity supply and investment (Lardy, 1978, p.141).

This was reflected, for example, by the fact that almost the entire output from the machinery industry remained under central control (Lardy, 1978, p.140). However, though the centre's power in exercising control over commodity flow, especially over inter-provincial transfer, continued, the establishment of the horizontal networks of administration had laid the foundation for the subsequent pursuit of a more self-sufficient industrial system at the local level.

In line with the emergence of horizontal partitioning in economic planning, organization for the supply system also changed. After 1958, specialized corporations which had previously handled commodity distribution covering several provinces were abolished (D.Yang, 1979, p.11). Secondary Supply and Purchase Stations, previously under provincial government administration, were 'sent down' to be managed by county commercial bureau.[2] A significant consequence of this development was that the boundary for the flow of commodities became increasingly constrained by the additional levels of administrative regions such as the counties. The establishment of horizontal 'blocks' often prevented flows of goods between provinces and between counties. These administrative regions, for all purposes, were often not the natural economic or trading regions.

With the readjustment policy coming into force after 1961, unified central control was emphasized again. The degree of autonomy in the management of manpower, finance, industry and commerce previously given to the provincial government was thus reduced. As far as enterprise control and the allocation and distribution of materials were concerned, the pattern prevailing in 1957 was said to have been basically restored by 1963 (J. He, 1979, p.37). In May 1962, an attempt was made to reestablish and expand specialized commercial corporations operating on a national level (State Council, 1962, pp.138-40). In September of the same year (1962), a proclamation was enacted to allow inter-regional flow of resources according to economic regions (Central Committee of the CCP, 1962).

However, the vertical structure of the central ministries had by then grown in such a selfsustaining way that corresponding agencies and branches at every level of the local government had been established. The skeleton of an integration of horizontal and vertical structures for material allocation had already been set up, although the power of the horizontal partitions was thus reduced. Therefore, the recentralization did not fundamentally change the new form of material flows. Even in the May 1962 resolution, it was stated that the system would still continue to operate under the dual structure of vertical ministry and horizontal local government administration (State Council, 1962).

The move to organize material flow according to economic regions, as against administrative territories, seems to have had only very limited success. In 1963, about 200 counties, or less than 10 per cent of the total number, were said to have broken through provincial boundaries in organizing their purchase and supply flows of commodities (D. Yang, 1979, p.11). On a national level, little had been changed. Nevertheless, the experience of Tangshan Prefecture (in Hebei Province) in eliminating inter-county barriers for the flow of commodities was officially promoted as a model and was said to have been tried in some 56 prefectures in China with good results.[3]

Perhaps the most remarkable step in the endeavour to improve efficiency in commodity flow might have been the ill-fated attempt to establish national trusts. National trusts, by definition, would have resulted in a pattern of commodity flow not bound by any territorial restrictions. It should be noted that these 'recentralization' measures were designed in accordance with the policy of using economic methods to achieve fast recovery and growth in production. The objective was clearly stated:

> the first priority for the supply of materials and equipment should be given to key industries and enterprises, so that the limited amount could be utilized for greater economic results. Proportional allocation without assigning priorities will, broadly speaking, lead to waste (Editorial, <u>Renmin Ribao</u>, November 14, 1961).

In order to facilitate reaching the objective of centralizing and unifying management of the country's material resources, the State Bureau of Material Management was established in March 1963 (State Council, 1963). A year later (October 1964), the Ministry of Allocation of Materials was reported to have been set up (Donnithorne, 1967, p.523).

At the same time, material allocation conferences were being used as a practical means to help distribute and balance material supplies via the vertical structure of ministry control.[4] Such regular conferences brought together suppliers and users of certain commodities from all over the country. Normally organized by the central ministries on a sectoral or commodity basis, the conference would arrange a system of fixed supply relations among enterprises and set out details for their co-operation in production (X. Wang, 1964, p.52; S. Wang, 1964, pp.29-36; Liang and Zhang, 1964, p.40; Richman, 1969, pp.712-20). Long-term supply contracts were drawn among the participating enterprises to serve as the formal link. In this way, these conferences also provided a mechanism for continued central government control of inter-provincial transfers of

103

resources. However, not all materials required for production were handled in such conferences, and there was no evident enforcement mechanism for the contracts thus signed (Liang and Zeng, 1964, p.63; Renmin Ribao, April 2, 1963).

During the Cultural Revolution, few details were available on the development and changes in the system of material allocation. But given the rapid development of local industries, and the political conditions prevailing in the 1970s, it is reasonable to assume that there had been a shift away from building a more centralized and vertical framework. In fact, by the end of 1969, the movement to hand over more responsibility for material allocation to the regional governments had reached a stage where some action was required to formalize the arrangements.[5] Again, this move to enhance the local regions (provinces) did not mean that the vertical structure for material allocation was to be abandoned. What it really meant was that vertical structures were practically instituted in a regional context.

Some ideal combination between vertical and horizontal structure was sought. That, in effect, led to a period when a variety of material allocation channels co-existed for different regions and for different commodities.

Table 5.1:   *Number of Commodities Under Direct Central Distribution*

Year	Number
1952	28
1953	112
1957	231
1958	417
1959	132
1964	370
1966	357
1972	146
1978	53

Source: *For the years 1953, 1957, 1966 and 1978: S. Wang, 1979, p.118; for 1952, 1958, 1959: Lardy, 1978, p.146; for 1964: S. Zhang, 1979, p.16; for 1972: J. He, 1977, p.37.*

In 1970, major new changes to the system of material allocation were formally introduced (Yang Deying, 1979, p.12; He Jianzhang, 1979, p.37). The changes took place at the same time as changes were made in investment policy, enterprise management and budgetary arrangements. The changes signalled a formal reversal of commodity allocation policies that had prevailed during the early 1960s, particularly those of 1964 and 1965. As a result, an 'overwhelming majority' of enterprises were decentralized to local control so as to 'restrengthen' local Party Committees and their centralized leadership over economic work and thus 'playing an outstanding part in industrial development' for the region (X. Deng, 1975-6 p.99, (The 18-points)). The proportion of critical materials planned for allocation by the local government has gradually increased. By 1978, about 28 per cent of steel products, 35.9 per cent of cast iron, 66.6 per cent of coal, 22.7 per cent of timber, 48 per cent of ferrous metals, 32.8 per cent of motor vehicles and 32.4 per cent of machine tools were reported to be under local allocation plans.[6]

The essence of the 1970 change was that, under the unified control of the centre, planning would be carried out mainly by the provinces while this local horizontal framework was to be integrated with the vertical structure controlled from the centre (J. He, 1979, p.37). As indicated in Table 5.1, the number of centrally distributed commodities was thus greatly reduced. Perhaps even more important was the report that almost all the centrally managed enterprises, such as the huge Anshan Steel Works or Daqing Oilfields, were also placed under local control.[7]

As far as material distribution was concerned, the 1970 reform strengthened not only the role of the provinces in building up their own system, but also that of the lower level governments. For instance, in Henan Province in 1970, not only was the power to allocate materials devolved to the prefectures, but the commercial profits from such commodity transactions were also assigned to the prefecture government (Renmin Ribao, March 31, 1978; Renmin Ribao, January 7, 1971; Hubei Renmin Chubanshe, 1977, p.13). At the same time, the majority of provinces had given up the management of secondary supply and purchase stations to their prefecture level government (D. Yang, 1979, p.12). Thus, with a vertical structure functioning within each horizontally partitioned administrative region, commodity flow had to go through each hierarchical level and region before it could reach the final users. For example, materials from one county could not go directly to another (even if neighbouring) county if they did not come under the same authority such as the same prefecture.

Having reviewed briefly the development in the formal organization for material allocation during the 1950s and 1960s, the situation of the 1970s can be studied against this background. It should be noted that, though not all materials had to go through the formal allocation and supply system, most of the input materials for the production of agricultural machinery did.

During the Fourth Five-Year Plan period, the basic principle for material allocation was 'unified central control' and 'decentralized administration'. In practice, materials were distributed in three basic forms (Zheng-zhi jing-ji-xue jiang-hua: she-hui-zhu-yi bu-fen (Talks on Political Economy: Socialism), 1976, pp.163-4):

    (1)   Centrally distributed materials. They were allocated directly by the state's planning organs under a unified scheme. Materials with critical importance, such as steel, copper, major machinery and generators belonged to this group.

(2) Ministerially distributed materials. Important materials with functional linkages and specialized materials were distributed and balanced by the central ministries in charge.

(3) Locally distributed materials. Materials not included in the above two groups were to be distributed by the provincial government concerned.

Such groupings of materials indicate clearly the characteristics of an integration of vertical and horizontal structures in the material allocation system.

The actual physical flow of the materials seems to follow three main routes. First, under the central plans, a fixed supply relationship was established among some enterprises so that goods could be shipped directly to the user-enterprises (J. Zhou, 1976, p.29). Secondly, supplies could be distributed by the material bureaux or departments at various levels. For any one enterprise, some materials might come through the vertical channels (from various levels of ministry branches) and some might come through horizontal channels (i.e., from the allocation given to the local governments).

Thirdly, enterprises could arrange supplies for themselves when there was a discrepancy between their requirement and their allocated quantities. Within the permitted areas, enterprises were supposed to be free to exchange materials or products among themselves under such situations.[8] In addition, in the case of specialized items in very small quantities, enterprises could buy directly from state commercial establishments.

Thus, the material allocation system during the period could be regarded as one in which there was considerable regional autonomy in deciding how to use allocated material supplies. However, the central government continued to exercise control over a wide range of commodities and over interregional (provinces) transfer of materials. Within the provincial system, a vertical structure based on smaller administrative regions (prefectures and counties) was the prevailing form. No more national material conferences seem to have been held during the period. In fact, it was reported that after 1966, even smaller-scale material conferences covering just a number of provinces and cities had already ceased.[9]

Because of the different sources and varieties of materials which any enterprise might need for production and with the cessation of material conferences, the practice of employing purchase agents (cai-gou-yuan) became very common in many enterprises.[10] Travelling around the country, the purchase agent's function was to chase after the supplies of materials which might have been promised allocation by the ministries, by the local governments, by the provincial conference or which were yet to be found.[11] The agent's work could either be part-time or full-time, but it seems that there were always a number of full-time agents in an enterprise. The number of full-time agents employed by each enterprise, from the limited evidence available, appears to have ranged between five and twelve often regardless of the size of the workforce of the enterprise (Mr Li, Xinhui County Agricultural Machinery Factory, Interview, December 23, 1977; Mr Li, Secretary, Office of Revolutionary Committee, Guangzhou (Canton) Heavy Machinery Works, Interview, December 21, 1977). Furthermore, the use of purchase agents was not limited to state (central, provincial or county) enterprises but also extended to collective (commune, brigade) enterprises (Renmin Ribao, May 29, 1978).

In such a mixed system of material allocation, it is perhaps not difficult to appreciate why agricultural machinery production (and repair services) had been organized on a regional basis with its own complete vertical hierarchy and with an increasing degree of self-sufficiency. Due to the fact that materials for spare parts and attachments probably did not have the same priorities as essential inputs for machinery production either in the horizontal or vertical channels, progress made in the provision of an adequate and effective service network for the repair and maintenance of agricultural machinery had thus been much slower. Furthermore, because of the limited range and quantity of material supply that each subprovincial regional government could command, the emergence of collaborative schemes of agricultural machinery production might offer a viable solution to ease the difficulties posed by lower-level regional material allocation and still achieve some self-sufficiency.

The Allocation and Distribution of Agricultural Machinery

Under the unified purchase and distribution system, output from enterprises should in principle first go to the higher planning authority for unified distribution. Except with special approvals, enterprisemanagement had no formal authority in the disposal of its output. In other words, production and distribution were separate and were carried out by different organs.

Although the number of centrally distributed commodities had been greatly reduced during this period, the local provincial governments continued to take responsibility for unified distribution within their administrative regions. Thus, as in the case of grain output, the central government was directly involved in the inter-provincial flow of essential materials, leaving their intra-provincial distribution mainly to the provinces.

As far as the distribution of agricultural machinery was concerned, it was ultimately the rural collectives which acquired the majority of the outputs since no groups or individual peasants were allowed to own major machines (such as tractors) at that time. In this regard, the county-level administration played a major role in getting the machinery for the county as well as in deciding how it was to be allocated and delivered. In general, whether the products came from allocation by the central ministries or from enterprises producing for the province, agricultural machinery supply would be centralized first in the provincial departments or companies which specialized in the allocation of agricultural machinery (Bureau of Agricultural Machinery Administration, 1975, p.65; SWB,

FE/W716/A1-2, March 21, 1973). From these departments and companies, machinery would then be passed downward through the hierarchy of the various levels of local government.

To outline the supply mechanism of agricultural machinery in actual practice, the allocation of one of the most important items, tractors, will be examined here. In general, the production teams were the main customers for small hand-held type tractors. The brigades and communes would acquire mediumand large-size tractors with their own reserve funds or with direct contributions from their member production teams.[12]

The collective that wished to acquire a tractor first had to file an application for its purchase with the appropriate higher level of authority, which would in turn activate a chain of applications through the collective system to the local government hierarchy. The disorganized and hectic rush by some communes and brigades to acquire tractors during the late 1960s was not repeated.

The decision on which commune (or brigade or team) should get tractors and at what time was firmly in the hands of the lowest effective rung of this link, i.e., the county government. There were reported cases where the county government might allocate tractors to communes which had not lodged a request or which had not yet found the necessary funds to make the purchase.[13] With the county also being the centre of the local repair and manufacturing network, it seemed quite natural that the county would also have the greatest influence over the distribution and delivery of agricultural machinery to the rural collectives under its jurisdiction.

FINANCIAL AND CREDIT CONTROLS ON AGRICULTURAL MECHANIZATION

While the material allocation system determined the ability of an enterprise or of a region to obtain inputs for the production of agricultural machinery, the supply system of agricultural machinery exerted an influence on the pattern and speed of acquisition of such machines by the rural collectives. In a centrally planned economic system such as China's, the financial control system, which reflected the patterned flow of financial resources rather than physical goods, had been installed as a necessary and complementary mechanism for the control of the flow in physical resources.[14]

The central-local budgetary arrangement, and the financial arrangements between manufacturing enterprises and the governments, were important elements of China's financial system. As in the case of material allocation, the financial system of the 1970s was also placed under the principle of 'unified central control and decentralized administration' (Zhu and Xiang, 1979, p.16; Lardy, 1978). The system was different from the one installed during the First Five-Year Plan period in which all revenues and expenditures were centrally administered by the state.

As discussed, that early system of strict central control was reformed in 1958. With the severe downturn of the economy following the Great Leap Forward movement, a higher degree of centralized control was again restored. During the Cultural Revolution, decentralized administration had been greatly enhanced, though the precise extent is not known. However, it was disclosed recently that because of a tightening up of central control over all revenue and expenditure in 1968-9 (similar to the measures of the early 1960s), yet another reform in financial control was initiated in 1970 (Zhu and Xiang, 1979, p.17).

The financial reform in 1970 coincided with the reform in material allocation discussed earlier. This financial reform was indicative of the emphasis and determination placed by the government to pursue a 'walking-on-two-legs' policy and to build up 'small and comprehensive' industrial systems at the provincial level quickly. The essence of the 1970 financial reform was the increased local share in the revenue-sharing scheme and the increased freedom of the local governments to dispose of their own revenue (Li and Wu, 1978).

Thus, commensurate with the change in the material allocation system, the provincial governments gained a greater degree of financial freedom to arrange and expand production within the province. Another notable development was the rapid expansion in local industries, which was partly made possible by the relaxation in control over their financial resources.[15] A significant factor accompanying this development was the deterioration in the ability of the People's Bank to carry out a strict supervisory role over the supply of funds and loans to the local governments and their enterprises (Ta Kung Pao, April 24, 1978; Renmin Ribao, July 4, 1978).

The diminution of the supervisory role of the bank was caused by several factors. Although the People's Bank was theoretically a monopoly financial institution that acted as the only clearing house for all transactions and as the distributor of state funds and loans, there were many difficulties in fulfilling all its assigned functions. It is beyond the scope of the present study to look into the whole issue but two features need to be noted.[16]

First, it should be noted that the People's Bank had little discretion in granting credit for working capital (Hsiao, 1971, p.207; Donnithorne, 1974, p.18), as the bank was obliged to provide funds for any activity included in the approved economic plans.

The experience of the Great Leap Forward showed that in times of strong political pressure for higher output, all controls could be denounced as bureaucratic. Thus the credit funds to the banking system from the national budget in 1958 and 1959 got completely out of hand.[17] Secondly, the bank in itself had little quantitative control over loans in general, and the alternative to the bank was defensive, i.e. to absorb money already in circulation via measures such as the promotion of economizing campaigns (for materials and stock clearing) and rural saving campaigns.

The factors affecting the supervisory role of the People's Bank during the early 1970s were not divorced from the general difficulties outlined above.[18] First of all, the supervisory role of the bank during the period from 1970 until 1972 suffered as a result of the policy that made financial works subordinate to the needs of production. Therefore, when the banking institution's activities in checking and controlling the activities of enterprise came under attack as bureaucratic and oppressive, the supervisory function of the bank was weakened (Cai, 1971; Renmin Ribao, September 19 and July 20, 1971 and November 13, 1978; Writing Group of Ministry of Finance, 1972, pp.68-9). Thus, in the name of developing local industries, the bank had in some cases permitted illegal usage of funds. For example, enterprises used working capital for fixed investment or for unplanned diversification in production (Y. Gong, 1975; Renmin Ribao, April 22; July 20, 1971; S. Wang, 1978, p.34).

The loosening of supervision of financial management during 1970 to early 1972 also occurred in the rural sector. In dealing with the rural collectives, branches of the bank were also asked to give loans according to the 'actual needs' of agricultural production. In that way, the existing rules for loans and credits were sometimes discarded. For instance, in Xiangtang County of Hebei Province, in order to 'support' agricultural production, basic loan policies such as the following rules were discontinued by the county branch of the People's Bank (SWB, FE/W689/A1, September 6, 1972).

(1) No loans to a unit (of the rural collectives) for the purpose of purchasing machinery not included in the unit's current-year plan.

(2) No loans to an insolvent brigade or team.

The extent of such 'de-regulation' cannot be estimated, but it would have certainly provided an impetus to the development of rural collective enterprises.

However, the apparent failure of the bank to supervise effectively did not mean that everything was out of control. The situation in the 1970s was not the same as in the Great Leap Forward movement. Rather, it meant that the local governments had, in many instances, been able to expand their manufacturing activities by switching some uses of enterprise funds. This was feasible because local planning was given a certain leeway as a means to stimulate local initiatives.

The most important financial variables, such as total wage funds and fixed capital investments, were still made through direct budgetary process by the Ministry of Finance. The share of working capital, which was one of the main sources for local manipulation, remained relatively small (M. Xue, 1979). In fact, during the period, all profits and most part of the depreciation funds were remitted back to the central government for reallocation (though not necessarily in a physical sense) (Zhu and Xiang, 1979, pp.15-6; C. Liu, et, al, 1979, p.46). Therefore, the revenue retained by provincial government was not large and was said to be just sufficient to cover administration expenses and some fixed capital investment and social services. Since targets for local governments' budgetary revenue and expenditure were still assigned by the central government almost item by item every year, the size of mobile funds in each province was thus limited. Lardy's study also presented evidence that attests to the central government's ability to control the interprovincial transfer of fiscal and material resources (Lardy, 1978, pp.142-3; Lardy, 1975-a, 1975-b).

To conclude, some remarks on the development of credit institutions in the rural sector are in order. In general, the main source of finance in the rural sector did not come from grants from budgets of the various levels of government.[19] As Chapter 6 of this study will deal with the question of financing of agricultural mechanization, an attempt will be made here to investigate the various rural financial institutions through which central control was exercised.

First, a note on the past attempts to set up a national financial institution for rural development. Up to 1975, there had been three attempts to establish a specialized bank for the rural sector. In 1951, the first attempt was made to establish the Agricultural Cooperative Bank; the second attempt was in 1955 to establish the Agricultural Bank.[20] Both attempts did not last more than a year. In 1963, a third attempt was made, this time to reestablish the Agricultural Bank, being part of the readjustment policy during that time. The primary function of this specialized bank had always been intended to be an instrument whereby agricultural production could be raised through the centralized organization of savings and investment in the rural sector (Hsiao, 1971, pp.41-50). In this way, resources from within the rural collectives could be mobilized for the promotion of agricultural growth. However, in 1965 that third attempt was also abandoned.[21] Since the Agricultural Bank had been organized under the People's Bank, when it was abolished in 1965, its operations were to be subsumed by the People's Bank. In fact, one of the reasons why the Agricultural Bank was dissolved was that many of its daily operations were not clearly designated and distinguished from those of the People's Bank and the latter was reluctant to release resources and manpower for the operations of the Agricultural Bank. At the level of the rural collective, the function was performed by the associate of the People's Bank, i.e. the commune credit co-operative.

In theory, the commune credit co-operatives were an economic undertaking and they were thus collective organizations owned by their members and not a government organ. However, at the time when the commune was formed in 1958, it was stipulated that its credit co-operatives were to be at the same time the local business office of the People's Bank (State Council, 1958-b, p.158; Hsiao, 1971, p.60). Therefore, the People's Bank could exercise direct control over their operations. Although little information is available on the development of the credit co-operatives after the Cultural Revolution, it seems that progress has been rapid (Renmin Ribao, November 22, 1974).

111

In the 1970s, the rural credit co-operatives assumed a very significant importance. By 1974, it was reported that almost every commune had set up credit co-operatives and that one-third of the production brigades had also established credit service stations (Renmin Ribao, November 22, 1974; SWB, FE/W805/A2, December 11, 1974). A rural financial network was therefore said to have been formed.[22]   Two significant features about this network should be noted.

First, during 1971 to 1974, the main recipients of rural loans had changed from individual member households to the collectives, i.e. the communes, brigades, and teams. In 1974, 88 per cent of the loans from the credit co-operatives went to rural collectives and their sub-divisions for expanding collective production, with only 12 per cent to households or individuals.

Secondly, about 60 per cent of the credit co-operatives, during 1974, were able to provide all or most of the loans needed for production purposes by the rural collectives. In 1974, the total amount of agricultural loans supplied by rural credit co-operatives in Jiangsu Province was 46 per cent more than the amount provided by the People's Bank (SWB, FE/W807/ A4-5, January 1, 1975). Needless to say, the main source of credit funds in the credit co-operatives came from deposits by their own members.

An equally important fact was that, while the credit co-operatives were operated by the commune, they deposited all their 'surplus' money in the People's Bank to 'support socialist construction' (NCNA, November 27, 1974). In other words, the rural credit co-operatives had become the major source of production funds for the member collectives, and the credit co-operatives were in turn closely linked to the People's Bank. Thus, the government maintained control and influence over this increasingly important but nominally nongovernment credit institution.

Along with the establishment of a rural financial network, a cash control system for the rural collectives was being promoted towards the end of the Fourth Five-Year Plan. Under the cash control system introduced in the 1950s, all industrial and commercial enterprises had to have an account with the People's Bank and deposit with it all spare cash above a predetermined small amount, and all transactions were to be settled by cheques (Tsiang, 1967, p.335; Donnithorne, 1978, p.9; Cassou, 1976, pp.82-97). However, this cash control system did not appear to have been rigorously applied to the rural collectives. When Cassou visited China in June 1973, he was told that the communes, including brigades and teams were not subject to such rules and that they had access to the sum total of their cash balance (Cassou, 1976, p.87). This was also confirmed indirectly in an article by a Chinese economist, who stated that it was only during the 1970s that the cash control system was gradually extended from the cities to the rural villages and from state enterprises to collective enterprises in the rural sector (P. Yang, 1979, p.50).

In summary, while the financial control system in the early part of the period seems to have provided a certain freedom to the local governments to expand their productive capability, the dominant position of control by the centre was not seriously challenged. As far as rural financial control was concerned, the commune credit co-operative was to act as the link between the government and the rural collectives.

INDIRECT CONTROLS OVER RURAL COLLECTIVES' ABILITY TO PURSUE AGRICULTURAL MECHANIZATION

In the foregoing section of this chapter, the study focused on the broad macro-framework on which the manufacturing and availability of agricultural machinery depended. In this section, it will examine the mechanism through which control over economic activities of the rural collectives was made. With a control mechanism, the government could affect the ability of the rural collectives to acquire modern inputs including agricultural machinery. This ability consisted of the financial capability of the collectives, and the ability or freedom to reallocate resources within the collectives to attain and to accommodate the use of agricultural machinery. Therefore, the control mechanism over those relevant economic activities exerted an indirect control over the potential demand for agricultural development and mechanization.

The most important indirect controls in this respect were the constraints placed on the production mix for grain and non-grain commodities and on the activities of collective enterprises run by the various levels of the communes. These constraints will be examined here. However, it should be noted that controls over demand for agricultural mechanization were not limited to these constraints. The relative prices between industrial and agricultural output as well as the availability of complementary inputs also played an equally important part.[23] The main concern in this section is with the controls over the output mix of the collectives, which directly affects the input mix, though very often the input mix was also subject to direct governmental regulations.[24]

On paper, the production teams, or brigades in some cases, were the basic accounting units in the commune system. Basic accounting units were responsible for their own profit or loss made from their production. They nominally owned the land they cultivated and were supposed to have autonomy in making decisions on how production should be made. However, the most fundamental decisions on what to produce, and indeed how much to produce, were almost completely under the direction of the government.

Indeed, the primacy of grain output practically dictated the output and input mix for most production teams, especially those teams which were less favourably endowed and had little margin over and above their own basic grain requirement for consumption and delivery to the state. First, grain production targets, though subject to a certain degree of revision (which normally could only be upward), were handed down by the provincial government through the county to the commune and brigade then to the teams (Su, 1976, pp.108-26;

Lippit, 1977; Crook, 1975). Diversification of agricultural production was only politically feasible when the grain output targets were met.

Despite the continuous campaign to persuade government units to respect the 'rights' of the production teams and to implement Party policy since 1971, the problem of violating the property rights of the production team continued.[25] In fact, very often, those violations were not considered illegal but were regarded as a legitimate and necessary part of socialist construction. Thus, the autonomy of the basic accounting unit was often a qualified one, its property rights were pre-conditioned on complying with state plans and directions from various government agencies.[26]

Thus, the grain output target, though in theory not the actual method of production, was the primary concern of the government. In fact, most non-grain production of the commune was also placed under various controls by the government. As will be investigated in the next chapter, non-grain production determined the financial ability of rural collectives to acquire modern inputs including agricultural machinery. Furthermore, these non-grain production activities were the main determinants of the possibility and effectiveness of efforts to modernize and mechanize agriculture.

On the one hand, the possibility and profitability of these activities were the basis for reallocation of resources within the collectives, especially in the case of the redeployment of labour which resulted from the use of machinery. On the other hand, non-grain activities such as repairs and establishing infrastructure also provided the necessary support services for the effective use of agricultural machinery. It should be noted that most of the non-grain production in the commune system would be undertaken by the rural collective enterprises run at the commune and brigade levels.

In general, rural collective enterprises were set up only at the commune and brigade levels (Tianjin College of Finance and Economics, 1977, p.8). Indeed, it was essentially the existence of those enterprises that made the economic presence of the commune and brigade felt. The production teams were considered too small a unit to run their own collective enterprises although it did not mean that they could not engage in non-grain production. While conditions varied from place to place, the general rules regarding whether enterprises should be set up by the commune or the brigade were: the more capital they required, the more complex the production and the larger the area they served, the more likely they would be run by the commune administration.

In most cases, the expenditure and revenue accounts of the rural collective enterprises were consolidated into the general account of the controlling collective, i.e., the commune or brigade (Renmin Ribao, February 17, 1975; Tianjin College of Finance and Economics, 1977, p.205). Thus, the profit or loss of a collective enterprise was directly under the control of the commune or brigade running it. The profits from the operations of the enterprises were used by the collectives for investment and for subsidizing those enterprises which were, or had to, run at a loss (Bureau of

Agriculture, Revolutionary Committee of Jiangsu Province, 1974, p.31; Agricultural Office of Zhejiang Province (ed.), 1977, p.136). The profits of the collective enterprises were normally not distributed to their member households. Furthermore, the profit (or loss) of a collective enterprise was often not the most important formal criterion for justifying an enterprise's existence or judging its performance. There were cases where enterprises were closed down in spite of their high profitability. These enterprises had to cease operations if they were considered to be following a 'wrong' orientation such as not gearing themselves to the perceived agricultural production needs of the rural collectives they served or competing for supplies and markets with state enterprises (Renmin Ribao, March 28, 1972 and August 5, 1973). In some places, it was even stipulated by the local county government that profits of such enterprises should not exceed a certain percentage (Editorial Department of Nongye Jixie (Agricultural Machinery) (ed.), 1978, p.87).

Thus, though the enterprises were collectively owned and managed by the brigades or communes, they were not cut off from supervision and control by various levels of government. The basic guideline from the government for developing rural collective enterprises was that they must give first priority to serving agricultural production. The general constraint placed on rural collective enterprises was that they must not compete with state enterprises for material supplies, funds or labour (Hubei Renmin Chubanshe, 1977, p.48; SWB, FE/W799/A6, October 30, 1974).

Since 1973, the control over rural collective enterprises by local government appears to have assumed a much greater significance. If not for other reasons, the tax revenue from such enterprises alone would have been sufficient to prompt local governments to take more notice of their activities. In Liling County (Hunan Province), for example, total tax paid by rural collective enterprises to the county government accounted for 80 per cent of the county's share of agricultural tax revenue for the year and for 13 per cent of the county's total tax revenue (Renmin Ribao, July 20, 1975).

Therefore, to strengthen control over the activities of these enterprises, economic targets similar to those applicable to state enterprises started to be imposed on collective enterprises.[27] Plans for the expansion or the establishment of collective enterprises by the brigade or commune were to be approved by the appropriate department or ministry in charge in the locality. Approval had also to be obtained for the use of labour and land, for the desired scale of operations, and for the marketing arrangements of such enterprises. The control over the use of labour was especially strict. The reason for this seems to rest on the perceived need of ensuring an adequate labour supply for grain production at all times. Thus, the development of rural collective enterprises was not allowed to affect the state targets for labour, wage fund or commodity grain (Hubei Renmin Chubanshe, 1976, p.71 and 1977, p.48; X. Xue, 1977, p.25-6). In fact, the official policy after 1973 seems to have favoured the setting of a maximum percentage of the total rural labour force that could be employed by such enterprises.[28]

In order to exercise such controls effectively, local government began to establish specialized administrative organs to look after the activities of rural collective enterprises. However, the real responsibility for supervision in all cases rested basically with the county. In some cases, specialized organizations such as management bureaux for rural collective enterprises might be set up; in other cases, existing county government organizations were utilized to take up the control of the activities of those enterprises which were related to their functional responsibility (Editorial Department of Nongye Jixie (Agricultural Machinery) (ed.), 1978, pp.86-7; X. Xue, 1977, p.54).

Regardless of the forms of administrative organization, the aim was to incorporate, as much as possible, the activities of the rural collective enterprises into the system of economic planning. In this way, it was hoped that a more rational distribution of enterprises could be set up among the rural collectives under government plans (Tianjin College of Finance and Economics, 1977, p.7; Hubei Renmin Chubanshe, 1977, Volume 3, pp.45-50). In fact, the way that rural collective enterprises were being brought into the planning framework is reminiscent of the strategy used to control private industrial enterprises during the period preceding the complete socialization of industry in the 1950s.

Thus, the rural collective enterprises were to establish direct production links with the county's factories, while the collective enterprises might also receive assistance from the government in terms of equipment, know-how and materials (X. Xue, 1977, p.54). As a result, simple finished products or components, which rural collective enterprises were capable of producing, would be decentralized for production in these rural set-ups. On the one hand, this arrangement was expected to help promote the development of these rural enterprises by providing a source of technology and market outlet. On the other hand, it also placed them under control and planning.

While surplus grain output (after quota sales, tax and self-consumption) was not allowed to be sold in rural open markets, the flows of output from rural collective enterprises were also increasingly being placed under more restrictions. The abovementioned trend of linking production between state and collective enterprises was an indication of this general pattern of development. The underlying idea for the establishment of collective enterprises, like that of local industries in the counties, was to utilize local materials for local use. Therefore, output from rural collective enterprises could normally be sold within their own area for local uses. However, products which were to be sold outside the local county had to go through state marketing and supply agencies (Renmin Ribao, October 4, 1978; Hubei Renmin Chubanshe, 1976, p.84; Agricultural Office of Zhejiang Province (ed.), 1971, p.135).

By 1975, some kind of formal control system for agricultural subsidiary production was being discussed and promoted. The emphasis seems to have been centred on the setting up of special organizations such as the Office of Rural Subsidiary Production in the counties (Renmin Ribao, July 31, 1975; An, 1976, p.65; Jiang and Lu, 1976, p.29; J. Xie, 1976, p.64; Bureau of Agriculture, Revolutionary Committee of Jiangsu Province, 1974, p.80). The new organization was to promote this kind of production and at the same time regulate the inputs and output of rural subsidiary production activities whether they were carried out by the various levels of the commune system or by individual commune members. In fact, the indication was that this subsidiary (or sideline) production, was to be placed under the control of the county via the rural collective administration so that income from such activities would go directly to the collectives and not to the individuals. As a result, specialized labour teams for the purpose of subsidiary production, and even production bases, were being promoted and organized at each level of the communes (F. Lin, 1976, p.60). This move would effectively transform the nature of such production into a more permanent and regulated form of organization. This clearly would have had significant implications for the development of agriculture, including the financing of modernization of agriculture in China.

One direct consequence was that the sales and allocation of intermediate inputs for subsidiary production were to be put under the influence and control of state commercial departments. The purpose was to place this aspect of rural production under some form of planning as far as possible. Therefore, not only grain output, but collective production as well as subsidiary production were all to be brought under the control of government plans. The effect on production in the collective could therefore be quite serious if such links were ineffectual and restraining.

These developments concerning rural collective enterprises and subsidiary production were consistent with an earlier policy development towards more government regulations and restrictions of commodity exchange activities in the rural sector, particularly exchanges through the rural open market or rural fairs. The basic level of the state commercial organ, the commune marketing and supply cooperative, had been extending branches to the brigade level in a bid to supervise and control all types of commodity exchanges among rural collectives, between collectives and members and between collectives and the state (Ban-hao nong-cun dai-guo dai-xiao-dian (Do a Good Job In Running Rural Supply and Marketing Shops), 1975; Jiang and Shu, 1975, pp.78-9; Yong Dazhai jing-shen ban cai-zheng jin-yong (Use the Spirit of Dazhai to Carry Out Works in Finance), 1977, p.31). Thus, the rural supply and marketing co-operatives were urged to exercise their guidance over the supply of materials for subsidiary production and thereby 'strengthen their market control in a positive way' (Jiangsu Provincial CCP Committee, 1974).

MANAGEMENT OF AGRICULTURAL MACHINERY IN THE COMMUNE

The provision of agricultural machinery repair and maintenance service, being a necessary condition to advance agricultural mechanization, had developed from the initial phase of temporary mobile service teams to the establishment of the county-commune brigade network organization. However, the development of a management system for the use of agricultural machinery within the commune proved to be a much more difficult task.

Systems of management and ownership of agricultural machinery (then basically tractors) had been the subject of political struggle during the early 1960s. After 1966, county-run state agricultural machinery stations' machines were gradually being sent down to the rural collectives.[29] After 1968, some preliminary attempts to set up management systems for use of agricultural machinery, with the commune operating machinery stations, began to appear in some communes.[30] That signalled a move towards a system of division of work within the commune system for the management of agricultural machinery, which sought to achieve compatability with the pattern of machinery ownership in the commune.

Since the state was no longer responsible for the running of agricultural machinery in most rural collectives, the establishment of commune agricultural machinery stations[31] was an important step in the new process of agricultural mechanization. Stavis quotes an official statement which claimed that by the spring of 1972, the transition of tractors to a commune ownership system had been 'basically' completed (Stavis, 1978, p.246).

In fact, it appears that by 1970, the pace in establishing commune agricultural machinery stations had accelerated (Hubei Renmin Chubanshe, 1976, pp.57, 91; Bureau of Agricultural Mechanization, 1976, Volume 2, p.39; Bureau of Agricultural Machinery Administration, 1975, p.84). For instance, Hua Guofeng, then in charge of Hunan Province, was said to have pushed forward a programme in 1970 aiming to have 80 per cent of the communes in Hunan Province establish agricultural machinery stations (Editorial Department of <u>Nongye Jixie</u> (Agricultural Machinery) (ed.), 1978, p.121). Although there is little available information on the subject, the establishment of commune agricultural machinery stations could have provided the basis of policy formulation for the 1971 Mechanization Conference. However, while commune agricultural machine stations were being established in most places by 1972 (Stavis, 1978-a, p.246; <u>SWB</u>, FE/W693/A8, October 4, 1972; Bureau of Agricultural Machinery Administration, 1975, p.78), there was no universally adopted management system for use within the commune. Even in 1977, it was admitted that management systems for the utilization of agricultural machinery in the rural collectives were varied and confusing (Editorial Department of <u>Nongye Jixie</u> (Agricultural Machinery) (ed.), 1978, p.112). Indeed, as of 1979, about

30 per cent of China's communes had not established any system or organization for the management of agricultural machinery.[32]

The problems with building a management system for the use of agricultural machinery were many. The core lay in the difficulties of reconciling the efficient utilization of the machinery and establishing accountability of cost and benefit associated with the ownership pattern of the machinery by various levels of the communes. Unlike the repair and maintenance network, which generally provided standard services at fixed locations, an appropriate and acceptable management system for the utilization of agricultural machinery had to handle a wide variety of agricultural works with different technical and seasonal demands.

The task of a management system was further complicated by the need to balance the need for effective utilization and the property rights of the owner-members. With the development of local selfreliance in agricultural machinery production and the large number of medium and small agricultural machines such as hand tractors and water pumps, the situation in the early 1970s was made more complex. Unfortunately, though the forms of management system might vary from place to place, there is very little comprehensive information on the actual set-up of any individual system except for the case of Xinzhou county in Hubei Province.

In Xinzhou County, the form of management system for agricultural machinery was based on the pattern of machinery ownership, and the acquisition of agricultural machinery by the rural collectives was said to follow certain set principles (Xinzhou County Communist Party Committee, 1974, p.58). For Xinzhou County, it was the production brigade which had become the dominant form of basic accounting unit. While the production team was still the basic accounting unit in 239 production brigades of the county, there were 292 production brigades operating as basic accounting units.[33] In addition, there were two communes in the county which had become the basic accounting units. The pattern of ownership in the county no doubt differed from the majority of rural collectives where the production teams were the basic accounting units at that time. However, since there were nearly as many production teams operating as basic accounting units in this county, this example could still provide some valuable insights.

A system of decentralized management within the commune for the use of agricultural machinery was adopted in Xinzhou County. The first basic principle was that if the commune was the basic accounting unit, then all agricultural machines of the commune would naturally be acquired and managed by the commune, since all means of production and land would be owned by the commune as one unit. However, semi-mechanized tools and small hand tools would still be kept and used by the production teams. The second principle stated that, if the production brigade, or the production team, was the basic accounting unit, all major agricultural machinery would still be acquired and managed at the commune level, whereas medium and small machinery would be acquired and managed at the brigade level and semi-mechanized and small hand tools by the production team.

In other words, the commune level assumed the management of all major agricultural machinery regardless of the ownership pattern. The given reason was that brigades varied in size and in wealth, so that only when the commune took over the management of large machinery could the machines be utilized effectively and, indeed, be acquired in most cases (Xinzhou County Communist Party Committee, 1974, p.58). Furthermore, it was argued that the commune would be in a better position to help those poorer member brigades and teams by extending their mechanized operations. In the case of pumping stations, or large tractors, it was also argued that only the commune level would possess the necessary technical back-up and the 'leadership' to resolve the conflicts arising from clashes of interest among different units of the commune.

Table 5.2:   *Agricultural Machinery Managed by Each Level of Administration Within the Commune in Xinzhou County*

Types of Agricultural Machine	Number of Machines Managed by the Collective Administration	
	At the Commune Level	At the Brigade Level
Large and medium agricultural machinery	374 units	153 units
Hand tractors	16 units	778 units
Large and medium pumping stations	98	5

Source: *Xinzhou County Communist Party Committee, 1974, p.58*

The operational instrument of the management system were the commune agricultural machinery stations and the brigade agricultural machinery teams (Xinzhou County Communist Party Committee, 1974; Editorial Department of <u>Nongye Jixie</u> (Agricultural Machinery) (ed.), 1978, pp.107-8; Z. Ji, 1977, p.74). Though the names might vary in different places outside Xinzhou, this basic structure appeared to remain the same.[34]

Some rural collectives also established a parallel organization that specialized in the overall management of agricultural mechanization. Thus, at the commune level, there were 'agricultural machinery management stations' or 'agricultural mechanization leading groups'; and at the brigade level there were 'agricultural machinery management teams' or 'agricultural machinery service (not repair servicing) stations' (Hubei Renmin Chubanshe, 1976, p.58;

Bureau of Agricultural Mechanization, 1976, Volume 1, pp.15, 52; Shang and Xiao, 1977, p.20). The actual set-up seemed to vary in different localities, sometimes making the operational commune agricultural machinery stations indistinguishable from the agricultural machinery management stations. In practice, some of their function might not be so clearly delineated.

The functions of these specialized management organizations were to co-ordinate and to formulate regulations for the machines' operation procedures, and to plan for the deployment of machinery and labour (Editorial Department of Nongye Jixie (Agricultural Machinery) (ed.), 1978, pp.107-8). They also set targets for various operations, material consumption (e.g. fuel), maintenance and safety measures of the machinery. This specialized management organization in the commune was very much a branch of the corresponding county organization which could be regarded as the real guardian of the collective organizations.

In fact, since 1973, there have been two important developments emerging on a small scale; both could have had significant implications for the process of agricultural mechanization. The first one was the establishment of special organs by the provincial and county government for planning and supervising the management and use of agricultural machinery for the communes. The second one was the attempt to adopt a highly centralized agricultural machinery management system by the commune administration.

The establishment of specialized organs at the county, prefecture and provincial levels was regarded as a concrete measure to strengthen the Party's leadership in speeding up agricultural mechanization. As early as 1971, in an advanced model such as Xinzhou County, the Agricultural Machinery Management Bureau had already been set up to exercise unified control over the rural collectives' agricultural machinery stations and agricultural machinery teams, the three-level repair network, and material supplies for agricultural machinery (Renmin Chubanshe (ed.), 1972, p.68).

Towards the end of the period, there were places where special supervisory groups to oversee the efforts of agricultural mechanization were being set up in a province-prefecture-county framework (Hubei Renmin Chubanshe, 1976, pp.16-17; Xinzhou County Communist Party, 1974, pp.74-5, 84; Renmin Ribao, October 19, 1974; Bureau of Agricultural Mechanization, 1976, Volume 2, pp.11-2; J. Xie, 1976, p.73; Editorial Department of Nongye Jixie (Agricultural Machinery) (ed.), 1978, pp.107-8, 111; Peking Review, August 19, 1977, p.34). The objective was to bring all major aspects of the mechanization of agriculture under the control of centrally formulated plans, in which the county seemed to play the vital part.

The supervision and control over the rural collectives' management of agricultural machinery, where they existed, extended beyond the mere deployment of machines. They included controls and plans for output and labour, as well as the administration of financial and accounting matters relating to the use of agricultural machinery. Thus, in actual practice, detailed administrative procedures for the rural collectives on how to run their machines were often drawn up by the county administration from a distance (Bureau of Agricultural Machinery Administration, 1975, p.77; Hubei Renmin Chubanshe, 1976, p.57; Editorial Department of Nongye Jixie (Agricultural Machinery) (ed.), 1978, p.97). It seems highly unlikely that such procedures would be so designed to suit all local conditions.

However, the imposition of a framework of more government controls did not produce a significant impact on alleviating the inherent problem arising from the conflicts between effective use and the property rights of ownership. During the Fourth Five-year Plan period, serious problems with the effective utilization of agricultural machinery persisted. Apart from inadequate repair services and the shortages of accessories, a main cause of the problem was in the pattern of machinery ownership. Even in the case of an advanced model such as Xinzhou County, many brigades continued to run large agricultural machines. Thus, the small size of the brigade in terms of production activities and the seasonal and limited nature of grain production, for which most of the machines were built and equipped, often led to their under-utilization.[35]

While the local self-sufficiency concept promoted growth in local production on an extensive scale, the numerous machine models and nonexchangeability of parts and components aggravated the problem of under-utilization. The problem was also exacerbated by the lack of technical operators and the inadequate training programmes. Inadequate training not only resulted in turning out insufficient numbers of operators but could also undermine the quality of operators (SWB, FE/W756/A12-3, January 2, 1974; Bureau of Agricultural Mechanization, 1976, Volume 1, p.43, and Volume 2, passim). Indeed, about one-third of the whole country's agricultural machine operators did not have any formal training at all (W. Zhan, 1979-b, p.9). In this way, not only were machines not fully used, but when they were used there were frequent accidents and breakdowns because of abuse and mishandling.

Partly as an attempt to solve this problem arising from the conflict between effective utilization and ownership of machinery and partly as a medium to strengthen government control over the rural collectives' modernization and mechanization process, a highly centralized management system operated by the commune administration began to appear in a small number of advanced units in 1975. The system was known as the 'four unifications' (si-tong-yi), a centralized management system operated by the commune level of administration. Under this system, management and control, despatching of machinery, maintenance and repair, pricing and payment for machinery services were all to be placed under the unified administration of the commune level (Ma and Tian, 1978, pp.42-6; Renmin Ribao, May 28, 1977; Z. Ji, 1977, p.74; Economic Reporter, No.22, July 7, 1978, p.14).

Initially, the system was meant to be operational only during the busy farming season. The stated objective was to improve utilization and efficiency of agricultural machinery within the commune and to make mechanized services more accessible to those brigades and teams which did not own any machines. Thus, during the busy seasons, the management of all machinery owned by different brigades within a commune was to be taken over by the commune level. The ownership of the machines was supposed to remain unchanged,[36] so that revenue earned from the machines could be channelled back to the owner-brigades or teams. This, in effect, required that for each piece of major machinery, such as a tractor, a separate account be maintained in order to portion cost and revenue according to ownership.

However, during that time, even in those advanced collectives where rural collective agricultural machinery stations had been established, the accounting system of such stations was still rudimentary and in most cases not functioning properly. Normally, the revenues and expenditures of these agricultural machinery stations were incorporated into their respective commune's or brigade's general accounts. It was only from 1974 onward that separate accounts began to be kept by some stations on a regular basis (Xinzhou County Communist Party Committee, 1974, p.59; Gong and Zhao, 1979, pp.34-6). The establishment of separate accounts by the stations was a vital step in the strengthening of management as it made clear the profit or loss from the running of agricultural machinery. This was necessary because a loss from the stations was generally subsidized by profits made from other enterprises belonging to the same brigade or commune.[37] With the four-unification system, one further step towards better accountability was made as the loss-subsidy relation had to be explicitly expressed on the basis of each individual item of machinery.

However, the major advantage of this new management system was expected to be found in its economies of scale and better quality of services. Based on the experience of a number of counties in Shandong Province and Guangxi Autonomous Region, the rate of utilization of tractors was thus raised by over 30 per cent, and the rate of liquid fuel consumption dropped by 18 per cent to 25 per cent.[38] As a result of better management and utilization, unit cost of operation was reduced by half (Ma and Tian, 1978, p.46). Furthermore, since machines were used more extensively over larger areas across different brigades and production teams, the average grain yield was also claimed to have been increased markedly so reducing the disparity between advanced and backward collectives (Editorial Department of Nongye Jixie (Agricultural Machinery) (ed.), 1978, pp.94-5). Indeed, one of the professed aims of installing a four-unification system was to promote the 'bigness and publicness' of the commune system and to advance socialist large-scale agricultural production.

On the other hand, there were several problems associated with the establishment of such a system, some of which were derived from conflicts between the need for efficient management of agricultural machines and the ownership pattern in the rural collectives at that stage of rural socialization.

First, the price charged to those units using the services of the machines often did not cover the true cost of running and maintenance incurred by the owner-collectives. From the whole economy's point of view, unified use of machinery would move closer to an efficient allocation of resources given the objective of the primacy of grain. From the viewpoint of individual owner-collectives, unified use may increase total revenue from field operations but not necessarily the aggregate profits from all uses of the agricultural machinery including alternative use such as transportation.

Secondly, the very idea that the use of machinery should be centrally administered at the commune level meant that despatching would be made according to the demands of various farming operations regardless of the ownership of the machinery. Although there might have been provision that collectives which owned the machines should get priority to use them, it could not be carried too far otherwise the whole unification system would break down. With direct subsidies or credits from the commune, those collectives that did not own any machinery could benefit from the use of machinery at a low cost to them. Indeed, this really constituted a redistribution of income in favour of those collectives that did not own the machines. In some cases, machines owned by the brigades were simply taken over by the commune level in the name of unified management without any financial compensations (Renmin Ribao, August 25, 1978).

In summary, the idea of collectively run systems of agricultural machinery had been firmly established during this period. On top of this collective management system were the state organizations which appeared to be exercising increasing influence over many aspects of the running of agricultural machines within the communes. However, the essence of the old question of efficient management for maximum utilization and an appropriate form of ownership for agricultural machinery continued to pose problems in this collective system of management. The setting up of the four-unification system was an attempt to solve those problems. The attempt, though in the initial stage, was clearly part of the economic policy of 1975 that placed emphasis on more central controls over industrial and agricultural activities and on applying more economic methods. Since the 1975 First Dazhai Conference which promoted the upgrading of the basic accounting unit in the commune system, this attempt to establish a four-unification system for agricultural machinery management could be considered as one measure which would have created conditions for such a move.

CONCLUSION

The development in the local manufacturing of agricultural machinery during the 1970s owed much to the changes in the material allocation system and in the financial arrangement that had taken place since the mid-1960s. A multi-layered horizontal partitioning in the allocation of materials instituted at all levels of the local authority, coupled with the complete vertical command channels originating from the central government, produced a highly complex framework governing the flows of inputs and outputs in the Chinese economy. Using this framework, the Chinese government intended to help establish local industrial capacity while at the same time maintaining an overall control by the centre over the rural collectives. The outcome, based on the experience during this five-year period, could be regarded as a mixed one.

While many provinces did manage to make claims that they were able to produce major agricultural machines within their own territories and while nearly all counties have established their own repair and manufacture networks, the real progress and the effectiveness of such capacities have been shown to vary widely among individual localities. However, in many important areas of agricultural machinery production, such as supplying adequate accessories and repair services, the performance has been unsatisfactory. One reason for this result could be attributed to the limitations of local resources and capacity. For the individual industrial enterprise, the problem was compounded by the fact that its required materials and inputs might come from many different channels managed by separate authorities and there was no guarantee that the quantity, quality and the timing of their supplies would be co-ordinated. The promotion of collaborative schemes of production among localities, despite its shortcomings, was clearly an attempt to circumvent these difficulties.

If the goal of local self-reliance in terms of production and utilization of agricultural machinery cannot be regarded as fully realized, the exercise of government controls on a national and local context was certainly maintained. This was evidenced by the vertical command framework in the allocation of key materials and outputs and by the various controls over the rural collectives' economic activities. Indeed, not only were the production and distribution of agricultural machines thus placed firmly under the direct influence of the government, but also the provision of essential complementary inputs for the mechanization efforts. For instance, the provincial government exercised direct control over the supply of electricity to the rural collectives and over the running of small hydroelectric stations.[39] As argued in Chapter 4, these factors were important determinants for the success of any mechanization attempt.

Though there had been no lack of attempts to promote the application of economic methods in decision making, the period as a whole still belonged to the era when the development of the productive forces was not permitted to, or be seen to, dominate over some desired forms of development for production relations.[40] As it was, 'class struggles' still held the key link in the formulation and implementation of economic policies. Therefore, the whole experiment in the mechanization of agriculture cannot be isolated from the demands for self-reliance, strengthening of the collective sector, reduction of income disparities and other preconceived socialist attributes such as putting group interest before individual interest.

After some years of experience with collective ownership of agricultural machines, no satisfactory system of machine management has yet been adopted by the majority of rural collectives. The later emergence of the four-unification system might have offered greater improvement in the utilization of machinery, but the fundamental conflict with the existing ownership pattern was not resolved. Clearly, while administrative rearrangements would help alleviate certain operational problems in the employment of the machines, the many-faceted nature of the problem involves more than the lack of accessories and the failure to establish a formal system of management. It also reflects the difficulties that resulted from the increasing restrictions placed on the commune's activities. This has affected the physical aspects for the allocation of resources within the collectives as well as the viability and profitability of any attempt to pursue agricultural mechanization. Together with other financial issues involved, a one-sided approach to the whole question of promoting the utilization of agricultural machinery was not likely to succeed.

Whether it was in the flows of inputs for production or in the supply of final products, it has been shown that a centralized approach managed by various levels of government had been adopted for efforts related to agricultural mechanization. The increasing control over the physical side of mechanization should have provided a basis for the introduction of modern inputs on a more comprehensive scale to selected regions and collectives. In fact, as the following chapter will demonstrate, this gradual though not always consistently implemented move back to a more selective and preferential treatment towards the question of rural development during this period was borne out by the financial aspects of the experience of agricultural mechanization by the communes.

NOTES

1. Since the main concern of the present study is the material allocation aspect, and since the reform and its measures have been well documented and analysed elsewhere, it will not be discussed here. See, for example, Donnithorne, 1967; Perkins, 1966; Y.L. Wu, 1967; Lardy, 1975-a, 1975-b, 1975-c, 1976-a, 1976-b.

2. D. Yang, 1979, p.11. Yang stated that, by early 1962, the number of secondary stations was thus increased to 874.

3. D. Yang, p.11-2; Renmin Shouce (People's handbook), 1965, pp.528-9. However, the Tangshan experience seemed to apply only to intercounty flow of commodities.

4. It should be noted that in the 1958 reform, provision had already been made where, under special circumstances, central ministries could convene national material production and supply balance conferences. See, Central Committee of the CCP, the State Council, 1959, p.100.

5. However, information on this subject was scarce and only recently was it mentioned in discussions on the proposed changes for the economic system. See, for example, Renmin Ribao, March 31, 1978; D. Yang, 1979; J. He, 1979.

6. S. Zhang, 1979, p.16. The units of measurement for the reported proportions were not given.

7. J. He, 1979, p.37. However, it is not clear whether they were placed under complete local control or under joint control. But it seems that the likelihood of joint control was greater.

8. J. Zhou, 1976, p.29. However, it is not clear what the rules were.

9. Renmin Ribao, January 12, 1979. Although provincial level material conferences were still being conducted during this period.

10. Official explanations for the widespread use of purchase agents attributed it to the closure since 1966 of special provincial level offices which were responsible for the following up of allocated supplies, contracts and purchasing of certain materials. However, as the number of enterprises increased and the variety of materials being handled expanded, and more importantly, with the basic organization and system for material allocation changed, the use of purchase agents became popular. See, Renmin Ribao, May 29, 1978.

11. Mr Li, Cadre of Xinhui County Agricultural Machinery Factory, Interview, December 23, 1977; Mr Li, Secretary of the Office of Revolutionary Committee, Guangzhou (Canton) Heavy Machinery Works, Interview, December 21, 1977.

12. Natang zai xue Dazhai zhong kuo-bu qian-jin (Natang Brigade Marches Forward in Learning from Dazhai), 1973, p.39; Renmin Ribao, January 17, 1978; Hubei Ribao (Hubei Province Daily), November 20, 1975; Mr Li, Cadre of Xinhui County Agricultural Machinery Factory, Interview on December 23, 1977; Mr Lei, Cadre of Nancu Production Brigade Revolutionary Committee, Gongnong People's Commune (Loyang), Interview on December 31, 1977. As will be discussed, this form of tractor acquisition and management was not without problems.

13. Hubei Ribao, November 20, 1975; Natang zai xue Dazhai zhong kuo-bu qian-jin (Natang Brigade Marches Forward in Learning from Dazhai), 1973, p.39. This is probably additional evidence that it was the county level that really determined the availability of agricultural machinery to the rural collectives.

14. For studies on financial planning and production planning, see for example, Ecklund, 1967, p.17; Donnithorne, 1974, p.18.

15. It was recently claimed that the financial reform in 1970 had probably overshot the reform in material allocation so that there were many inconsistencies between production and financial planning. Zhu and Xiang, 1979-a, p.18; S. Wang, 1978, p.34. Indeed,

the misuse of funds by government enterprises had its beginning in the 1950s. See, for example, Y. Wu, 1965, p.70; Perkins, 1966, p.198.

16. For discussion on the 'softness' of the budgetary constraints of the socialist enterprises in general, see the excellent work by J. Kornai (1980-a). The Chinese banking system has undergone major reforms in the 1980s and more changes are expected.

17. For details of the divergence between actual and planned credit funds, see Donnithorne, 1974.

18. For discussion of the supervisory role of the People's Bank and loan policy during those years see, H. Yi, 1979, pp.40-4; Q. Tang, 1979, pp.45-51.

19. Donnithorne, 1978, p.5. For analysis of the financing of agricultural mechanization, see next chapter.

20. For detailed analysis of the setting up and the subsequent quick abandonment of them, see K. Hsiao, 1971, pp.41-50.

21. Ta Kung Pao (Ta Kung Daily), March 3, 1979. In 1979, the Agricultural Bank was reestablished for the third time; this time the Agricultural Bank became a department directly under the State Council with the same status as the People's Bank although it would again be managed by the People's Bank.

22. Renmin Ribao, November 22, 1974; SWB, FE/W805/A2, December 11, 1974; SWB, FE/W808/A2, January 8, 1975. In fact, the number of commune credit co-operatives, about 50,000 (assuming there were about 50,000 communes), far exceeded the number of branches of the People's Bank which numbered 33,000 in 1977. Ta Kung Pao, March 27, 1977. For estimates of number of communes, see F.W. Crook, 1975.

23. The first factor will be studied in the following chapter while the second one has been examined in Chapter 4.

24. Given the lack of information, and the many restrictions placed on the production decisions of the rural collectives, no attempt will be made to derive their 'demand function' for agricultural mechanization. It is perhaps sufficient to note that the output-input decisions were very much affected by the ruling economic and political priorities as by the desire of the collective to improve its members' economic welfare. For discussions on the optimizing behaviour of rural collectives in their production decisions, see for example, Vanek, 1975; Ishikawa, 1967; Kelley, Williamson and Cheetham, 1972.

25. See, for example, Renmin Ribao, May 13, 1978 and October 6, 1979; Central Committee of the Chinese Communist Party, 1978. The drafted resources might be used in various projects, mainly land improvement construction projects, which might not benefit the participating team directly.

26. Natang xai xue Dazhai zhong kuo-bu qian-jin (Natang Brigade Marches Forward in Learning From Dazhai), pp.47-8; see also Chapter 3 of this study.

27. Tianjin College of Finance and Economics, 1977, p.242. These economic targets were: output value, quality, variety, material consumption, labour productivity, cost, profit and turnover rate of working capital.

28. The maximum percentage was 5 per cent of total rural labour force of the collective concerned. See, Hubei Renmin Chubanshe, 1977, p.59; Sigurdson, 1975, p.412.

29. Most of the state agricultural machinery stations were located in key agricultural regions.

30. The agricultural machinery might have been acquired from the state stations or newly bought.

31. Agricultural machinery station is a general term, for it had been used to include machine cultivation station, mechanized irrigation station or tractor station. See, for example, Hubei Renmin Chubanshe, 1976, p.91.

32. W. Zhan, 1979-b, p.9. Of course, part of the explanation was that some communes did not own any machines.

33. Xinzhou County Communist Party Committée, 1974, p.57. However, there is no information on the relative sizes of these different brigades.

34. They may take names such as mechanized cultivation teams, machinery working teams, etc. See for example, Editorial Department of Nongye Jixie (Agricultural Machinery) (ed.), 1978, pp.1078; Z. Ji, 1977, p.74.

35. Some big tractors were used only for three months each year. See, Editorial Team of Ren-min gong-she zai yue-jin (ed.), 1974, pp.110-1. See also Chapter 4.

36. Ma and Tian, 1978, pp.42-6; Renmin Ribao, May 28, 1977; Z. Ji, 1977, p.74; Economic Reporter, No.22, July 7, 1978, p.14. However, there were also cases where machines of the brigades were being sold or 'transferred' to the commune level. See, Renmin Ribao, August 25, 1978.

37. Bureau of Agricultural Machinery Administration, 1975, p.12; see also Chapter 6 of this study.

38. Ma and Tian, 1978, pp.44-5; Editorial Department of Nongye Jixie (Agricultural Machinery) (ed.), 1978, pp.94-5. The rate of utilization was measured as the average annual standard mu per horsepower of the tractor; the rate of liquid fuel consumption was measured as the weight of liquid fuel (in kilograms) required for completing each standard mu over a period of time. A standard mu is a uniform unit used to measure the amount of work done by a tractor engaged in different operations. It assumes a tractor in normal use and proper technical state, pulling a complex plough to cultivate land (the soil having a specified resistance of 0.45 to 0.5 kg per square cm) to a depth of 20-2 cm over an area of 1/15 hectare. See, Donnithorne, 1967, p.116.

39. Perkins et al., 1977-a, pp.107-8. In addition, the provincial government also exerted direct control over the construction of fuel storage tanks in the rural villages. Thus the control over the energy source for agricultural machinery was almost complete. SWB, FE/W769/A2, April 3, 1974.

40. It was only in 1978 that the pursuit of four modernizations was made the central task of the country so that growth in material output was given much greater emphasis than consideration of political struggles. However, even at the present moment, the interpretation of socialist development still appears to be a subject for debates among Chinese leaders and economists.

Chapter Six

FINANCING THE MECHANIZATION OF AGRICULTURE

The creation of an effective demand, and the generation of sufficient funds for productive investment form a vital link in the pursuit of economic development. In China, being a developing economy, there has certainly been no lack of demand for investment funds and indeed organizational and institutional arrangements have been designed to ensure such demand will be made. In essence, investment funds come from the surplus of total production after meeting consumption requirements and production costs when no external source of assistance is available. As explained earlier, under China's then existing economic system, production was primarily carried out by two types of production units, i.e., the state and the collective enterprises.[1]

As far as the state sector was concerned, profits and depreciation funds of the state enterprises were remitted to be centralized by the state, and most investment funds were in turn allocated and distributed by the various administrative organs of the government.[2] However, such arrangements did not apply to the agricultural sector where the rural collectives were the basic economic entities. As these collectives had nominal power over the distribution of their own production and income, other methods were used by the Chinese government to maintain a high rate of investment within the rural sector.[3] Indeed, since the days of the land reform programme, the Chinese government had been trying to initiate a continuous stream of institutional changes in the rural sector, mainly through increasing the degree of socialization, in order to ensure that a high level of savings and investment was made by the rural collectives.

It was clear that in order further to transform agricultural production, a substantial increase in the level of investment in agricultural production, whether by the government or by the rural collectives, would have been required. In this chapter, an attempt will be made to study the finanical issues involved and their implications in the agricultural mechanization efforts during the Fourth Five-Year Plan period. The questions of the sources of funds for mechanization and the economics of mechanization from the viewpoint of the communes will be examined. This study does not attempt to investigate the whole issue of China's approach and overall strategy towards the generation, distribution and utilization of investment funds for the pursuit of its objectives of socialism and economic development. However, by studying the financial side of the mechanization issue it is hoped that some light may be shed on its overall approach to development finance. In addition, the problems in the physical aspects of the mechanization process such as the unbalanced progress in production and utilization and the conflict between management and machine ownership could thus be better understood.

MAINTENANCE OF ACCUMULATION

By the late 1970s, the rural collectives produced over 90 per cent of all food grains and economic crops in China, and they bought about 70 per cent of the agricultural machinery produced in the country with their own funds (C. Liu et. al, 1979, p. 39; Peking Review, No. 9, February 25, 1977, p.26). Under China's economic system, agricultural mechanization has been a process which required the state to build factories which manufacture the machines and to provide some necessary infrastructure. On the other hand, it also required the final users, i.e. the rural collectives, to accumulate the necessary funds to purchase those machines and their complementary factors of production. However, it is not possible to determine here whether the agricultural sector has been a net recipient or a net supplier of resources to the rest of the economy during this time. Thus, on a macro level, the net flows of finance and expenditure cannot be ascertained and therefore a question such as which sector actually financed the mechanization of agriculture cannot be fully answered.[4]

Table 6.1:   *Annual Rates of Accumulation in China*

1953-57	23%-25%
1958	30%
1959	40%
1969	21%-22%
1970	30%
1971-75	30%

Source: See Appendix B

On the other hand, the generation of sufficient funds from within the commune system for investment in agricultural development and mechanization have been an equally, if not more, important and immediate issue. In fact, the way that funds are being extracted from the commune system has been an integral part of the desired form of socialist development as perceived by the Chinese leadership.

In this section, the general framework governing the generation of investment funds within the commune will be investigated. The first part of the section is a brief outline of the concept of investment funds used in China and an examination of some relevant data. The second part is a study of the mechanism imposed on the commune system for the realization of the maximum extractable accumulation funds.

Table 6.1 presents a set of official figures on the rate of accumulation for selected years. It was claimed that the accumulation rate during the 1970s had been consistently maintained at a level over 30 per cent annually (Z. He, 1979, p.9).

Unfortunately, the figures in Table 6.1 do not indicate the shares of accumulation contributed by each sector of the economy. However, such a high level of accumulation does imply a high level of achieved savings and thus a lower level of consumption than would otherwise have been.

For the basic accounting unit, i.e. the production team, the principle for distribution of income within the collective was normally straight-forward (Su, 1976, pp.115-8; Department of Agricultural Economics, Liaoning College of Finance and Economics (ed.), 1973, Chapter 7; Bureau of Rural Finance, 1977, p.129).

The net income (D) is the difference between total income of the collective (Y) and the sum of expenditures on material cost of production and other costs (C) plus the various taxes it has to pay (T). Having calculated (D), then a decision would be made to determine a suitable ratio, (P), to split (D) into two parts, one being the public accumulation (A) and the other the distributable income for remuneration of labour (W). In notation formulation:

$$Y - (C + T) = D \qquad \text{... (1)}$$
$$Y - (C + T) = \ell \cdot D + (1-\ell) \cdot D = W + A \qquad \text{... (2)}$$

where $\ell \cdot D \equiv W$
$(1-\ell) \cdot D \equiv A$
$0 < \ell < 1$

As far as the public accumulation (gong-gong-ji-lei), (A), is concerned, it would be split further into two major components, i.e. public reserve of the collective (K), and welfare fund of the collective (H). Thus

$$A = K + H \qquad \text{... (3)}$$

The public reserve (gong-ji-jin), (K), is used for investment purposes, whereas the welfare fund (gong-yi-jin), (H), is used for socialized consumption such as education, health, pension and cultural activities. In some cases, a portion of the public accumulation (A) may be used to build up a grain stockpile for the collective. The distribution mechanism within the rural collectives therefore clearly provided for the systematic withholding of income for raising accumulation.

MECHANISM FOR ACCUMULATION WITHIN THE COMMUNE SYSTEM

Writing on the subject of self-managed firms in England, Vanek argued that the principle of mandatory accumulation was the single most important condition for a successful self-managed firm or economy (Vanek, 1975, p.24). Of course, one <u>raison d'etre</u> for organising rural households into co-operatives and collectives was to facilitate mobilization of investment funds and the better utilization of resources. It should be noted that, during the formation of the elementary agricultural co-operative in China, the model regulations stipulated that the public reserve (K) of the co-operative should have a maximum level of 5 percent of annual income in the initial stage (D. Xu, 1962, p.94). As production developed, the maximum level was to be raised to 10 per cent.[5]

By 1957, the contribution to the public reserve of the agricultural co-operative was formally set at the level of 8 per cent of total annual income. It is quite clear that the Chinese government has from the start tried to intervene directly and indirectly in the agricultural collective's decision-making process concerning its internal distribution of income.

There were basically two courses of action which together made up some kind of institutional mechanism to guarantee that the desired level of accumulation would be maintained within the commune system. The first course worked through an informal ceiling placed on the growth of personal income of the commune members. Such informal limits seemed to be enforced by political pressure rather than by formal rules. The second course was to reduce the share of distributable income (W) by expanding the claims on the collective's total income for use in various investment projects. As will be shown, the rates of growth of distributable income in many collectives seem to have lagged consistently behind those of accumulation.

Direct Informal Actions

Consider the case of the model brigade Dazhai. During the ten years between 1966 and 1975, the monetary value of each workday had been consistently maintained at 1.5 yuan (Reporting Team Stationed at Dazhai, 1977, pp.20-1, p.145, p.166; Zhongguo Caizheng Jingji Chubanshe (ed.), 1977, p.92). Meanwhile, the total income of the collective had increased by well over 200 per cent with only a small increase in the workforce.[6]

It should be noted that 1.5 yuan per workday was still a relatively high level among China's grain-producing collectives. In 1976 the value of each workday in Dazhai was voluntarily reduced to

133

1.4 yuan so as not to exceed by too large a margin the average level achieved by neighbouring collectives.[7] In fact, at Dazhai's reported level of production, the value of each workday could have been as high as 3 yuans (Zhongguo Caizheng Jingji Chubanshe (ed.), 1977, p.92). Of course, 1.5 yuan was not the official norm as an upper limit on the value of one workday, there were collectives that maintained their value of one workday for many years at the level of 1.2 yuan (Renmin Ribao, January 18, 1979), or 0.9 yuan (Chinese Communist Party Committee of Pingshun County, 1976, p.67). In general, these limits appear to depend on individual conditions and the development in surrounding collectives. Two broad guidelines for determining the distribution of collective income were employed.

First, the relationship between the state, the collective and the individual members was to be handled 'correctly'. Attempts were to be directed towards making more contributions to the state, towards expanding continuously the accumulation of the collectives, and raising gradually the standard of living of commune members (Renmin Ribao, August 18, 1975).

Secondly, the accumulation of the collectives was to be used to expand collective production, to develop collective enterprises, to purchase agricultural machinery and tools, and to help develop production in the poorer member units (Jiang and Lu, 1976, p.32).

However, accumulation could at times be sacrificed in order to maintain a stable minimum level of consumption when faced with severe downturn in total production and income. In Table 6.2, the growth of public accumulation and income in a number of collectives is compared. Though the data are based on scattered and incomplete information from various places at different points in time, they do indicate that the rates of increase in public accumulation of the collectives were generally greater than the increase in distributed income in nearly every case. Since most of the samples in the table were from advanced units, the rates of increase in accumulation may have been much higher than the average because most of them would have already met the basic food requirements of their members. Furthermore, the rates of increase were calculated over a long period of time. Since the initial level of accumulation would generally be very low, the subsequent rate of increase would thus appear to be very high. It should also be noted that the figures for public accumulation in Table 6.2 include both public reserve and welfare funds of the collectives. Since they do not indicate the relative weights between the public reserve and welfare funds, it is not possible to estimate the share of increase in public reserve which was the main source of funds for investment in the collectives. However, the greater portion of the public accumulation is generally taken up for public reserve (see Table 6.3).

To examine in more detail the characteristics of the dynamic adjustment process between these rates of increase, consider the case of Xipu Production Brigade in Zunhua County (Hebei Province).[8] The relevant data on this model brigade, with the derived rates of increases, are presented in Table 6.3.[9] The evidence indicates that both per capita income and total distributed income in the brigade have increased by over 50 per cent in five years with an average annual growth rate of over 9 per cent. However, the increase in members' income was due mainly to the two major increases in 1972 and 1973, the two years when the campaign urging cadres to realize the Party's rural economic policies

Table 6.2: *Comparative Rates of Increase in Collectives' Income, Public Accumulation and Distributed Income to Commune Members*

Place	Time Period	Δ Y	Δ A	Δ W (a)	(b)
Heilongjiang Province	1965–75	110%	150%		34.4%
Shanghai City Rural Outskirts	1965–73	37%	130%		
Xingzi County Jiangxi Province	1966–75	103%	(360%)	63%	
Dazhai Brigade	1966–75	270%*	380%	100%	
	1974–76	–	19.6%	-1.5%	
Chaoyang Commune Jiangsu Province	1957–72	400%		200%	
Malu Commune Shanghai	1965–74	96%			50%
Nancheng Brigade Shanxi Province	1965–74		179%	119%	
Niejia Brigade Shandong Province	1966–74		500%		64%
Natang Brigade Guangxi Province	1970–72		101%		18.7%
Nanchaotai Brigade Hebei Province	1971–72		11.4%	10%	

Δ Y   Increase in total collective income;
Δ A   Increase in the public accumulation of the collectives;
Δ W   Increase in the distributed income of collectives;
  (a) Changes in total level (b) Changes in per capita distributed income
* For the period 1964-74; ( ) for change in public reserve of collectives
Source: See Appendix B

Table 6.3: Growth of Collective Income and its Distribution in Xipu Production Brigade, Zunhua County, Hebei Province (1969-74)

Year		(Y)	(A)	(K)	(H)	(W)	(W/pop.)	(C+T)
1969	i	136,231	13,280	9,500	3,780	82,388	75	39,563
	ii	+18.9%	+17%	+18.8%	+12.7%	+20%	+17.2%	+16.4%
	iii	(100)	(10)	(7)	(3)	(61)	-	(29)
1970	i	139,488	11,186	8,396	2,790	83,539	74	44,763
	ii	+3.2%	-15.8%	-11.6%	-26.2%	+1.4%	-1.3%	+13.1%
	iii	(100)	(8)	(6)	(2)	(60)	-	(32)
1971	i	149,459	11,864	7,417	4,447	85,015	75	52,580
	ii	+7.2%	+6.1%	-11.7%	+59.4%	+1.8%	+1.4%	+17.5%
	iii	(100)	(8)	(5)	(3)	(57)	-	(35)
1972	i	190,330	19,033	13,323	5,710	106,284	94	65,013
	ii	+27%	+60.4%	+80%	+28.4%	+25%	+25.3%	+23.8%
	iii	(100)	(10)	(7)	(3)	(55)	-	(35)

Table 6.3: *Growth of Collective Income and its Distribution (Continued)*

Year		(Y)	(A)	(K)	(H)	(W)	(W/pop.)	(C+T)
1973	i	235,260	40,537	35,300	5,237	125,807	111	68,916
	ii	+23.6%	+113%	+165%	-8.3%	+18.4%	+18.1%	+6%
	iii	(100)	(17)	(15)	(2)	(54)	-	(29)
1974	i	273,975	39,155	32,993	6,162	132,160	115	102,660
	ii	+16.5%	-3.4%	-6.5%	+17.7%	+5.1%	+3.6%	+49%
	iii	(100)	(14)	(12)	(2)	(48)	-	(38)
Total change between 1969 and 1974 (in %)		+102.6	+195	+247	+63	+60	+53	+160
Average annual rate of growth between 1969-1974 (in %)		15.2	24.2	28.3	10.3	9.9	8.9	21

Table 6.3: Growth of Collective Income and its Distribution (Continued)

Y   = Total Collective Income
K   = Public Reserve
W   = Distributable Net Income
C + T = Cost and Taxes

A   = Public Accumulation of Brigade
H   = Welfare Fund
W/Pop. = Income Per Capita

$Y = A + W + C + T$ and $A = K + H$

i   figures are monetary value expressed in yuan at current prices
ii   figures in percentages are rates of increase over the previous year for that variable
iii figures in brackets are shares as a percentage of total collective income

Source: See Appendix B

was promoted. As Table 6.3 indicates, total income also had the largest increase during those two years. In terms of absolute level, however, per capita income was only recovering to a level achieved earlier in 1961-3.[10]   Only by 1973 could the increase in per capita income be considered to be a net real improvement. Nevertheless, the growth in personal income has been relatively stable.

On the other hand, the public reserve component has followed a more volatile pattern of change. While there was an increase of total collective income of 102.6 per cent between 1969 and 1974, public reserve increased by 247 per cent with an average annual growth rate of 28.3 per cent which was three times faster than the rate for per capita income growth. In fact, not only did public reserve achieve the highest average annual rate of growth against other claimants, it has almost doubled its share in the total collective income from 7 per cent in 1969 to 12 per cent in 1974. In contrast, the share of distributable net income (W) has been consistently reduced, from 61 per cent in 1969 to only 48 per cent in 1974.

As for the welfare fund, its share in the total collective income seems to have remained stable, and indeed the share had changed little over the whole period from 1955 to 1974. In 1969, the amount of income devoted to welfare funds was about a third of that devoted to public reserve, but by 1974 this had changed to only one-sixth. It is worth noting here that the rate of increase in the amount of income used for production costs and taxes was second only to that of public reserve. This reflected the increasing use of modern inputs and the cost of maintaining and operating agricultural machinery, though no doubt the amount of indirect taxes paid by the commune would also have accounted for a part of the overall increase.

The pattern in Xipu Production Brigade appears to have followed the two general principles for distribution of income within collectives quite well. Hence, the level of public accumulation had consistently grown at a faster rate while the total income of the collective achieved only a reasonable rate of increase. The only exception was in 1974 when the components of production costs and taxes suddenly jumped by 49 per cent. On the whole the case of Xipu also demonstrates that personal income was controlled and restrained in a gradual process of growth.

Finally, a note on the share of public accumulation in the total income of Xipu Brigade. After the Cultural Revolution started, this share was raised to and consistently maintained at (except for the years 1970 and 1971), over the 10 per cent level. However, the share of public accumulation achieved by Xipu (the highest level being 17 per cent in 1973) was certainly not the highest level in China. For instance, in Dazhai Brigade, this share has been maintained at over 20 per cent since 1970.[11]   In other cases, collectives were known to have achieved a higher or comparable level within a shorter period of time (Editorial Team of Xin yu-gong yi-shan ji, 1977, p.81; Long, 1976, p.30; Xin and Zhu, 1976, p.30).

Restraints on the Share of Distributable Personal Income (W)

Most of the measures in this category involved indirect suppression of the share of distributable personal income to commune members. At the same time, they were designed to build up and expand the permanent elements of public accumulation to be administered by the commune system. The real significance of the measures in this category was that, unlike the actions in the first course, they involved on-going claims on the collective's income so that no discretionary or public decisions on the assignment of relative shares for personal distribution and accumulation were necessary.

Judging from the available evidence, the building of agricultural basic construction projects can be considered as the most important and universally adopted measure in the Chinese rural collectives during the 1970s. Apart from this, several other measures were also being used in various places at the same time. Before studying this major measure of agricultural basic construction, some of the other measures will be examined below.

First, the provision of primary education and basic health care became an increasingly important responsibility shouldered by the commune system durning the 1970s. For instance, in Xiyang County, between 1966 and 1976, student numbers increased by more than 12 times but the education funding allocated by the state only doubled (Zhongguo Caizheng Jingji Chubanshe (ed.), 1977, p.71). The commune level had actually assumed the burden of providing not only primary education to the children of its members but also specialized agricultural training schools. With the increasing use of modern inputs and agricultural machinery, the role of training technical operators was also being taken up by the communes (Bureau of Agricultural Mechanization, Ministry of Agricultural and Forestry (ed.), 1976, Volume 2, p.14, p.40; J. Xie, 1976, p.77). In some places, 'training networks' involving the province, prefecture, county, commune and brigades were set up for this purpose (SWB, FE/W859/A7, January 7, 1976; Editorial Department of Nongye Jixie (Agricultural Machinery) (ed.), 1978, p.54). As is well known, many rural collectives have established health clinics of some kind, with full- and part-time paramedical personnel (e.g. the barefoot doctors). However, all such services have to be funded largely by the rural collectives themselves from their own welfare funds, public reserve or other expense accounts.

In addition to the provision of funds for education and health care, there were other measures to restrain growth of distributable income. For example, in some collectives incomes from all nongrain production were not even included in the income for distribution to members (Renmin Ribao, December 31, 1978). When the per capita income of a production team or brigade reached a certain level, that part of the 'excess' could be kept by the commune administration to be used as funds for the public accumulation of the commune. Production teams were also required to devote a certain proportion of their income to build up grain reserves in order to hedge against poor harvest and to prepare for war (Renmin Ribao, December 16, 1971).

According to the Revised NPAD, the target (originally intended to be reached by 1969) was to build up grain reserve levels of up to 18 months consumption in each collective, and for the state as a whole, one- to two-year reserves.[12]   The significance was that the grain reserve in physical form as well as the financial fund for maintaining the reserve were both supposed to remain untouched, i.e. they could not be utilized for any other purposes (Department of Agricultural Economics, Xibei Agricultural College, 1977, pp.162-3).   Therefore, all these measures discussed above were designed to bring down, or to hold steady, the share of distributable income and to increase the share of public accumulation in the collective's total income.   Though some of them can be regarded as investment in human capital, others are not directed towards expanding the productive capacity of the production units.   In contrast, the measure to be discussed below has been aimed solely, on the surface, at creating and improving this productive capacity and in actual fact also served to limit the share of distributable income in the collectives.

The building of agricultural basic construction projects was viewed as an application of the concept of 'labour accumulation' which was defined as:

> the labour expended by the collective economy of the people's commune for carrying out capital construction on farm land and cultivating resources for diverse undertakings.   The products turned out (e.g. reservoirs, pondembankments, forest land) with this portion of labour are not expressed in terms of value.   Even if they are so expressed, they are not for distribution (Y. Zhang, 1966, p.28) (emphasis added).

In fact, it is argued by some economists in the West that the only justification for the existence of collectivization rested on such projects (Fung, 1974, p.46).   Since the 1970 Northern Agricultural Conference, these projects have become a regular activity on a large scale for almost every rural collective during the winter season.[13]   The objective of these projects of labour accumulation was to utilize the seasonally under-employed labour resources and turn them into capital-formation activities, what Schran regarded as 'intrasectoral capital formation' (P. Schran, 1969, p.9), without having to increase the share of distributable personal income.   The way through which such projects achieved this objective in practice is examined here.   In general, the commune or brigade authorities would plan and organize these projects to which the production teams, the basic accounting units, contributed their labour.[14]   Thus, the extractive effect of labour accumulation is twofold in practice.

On the one hand, there is the 'voluntary' part of labour contribution which is not to be counted as workdays and thus is not rewarded.   It is appropriate to note that a workday is an accounting measurement, generally consisting of ten work points, for calculation of standard work of commune members for the purpose of income distribution. Hence a workday is not necessarily equivalent to a calendar day. On the other hand, though labour is the major input in such projects, materials and equipment are still needed. Regardless of how such expenditures on materials and equipment are treated in the accounting procedures in the immediate year (i.e. whether they are treated as part of production cost or accumulation), they would invariably exert a pressure to prevent the rising of the share of distributable personal income.[15]

Of course, when labour contribution exceeded the 3 per cent limit originally stipulated in the 60 Articles, and it is doubtful whether this ceiling has really been observed during the first half of the 1970s,[16] the excess labour contribution should have been rewarded accordingly. However, judging by all the available evidence, the value of the workdays thus awarded to the excess labour contribution was in fact calculated after merging with the normal workdays for routine farm work.[17] Therefore, the value of each workday would have to come down when the amount of distributable personal income is not raised. For instance, in a commune of Shanxi Province, it was calculated that if agricultural basic construction projects were not carried out, the value of a workday in 1973 would have been increased by 33 per cent (Renmin Ribao, October 8, 1974).

Though comprehensive information on the percentages of workdays being spent on such projects is scarce, a rough estimation of the magnitude of efforts exerted by the collectives towards this end can still be made.[18] Reports indicate that during the Fourth Five-Year Plan period, there were, on average, 100 million people and 1 million cadres working on agricultural basic construction projects during the winter slack season of each year (SWB, FE/W868/A2, March 10, 1976; SWB, FE/W880/A1, June 2, 1976). Normally, such projects would take two to three months each year (SWB, FE/W816/A4, March 5, 1975; SWB,FE/W815/A7-11, February 26, 1975 and FE/W852/A3-10, November 12, 1975). Since the rural labour force was about 300 million (W. Zhan, 1979-a, p.14), it is implied that about 5 per cent to 7 per cent of the total workdays were used in such projects each year.

Table 6.4 contains some scattered information on the labour used in such projects. It is clear that the percentage of the labour force employed in these projects varied from place to place, even from year to year for the same place. However, based on the information in Table 6.4, it seems that nearly all the cases have at least 40 per cent of the labour force participating in such projects each year.

In fact, towards the end of the Fourth Five-Year Plan period, rural collectives started to set up full-time specialized construction teams to carry out these projects. Based on discussions with commune cadres in China, it appears that the specialized teams were meant to improve the speed and efficiency of construction so that land improvements for agricultural mechanization could be better prepared. It should perhaps be noted that the establishment of specialized teams at that time was not meant to eliminate the mass mobilization of labour during winter slack seasons. Such teams would probably help to absorb some of the increased labour due to population growth and displacement from use of agricultural machinery. These teams could be organized by the county, commune or brigade level administrations (Renmin Ribao, January 9, 1976 and August 19, 1977; SWB FE/W815/A8, February 26, 1975; Revolutionary Committee of Fenglai County, Shandong Province, 1975, p.24).

Table 6.4:   Labour   Used   for   Agricultural   Basic   Construction
               Projects

	Area	Year	(A)	(B)
1.	Qinghai Province	1975 winter	40%	0.337
2.	Shaanxi Province	1975 winter	15–20%	2.2
3.	Xizang Autonomous Region	1975 winter	50%	0.4
4.	Jiangxi Province	1975 winter	29%	2.6
5.	Liaoning Province	1975 winter	(50%)	3.66
6.	Yunnan Province	1975 winter	40%	4
7.	Sichuan Province	1974 winter	40%	14.7
1.	Guangxi Autonomous Region	1974 winter	71%	8.1
9.	Guangdong Province	1974 winter	50%	10
10.	Kueizhou Province	1974 winter	(50%)	4.35
11.	Liaoning Province	1974 winter	(71%)	5.2
12.	Shaanxi Province	1974 winter	51%	4
13.	Hubei Province	1973 winter	(40%)	5.5
14.	Shanxi Province	1973 winter	(69%)	3.87
15.	Sichuan Province	1973 winter	50%	
16.	Guangdong Province	1973 winter	70%	11.9
17.	Shanxi Province	1972 winter	60%	3.8
18.	Suqian County	1971–1975	50%	
19.	Zhangding County	1971–1975	80%	0.13
20.	Xiyang County	1974	80%	0.07
21.	Linan Prefecture	1973 winter	70%	
22.	Menyuan County	1973 winter	(40%)	0.01
23.	Zhangchun Prefecture	1973 winter	65%	0.57
24.	Siping Prefecture	1973 winter	50%	0.4
25.	Xinxiang Prefecture	1973 winter	(51%)	0.4
26.	Qinglu County	1973 winter	67%	0.028

(A)   Percentage of total labour force working on projects
(B)   Number of people working on projects (million)

Note: Figures in brackets indicate percentages as a proportion of total rural labour force.

Source: See Appendix B

The amount of the rural labour force being organized into such teams seems to have been generally fixed at 10 per cent of the total (Renmin Ribao, August 19, 1977; SWB, FE/W845/A8, September 24, 1975; SWB, FE/W830/A3, June 11, 1975; SWB, FE/W815/A8, February 26, 1975), although it could range from 3 per cent to 15 per cent (SWB, FE/W824/A4-5, April 30, 1975; SWB, FE/W815/A8, February 26, 1975; Renmin Ribao, January 9, 1976).

In carrying out various forms of action to maintain some desirable levels of accumulation in the collectives, it is clear that the upper levels of the commune system, i.e. the brigade and the commune, have to assume a more significant role in the affairs of the production team. Thus, it is not difficult to see why the control and management of many aspects of the economic activities of the collectives were coming under increasing direct supervision, and even execution, by the brigade and commune administrations.

To recapitulate, it has been shown that there existed a number of measures designed to ensure that a high level of accumulation was generated within the commune system. In order to carry them out successfully, the property rights and autonomy of the basic accounting unit appear to have been undermined to various extents. Thus, the emergence of repair and management networks for agricultural machines in the rural collectives, coupled with the vital role played by the collective enterprises, has made the maintenance of high accumulation within the collectives an integral part of the whole development process. While it has been established that there existed a mechanism to maintain a high share of the collective income in the form of accumulation, the next question is to find out how the accumulation funds were actually used and what the activities were that generated these funds. As will be discussed in the following section, the efforts in agricultural mechanization would not have been feasible, under the prevailing economic policies and conditions, without such a mechanism to guarantee accumulation funds from the distribution of collective income.

FINANCING OF AGRICULTURAL MECHANIZATION BY THE RURAL COLLECTIVES

In studying the way the commune system actually financed its efforts in agricultural mechanization, this section will be divided into three main parts. In the first part, the role played by the commune system in generating funds to mechanize agriculture is investigated. In the second part, the source of finance for mechanization in the collectives will be examined in terms of the types of production activities and the organizational forms of production. The third part of this section deals with the control mechanism over the major source of funds for mechanization.

Table 6.5: Relative Economic Strength of the Three Levels of the Commune System

Area	Year	Income Shares			Fixed Capital Shares		
		C %	B %	T %	C %	B %	T %
Shanghai Rural Suburbs	1974	C+B = 47.7		52.3	C+B = 49.3		50.7
	1977	C+B = 65		35			
Peking Rural Suburbs	1977	C+B = 57		43			
Tianjin Rural Suburbs	1977	C+B = 55		45			
Jiangsu Province	1977	C+B = 46		54			
Shandong Province	1977	C+B = 41		59			
Wuxi County	1965				C+B = 4.3		
	1976	C+B = 65		35	C+B = 65		35
Wangpo County	1974	15.6	8.6	75.8	20.6	26.4	53
Liangzun Commune	1965	0	9.7	90.3			
	1975	30.8	32	37.2			
Yantai Prefecture	1975	C+B = 32					

Notes: C - Commune, B - Brigade,
T - Production Team
Income share as percentage of total income of the commune system.
Fixed capital share as percentage of total value of fixed capital of the commune system.

Source: See Appendix B

Table 6.6: Provision of Funds by the Commune System and by the State for Investment in Projects of Agricultural Mechanization

Area	Year	(A)	(C)	(S)	Use of the Funds
Wuming County	1971 1975		73%	27%	Purchase of agricultural machinery
Haining County	up to 1975		88%	12%	Irrigation projects
Shangzhuang Commune	1969 -1974	3.05	92%	8%	Agricultural machinery
Mencheng County	1970- 1973	12.16	82.2%	17.8%	Agricultural machinery
Licheng County	1974- 1975	6.6	83%	17%	Water control projects
Xinzhou County	1956- 1971	25	82.5%	17.5%	Agricultural machinery
Qingchuan County	1975	3.31	73%	27%	Agricultural machinery
Chuansha County	1971- 1975	25	85.5%	11% (loans) 1.5% (grant)	Agricultural machinery
Yantai Prefecture	1970- 1975		85%	15%	Agricultural machinery
Xiyang County	1967- 1976	18.3	87%	13%	Agricultural machinery
Natang Brigade	1971- 1973 1974-75	0.18 0.02	97.7% 100%	2.3% (loans)	Agricultural machinery
Fangang Commune	1970 -1975	0.55	100%		Agricultural machinery
Taoyuan County	1971- 1975		71%		Small hydro-electric stations
Meixian County	1973		85%	15% (loans)	Small hydro-electric stations

Table 6.6:   Provision of Funds (Continued)

Area	Year	(A)	(C)	(S)	Use of the Funds
Luchuan County	1974		65.7%		Small hydro-electric stations
Xinglongjie Commune	1971 1975	2.48	83%		Small hydro-electric stations

(A)   Amount (in million yuan)
(C)   Share of total funds provided by the commune system
(S)   Share of total funds provided by the state

Source: See Appendix B

The Role of the Commune System in Financing Agricultural Mechanization Investment

As of 1975, it was reported that 90 per cent of China's cultivated land, irrigation and drainage equipment and machinery, and 80 per cent of all tractors belonged to the rural collectives (C. Zhang, 1975; Editorial Team of Talks of Political Economy: Socialism, 1976, p.56). It was also reported that the production brigades and the production teams owned 64 per cent of the country's large and medium tractors and 96 per cent of small tractors.[19]   Though no further breakdowns on these figures are available, the 64 per cent of large and medium tractors would probably be owned mainly by the brigades.

In general, ownership and management of agricultural machinery were determined by who funded the purchase, with the possible exception of small hydroelectric stations. The ability to put up such funds depended in turn on the economic strength which the three levels of organization in the commune system had achieved. In 1977, income of the commune and brigade levels accounted for 32 per cent of the total income of the whole commune system in China, while income of the production teams accounted for 68 per cent (M. Xue, 1978, p.8). Unfortunately, there is little information on how these shares have changed over the preceding years.

In Table 6.5, some scattered figures on the relative economic strength at the various levels of administration within the commune system are presented. Although the data contained in this table are limited and probably came from advanced units, they nonetheless point to a situation where the economic strength of the upper levels of the commune system has become a major moving force of development. That is so because the incomes of the upper levels are generally used for production and not for distribution to members.

147

Most of the figures in Table 6.5 exceeded the national average for 1977 noted earlier, but even the national average (32 per cent of total income coming from the commune and brigade level) was not an unimpressive 'achievement'.

Consider next the actual pattern in the financing of agricultural mechanization in the rural sector. From the available figures contained in Table 6.5, the indication is that over 70 per cent of the funds needed to build small hydrolectric stations and to purchase agricultural machinery for field operations as well as for water control, were provided by the communes, brigades and teams. As for the share coming from state assistance it is not clear whether the contents included grants, loans or other forms of assistance. Furthermore, no information is available on the manner in which such assistance was given. For instance, the timing, the structure of payments and repayments could be vital to the viability, and indeed the reason, for the investment on mechanization by the communes. In any case, there should be little doubt as to the fact that is was really the commune as a whole that contributed the substantial part of the funds for investing in agricultural mechanization, though Table 6.6 does not indicate the relative share of contribution by each level in the commune system. Together with the direct and indirect costs associated with the farmland construction projects, which were viewed as a necessary preparation for the effective introduction of agricultural machinery, the proportion contributed by the commune system would have been much higher. In summary, as far as the purchases of agricultural machinery (at statedetermined prices) are concerned, available evidence suggests that the rural collectives themselves have to provide most of the needed funds.

Sources of Collective Funds for Mechanization

Given that the communes and their member brigades and teams are the main source of funds for investment, it is necessary to investigate from what types of activities and through what kind of production organization such funds are obtained. As the commune, brigade and production teams differed in their economic strength, output mix and responsibilities, the types of agricultural machinery they bought and the way they generated the necessary funds were not therefore all the same. However, in terms of formulating production strategy, the primacy of grain self-sufficiency generally had the overriding priority. Thus, in a lot of cases the expansion of grain output has even been promoted in official campaigns as the <u>first step</u> to generate funds for agricultural mechanization.[20] However, most practical methods were not centred on grain production. Indeed, grain production was meant to be improved via the pursuit of mechanization. In practice, the many ways in which rural collectives have sought to generate funds for the purpose of agricultural mechanization fall into two categories (<u>Renmin Ribao</u>, September 2, 1971, and February 21, 1975; Bureau of Agricultural Mechanization, 1976, Volume 1, pp.41-2, pp.47-8; Shang and Xiao, 1977, p.27;

Editorial Department of Nongye Jixie (Agricultural Machinery) (ed.), 1978, pp.78-80): development of rural collective enterprises and development of (non-grain) sideline production. The former is characterized by the form of production organization, whereas the latter is identified by the production activities (or outputs) undertaken by the collectives. However, as noted in Chapter 5, the two categories are not entirely separate. Before they are studied in more detail, a brief digression to examine the ability of the commune and brigade to 'tax' the production teams is appropriate.

A Digression: Intra-commune Redistribution of Funds.

As discussed earlier, though the production team is in general the basic unit of accounting, the property rights of the team have been qualified. In addition to the direct and indirect constraints placed by the state, the production teams were also subjected to a variety of extractive measures imposed by the commune and brigade in which they belonged.

One of the most important extractive measures, or intra-commune taxation, was the ability of the upper levels to transfer accumulation funds from the lower units (i.e. from the teams to the brigade, from the brigades to the commune). The ability of the upper levels to transfer public reserve from the basic accounting units was actually written into the Revised Draft Work Regulations for the People's Commune (The 60 Articles) adopted in 1961.[21] However, under that stipulation, the proportion to be transferred was supposed to require the approval of the County People's Assembly. Since the Cultural Revolution, such freedom to transfer seems to have been greatly expanded. In spite of a series of proclamations to urge that the Party's rural economic policies be respected,[22] the transfer of funds has become a matter-of-fact 'right' of the upper levels (Hubei Renmin Chubanshe (ed.), 1976, Volume 2, passim; Renmin Ribao, July 5, August 25, 1978; Xinzhou County Communist Party Committee, 1974, pp.23-4). In fact, some commune administrations were bypassing the brigades in transferring accumulation funds directly from the production teams. During the 1970s, such transfers were often made in the name of agricultural development and mechanization.

In addition to the direct transfer of accumulation funds, the higher levels of the commune were also able to impose quotas of contribution ('tan-pai') for materials, money and labour that the lower levels had to make (Bureau of Agriculture, 1974, p.30; J. Xie, 1976, p.57). In fact, contributions could be demanded in a variety of fashions. For instance, when a commune decided to purchase tractors, member production teams could be asked to give contributions, say, at the rate of 1.5 yuan per mu (or 22.5 yuan per hectare) of cultivated land (Renmin Ribao July 5, 1978). In other cases, demands were made by the commune to the teams to pay the commune a surcharge on the teams' purchase of agricultural machinery, or to pay management fees (for agricultural machinery, reservoirs, collective enterprises, etc.). Feedstock, timber, steel and other materials were also demanded by the brigade and commune administrations (from the teams) for their economic undertakings (Renmin Ribao, July 22, 1978). Of course, all these contributions, as with transfer of accumulation of funds, were not repaid or compensated.

On the other hand, the commune system was of course initially conceived as an organization to bring about more equality among the members, to reduce the 'three great differences', and indeed as a transitory step towards communism. Thus, some sort of redistribution of income and wealth within the commune became inevitable under these presumptions, though the degree and emphasis of such redistribution seems to have depended very much on the political orientation of the Chinese leaders in power. With such redistribution, resources were being transferred out of some collectives. The resources thus transferred were being used partly to assist projects that benefited all member teams, and partly to help, via subsidy or low-interest loans, to develop production in other poorer teams (Bureau of Agricultural Mechanization, 1976, Volume 1, p.11; Hubei Renmin Chubanshe, 1975, p.72). Nevertheless, intra-commune redistribution has clearly served as a means to maintain a certain level of accumulation within the commune system (since resources 'taxed' by the upper level were mainly used to expand production), apart from the possible effects of bringing about more equality. As for immediate increase in the absolute level of collective income (and thus of accumulation) which really determines the ability to invest in mechanization, redistribution would have little impact other than changing the composition of it. In the longer run, such redistribution might have a greater impact but the direction of change is not predetermined. It is sufficient to state that, in the shorter term, it was really through profitable production that new funds for agricultural mechanization could be generated.

Rural Collective Enterprise and Sideline Production.

The two types of activities are characterized, one by the fact that they belong to non-grain agricultural production and the other by the form in which production is organized. If they are judged simply by their outputs, these activities are not mutually exclusive. Most of the activities under sideline production were in fact organized in the form of collective enterprise production. On the other hand, industrial production (such as repair and assembly of machinery) by the collective enterprises was not part of sideline production activities, whereas many small-quantity and seasonal sideline production activities were not organized into enterprises.

Judging from the available information on the share of value of output from collective enterprises and from sideline production contained in Table 6.7, these activities seem to have contributed quite a significant share of the total income of the collectives in the samples. In comparison though, the contribution to total collective income by sideline production appears to be significantly greater than that by the rural collective enterprises. In fact, in 1972, about one-third of the total value of output from the agricultural sector in China was reported to have come from sideline production (<u>Renmin Ribao</u>, July 18, 1972).

Table 6.7:   Relative Shares in Total Collective Income from Sideline Production and from Collective Enterprises

Place	Year	Sideline Production	Commune- & Brigade- Run Enterprises
Liuji Commune	1971	34%	
Jixing Brigade	1971	61%	
Qianan County	1971	25%	
Xigou Brigade	1971	20%	
Gangyao Brigade	1971-3	40%	
Dongguan County	1971	54.6%	
Tuanpiaozhuang Commune	1974	40%	
Hunan Province	1973 1975-6		12.2% 20%
Sifang County	1975		11%
Zhaodong County	1973		28%
Xiyang County	1973		10%
Peking Red Star Commune	1975		20%
Yangsi Commune	1975		40%
Shanghai July 1 Commune	1975		32%
Helie Commune	1975		50%

Source: See Appendix B

However, generalized interpretation of this limited range of available samples in Table 6.7 should be made cautiously. As noted earlier, much sideline production may well have been organized into collective enterprise, and then it is not clear to what extent this has happened in the samples of Table 6.7. For instance, in Zunhua County, income from sideline production contributed 90 per cent of the investment in agricultural mechanization by the rural collectives of which 70 per cent actually came through the collective enterprises (J. Xie, 1976, p.66). It should also be noted that some of the sideline production activities were carried out by the production teams and by individual commune members on a private basis, and it is not clear whether the figures in the table include this private income of the members of collectives. If so, then the share of sideline income that actually went to the collectives for collective use would be smaller.[23]

However, existing evidence suggests that many of the sideline production activities which did contribute directly to investment funds for agricultural mechanization were actually organized in the form of collective enterprise production. Whether they were tea growing, bee-keeping, embroidery, or woodwork, brick-making, fish farms and poultry farms, such sideline production has in many cases provided nearly all the funds required for any attempt towards agricultural mechanization and they were all productions organized by collective enterprises (Renmin Ribao, August 30, 1971, August 28, 1972, May 28, 1973, October 30, 1975; Bureau of Agricultural Machinery Administration, 1975, pp.73-4). The main reason for this outcome can be attributed to the control set up over the profits generated from these collective enterprises. Before studying this control mechanism over the collective enterprise in the next section, a few notes on these enterprises are in order.

The scattered data contained in Table 6.8 seem to support the view that collective enterprises had played a major role in the provision of funds for investment in agricultural mechanization. If the figures in Table 6.8 were representative of China's rural communes, then an important conclusion can be drawn. That is, agricultural mechanization would have been impossible without the development of these enterprises since over 80 per cent of the required funds were self-financed by the collectives (see also Table 6.6).

However, it is not possible to ascertain the relative importance between the brigade-run and the commune-run enterprises in terms of their relative contributions to mechanization investment due to the lack of appropriate information. Perkins argued that commune-run enterprises usually made a greater profit than brigade-run enterprises because the former sold more sophisticated products to wider markets and thus obtained a reasonable return, whereas the brigade-run enterprises managed only repair shops, grain mills and brick kilns and sold only to agriculture at a minimum level of profit (Perkins et al., 1977-a, p.224). However, there seems to be no substantial evidence to support this hypothesis. In fact, brigade-run enterprises, particularly those engaging in sideline production, were often quite profitable. There were many reports which claimed that the brigades were able to obtain their entire funds for mechanization from such production (Renmin Ribao, June 18, 1972; J. Xie, 1976, p.56; Renmin Chubanshe (ed.), 1972, pp.34-5; 1975; Bureau of Agricultural Mechanization, 1976, Volume 1, p.84).

Table 6.8:   *Role of Rural Collective Enterprises in Financing Agricultural Mechanization Within the Collectives*

Place	Year	Percentage of Mechanization Investment made by Rural Collective Enterprises	Share of Enterprise Accumulation Fund used for Mechanization
Jiading County	1971-4	56%	
Wuxi County	up to 1977	90%	
Chuansha County	1971-4	87.5%	
Malu Commune (Shanghai)	up to 1975	62%	
Wuxi County	1971-4		58%
Hunan Province	1974		31%
Jinkou Commune (Guangdong Province)	1965-74		51.8%
Lijiazhuang Commune (Shanxi Province)	1973		62%
Caijianjian Commune (Hunan Province)	1966-74		50%

Source: See Appendix B

Towards the end of the Fourth Five-Year Plan period, a new direction for development of the rural collective enterprises emerged. As discussed in Chapter 5, the production activities of these enterprises became directly linked to factories in the cities, and many had thus effectively become sub-contractors or processing plants for simple parts and intermediate inputs.[24] In this way, both inputs and outputs for the collective enterprises were assured of a certain degree of stability. Such arrangements often involved the commune-run as well as brigade-run enterprises. For example, in Zunhua County, it was the brigade-run enterprises which participated most actively in this link-up with the city factories (J. Xie, 1976, pp.45-6).

The development was closely associated with the conception and establishment of the agricultural machinery repair and assembly networks already being promoted and developed. It is sufficient to note here that such a development in linking up the rural enterprises presented a good opportunity for faster modernization in the rural collectives with the prospect of additional jobs that might be created and for providing an effective form for the transfer of technology to the agricultural sector. The problem with this development was the dependence on the proximity of the rural collectives to a prosperous and growing industrial city, without which successful development could be seriously undermined. Another probable obstacle would be the resultant shortage of adequate repair and agriculture supporting services for the communes if collective enterprises were all turned into subcontractors of city factories.

Control Mechanism over Funds Generated by Rural Collective Enterprises

The most important feature in the financial management of a rural collective enterprise was that its profits were not distributed to the commune members as personal income (Tianjin College of Finance and Economics, 1977, p.7; Hubei Renmin Chubanshe, 1976, p.70). Workers in the collective enterprises, whether they were fulltime or part-time, were mostly peasants from the production teams. In general, the remuneration for these workers was paid by the enterprise according to the same workpoint system of the production team to which the workers still belonged (Hubei Renmin Chubanshe, 1977, p.59). Normally, some additional subsidies to compensate for the workers' extra expenditure on meals and travel would be paid.[25]

When a separate accounting system has been set up in the rural collective enterprise, its profit could be properly calculated. Profit is calculated as the difference between total income from sales of products (and services) and total expenditure. Expenditure included cost of materials, administration costs, sales tax, administration fees (to the administrative level, brigade or commune, that managed the enterprise), and labour remuneration when applicable (Tianjin College of Finance and Economics, 1977, p.203). The government usually provided some concessions in the collection of sales tax for encouragement. For instance, all agriculture-related products such as chemical fertilizer, insecticide and processing machinery that were produced by rural collective enterprises were exempt from sales tax.[26] Other agriculture-supporting services such as repair and processing provided by the collectives were also exempted from sales tax. As for other commodites produced by the enterprises, a five per cent sales tax was applicable; and for other repair and processing services not considered to be related directly to agriculture, a three per cent tax was applied (Tianjin College of Finance and Economics, 1977, p.180).

For Tianjin's rural suburbs, the profit tax scheme was as set out in Table 6.9.

The first claimant on the profits of a rural collective enterprise was the profit tax, which need not go to the central government but might be payable to the provincial or county government.

The tax scheme for Tianjin was a progressive one, but the taxable base of 2,400 yuan seems to be much higher than the general average level of 600 yuan that prevailed during the Fourth Five-Year Plan period (Renmin Ribao, February 10, 1979). However, the starting rate, 20 per cent was the same as the national standard.

Table 6.9:   *Profit Tax Scheme for Rural Collective Enterprise*

Annual Profit (in yuan)	Rates of Profit Tax (in %)
2,400 - 30,000	20
30,001 - 60,000	25
60,001 - 100,000	35
100,001 and over	45

Source: *Tianjin College of Finance and Economics, 1977, p.192*

After paying the profit tax, the remaining part of the enterprise profit, or net profit, would then be ready for distribution though not as personal income to commune members. There were two basic methods of distribution. One method was for the enterprise to hand over the entire sum of the net profits to its controlling unit, i.e. the revolutionary committee of the brigade or the commune (Tianjin College of Finance and Economics, 1977, pp.188-9). The controlling unit would in turn allocate, as it saw fit, the funds needed by the collective enterprise.[27]

There was another more elaborate method which split the enterprise's net profit into three parts:

(1)   Agricultural mechanization fund. This amount would be transferred directly to the controlling unit for investment. In Tianjin's case, it accounted for 35 per cent of the net profit.

(2)   Profit to the controlling unit. This amount would be sent back to the controlling unit for developing the collective's economy. It was 10 per cent of the net profit in Tianjin's case.

(3)   Public reserve of the enterprise. This amount would be retained by the enterprise for reinvestment purposes. The provision of a depreciation fund was included here. (Tianjin College of Finance and Economics, 1977, p. 188-9)

In this second method, net profit was thus distributed according to specified uses, of which agricultural mechanization was one. However, as in the first method, it was still the controlling unit which ultimately determined how the profit should be used. Regardless of the method used, it remained true that the amount of accumulation within the whole commune system was thus further guaranteed by this institutional framework.

Finally, it should be noted that, with increasing controls being put on the activities of the rural collectives and their enterprises, even the distribution ratios for the enterprise's net profits had come under government ruling. For example, in Wuxi County, the county government considered it appropriate to stipulate that 60 per cent of the profit of the collective enterprise should be used in agricultural mechanization (Peking Review, August 19, 1977, p.36; Renmin Ribao, July 25, 1978).

To summarize, the rural collectives were chiefly responsible for the financing of the agricultural mechanization expenditure within their collectives. As discussed in the previous section, there has been constant pressure to maintain a highlevel of accumulation within the commune system, and this appears to have been particularly important in ensuring that the basic accounting units (which did not operate collective enterprises) channelled the greater share of any real increase in income into investment projects. The kind of production activities which have become the major source of investment funds for the rural collectives was non-grain sideline production. In fact, the term 'sideline' should really be viewed in contrast to the primacy of grain self-sufficiency. In financial terms, such sideline activities were the primary moving force for agricultural development in the communes. Through the production organization of rural collective enterprises, the upper levels of the commune system (the commune and the brigade) did not only obtain funds for agricultural mechanization but also achieved increasing control over the economic activities of all units in the commune system. At the same time, the commune system was also subject to the control of various levels of government via production link-up and taxes on collective enterprises and restrictions on non-grain activities.

THE MICROECONOMIC ASPECTS IN THE FINANCING OF AGRICULTURAL MECHANIZATION

The primacy placed on grain production ensured that the efforts in mechanizing agriculture were geared towards this objective. It would be interesting to make a marginal analysis of the costs of mechanization and the benefits that would result. Such an analysis would determine, in a narrow sense, the efficiency of agricultural mechanization in achieving the goal of increasing grain output. It is narrow as it might not consider all the indirect costs and benefits, such as costs of diverting resources to build agricultural machinery or the benefit from the improved opportunities gained from diversifying production as a result of mechanization, etc. Furthermore, agricultural inputs do not work independently of each other and thus the production effects of agricultural mechanization need to be properly estimated and interpreted. Unfortunately, for the period under investigation, there are neither time-series nor cross-sectional data available (nor data on any experimental plots) to permit such a study. However, with the information that has been released, it would still be instructive to study a number of financial factors relevant to the agricultural mechanization process of the rural collectives. Firstly, the price of grains and their cost of production are examined. Then the costs of agricultural mechanization to the rural collectives will be discussed.

First consider the price of grain and the cost of grain production. The purchase price paid by the state to the rural collectives for compulsory quota sales of grain output was set by the state and it seems to have been uniform all over the country. A premium above the normal fixed price would usually be paid by the state for the over-quota grain delivery made by the rural collectives.[28] In Table 6.10, some reported figures for the state purchase price of food grains are presented. One major problem with these figures is that almost all of them were given without reference to the quality or the grade of the food grains in question. Since different grades of grains receive different prices, some of the figures may in fact not be comparable.

It should be noted in passing that the retail price of grain has not been changed much over the years. Grains were rationed to the urban population and stability in this price was an important measure for the control of wage funds and inflation. In fact, the retail prices of food grains had been subsidized by the state to avoid fluctuation, while the state purchase prices paid to the rural collectives were raised several times. In the case of rice, it was claimed that, on average, a subsidy of 0.048 yuan was granted for each kilogram by the state. The subsidy amounted to 0.12 yuan per kilogram of rice when transport, administration and other costs were taken into account . For the year 1979, it was reported that the subsidy on grain consumption for each city dweller amounted to 35 yuan per year (Ta Kung Pao, November 7, 1979). However, as far as the rural collectives were concerned, the retail prices of food grain were of little concern to them as they were not normally permitted to sell

157

their surplus grain in the open market during this period. Their main concern was centred on how much grain they could produce, what price the state paid for their grain sales and the cost of producing the grains.

Table 6.10:   *Purchase Price of Food Grains Paid by the State to the Rural Collective*

Year	Average Price	Price for Wheat	Price for Rice
1950	1.11 yuan/kg		
1957		0.146 yuan/kg	
1965		0.228 yuan/kg	
1975	0.26 yuan/kg	0.26 yuan/kg	
		0.284 yuan/kg	
1979			0.334 yuan/kg

Source: See Appendix B

Following Marxian usage, the cost of production in China is taken to be the comprehensive indicator of the labour time necessary to make a product, and includes the following: wages, material expenditures, depreciation and administration expenses (H. Xu, et al. (ed.), 1975, pp.151-2; Donnithorne, 1967, p.161). However, when production costs were calculated by the rural collectives, the remuneration of labour was normally excluded. In Burki's report on Chinese communes in 1965, none of the communes included labour remuneration in their calculation costs (S.J. Burki, 1969, pp.25-7). In fact, Burki's delegation was given the definition that grain production costs included 'all those agricultural inputs which a production unit has to purchase from the outside', for instance: seeds, animal feed, chemical fertilizer and insecticide, tractor ploughing charges, electricity, fuel and workshop charges. Indeed, in all the available accounting manuals and textbooks for the production teams during the period labour remuneration has been excluded in cost calculation.[29] Actually, it was confirmed recently that labour remuneration was generally omitted by the rural collectives in their production cost calculation (Z. Jiang, 1979, p.51). Such a situation was perhaps not unexpected since the remuneration of labour in the Chinese rural collectives was the only major source of distributable income which was regarded as a residue rather than a first claimant on the collective's revenue.

    Table 6.11 presents some official figures, mostly on a highly disaggregate basis, on the unit cost of production for food grains. Except for the figures in (1), all the data in Table 6.11 were on individual collectives at or below the brigade level. As is apparent from the grain yield figures, most of these collectives had relatively high levels of achievement. As all of the figures in Table 6.11 except

(1) were released during the Fourth Five-Year Plan period, production costs would have excluded labour cost. Thus, this relatively low unit cost of production (again with the possible exception of (1)) compared with the state purchase price of grains of around 0.26 yuan/kg would give the appearance that grain production was a profitable activity. However, such cursory interpretation may be misleading. If the unit cost of production was calculated exclusive of labour costs, then the fact that the state purchase price of grain was greater than the unit cost of production so derived did <u>not</u> necessarily imply that the total revenue from grain production would exceed the sum of total cost of production when labour remuneration and the agricultural tax were included.[30]

Table 6.11:   *Unit Cost of Production for Food Grains in Rural Collectives*

Area	Year	Unit Cost of Production (in yuan/kg)	Grain Yield (in kg/ha)
1. Survey of 2,162 production teams (6 food grains)	1965	0.226	1,740
	1976	0.256	2,370
2. Nanzhang Brigade (Shanxi Province)	1968	0.134	
	1972	0.0476	
3. Dazhai Brigade	1974	0.06	7,695
4. Daoyuanzhuang Brigade (Shandong Province)	1971	0.06	4,335
5. Jianggezhuang Brigade (Shandong Province)			
Production Team 1	1972	0.044	6,750
Production Team 2	1972	0.082	6,750
6. Zhuli Brigade (Jaingsu Province)	1965	0.052	
	1972	0.044	
7. Weijiazhuang Brigade (Shandong Province)	1965	0.2	
	1972	0.06	
8. Maosucun Brigade (Hebei Province)	1969	0.082	3,225
	1974	0.0576	8,250
9. Luozuaung Brigade (Peking)	1974	0.0279	12,383

Source: See Appendix B

On the other hand, if the figures from the sample survey contained in (1) of Table 6.11 were truly representative of the majority of rural collectives, then regardless of whether labour remuneration had been included in the reported unit cost of production, it would mean that grain production was an unprofitable or even a losing business. In light of the large sample size in (1) of Table 6.11 and the level of grain yield which approached the national average, it seems that the figures in (1) might indeed be more realistic and representative. The fact that grain production has seldom been seen as the practical means to finance agricultural development would also serve to demonstrate its low level of profitability.[31]

Table 6.12:   *Prices of Agricultural Machinery and Other Related Inputs*

Type of Machinery	Model	Year	Unit Price in Yuan
Tractors	Gongnong-10, 10 h.p hand tractor	1977	2,000
	10 h.p. crawler tractor	1975	3,600
	12 h.p. hand tractor	1975	2,000
	20 h.p. crawler tractor	1975	4,000
	Dongfenghong-28, 28 h.p. crawler tractor	1971	11,830
	30 h.p. 4-wheel tractor	1975	12,000
	35 h.p. 4-wheel tractor	1977	13,000
	55 h.p. 4-wheel tractor	1975	10,000-20,000
Diesel Engines	3.5 h.p.	1975	550
	12 h.p.	1975	700-800
	55 h.p.	1975	3,200
Water Pump	4 inch	1971	215.8
		1972	125
Husking Machine		1973	1,000
Mechanical Thresher	1.5 tons of peanuts per hour	1976	100
Boat Cultivator Without Engine		1976	1,000

Table 6.12:   Prices of Agricultural Machinery (Continued)

Type of Machinery	Model	Year	Unit Price in Yuan
Transplanter	Manually drawn	1966	199
		1972	69
		1975	60
	Power-driven, 14 row without engine	1975	1,000
Irrigation Equipment	Motor and pump price per h.p.	1975	210
		1976	130
Transmission Gear for Tractor			
Driver's Cover Compartment for Tractor		1973	780
Fuel, Diesel	for general use, per kg.	1975	0.40
	for agricultural use, per kg.	1975	0.27
Petrol	for general use, per litre	1975	1.42
Electricity	for household use, kWh.	1975	0.07
	for industrial use, kWh.	1975	0.06
	for agricultural use, kWh	1975	0.03

Source: See Appendix B

Next, consider the various expenditures for the communes to mechanize their agriculture. Although existing information does not permit a comprehensive study on how agricultural mechanization has affected the cost of production and profitability in individual collectives, under the then prevailing conditions, it will still be instructive to examine the relevant expenditures to estimate the necessary cost for the agricultural mechanization efforts by the rural collectives. We will examine first the prices of a number of agricultural machines. Table 6.12 presents the reported prices of some major items of agricultural machinery and prices of complementary inputs.

It has not been possible to establish whether the prices given in Table 6.12 were all retail prices or ex-factory prices. Unlike the prices of food grains, the retail prices of agricultural machines actually paid by the buyers were not completely uniform in all places.[32]   Since a large number of machines, particularly the smaller ones, were being manufactured locally, the local governments seem to have had a certain freedom to determine the prices of many of the machines made by their factories (<u>Renmin Ribao</u>, December

24, 1972; May 17, 1973; August 4, 1978). Differences in retail prices were probably a result of the production cost differentials and the varied rates of surcharge placed on the purchase of machines.[33] For instance, a hand tractor could be sold for 2,938 yuan to a production team with different rates of surcharge levied by the province, city, county and commune (<u>Renmin Ribao</u>, August 4, 1978). On the other hand, there seems to be little price variation in essential items such as fuel and electricity.

If each production team owned at least two hand tractors,[34] then it would cost the team about 4,000 yuan just to acquire them. It was reported that, on the average, total fixed capital assets in each production team in China amounted to about 10,000 yuan (W. Zhan, 1979-a, p.16). Therefore, the purchase of tractors alone would represent a sizeable investment. Of course, the mere acquisition of tractors is not equivalent to the realization of mechanization. The total investment cost of mechanization of agriculture could exert quite a burden on the commune member. For instance, in Dazhai Brigade, the investment in agricultural machinery cost 400 yuan per capita for each year during 1971-4, with another 100 yuan per capita for land improvement projects (Reporting Team Stationed in Dazhai, 1979, p.211).

According to a Chinese survey, to achieve mechanization of agricultural production, about 1,500-3,000 yuan need to be spent on each hectare of cultivated land (Zhang et. at, 1979, p.27). That 1,500-3,000 yuan was only for the purchase of equipment and materials; additional workdays which were required to accommodate the change to mechanization had not been included. For example, in Wuxi County, about 2,250 yuan was required to mechanize each hectare of cultivated land in order to achieve high and stable grain yield, with another 3,000 workdays needed on each hectare to make it work (P. Liu, 1978, p.21). If each workday was valued at, say, 0.5 yuan (not a high level for a prosperous region), it would mean that the total cost of mechanizing one hectare was about 3,700 yuan.

Such a magnitude of capital outlay is not within the easy reach of the majority of rural collectives. As of 1977, the average annual income for each commune member in China was only 65 yuan (W. Zhan, 1979-a, p.16). In fact, about 40 per cent of the rural basic accounting units (production teams or brigades) had average annual incomes of less than 50 yuan for each commune member. The average value of fixed capital per hectare of cultivated land as of 1977 was only 735 yuan (W. Zhan, 1979-a, p.16). Thus, it is apparent that, for any average rural collective or commune member, the pursuit of agricultural mechanization would represent a major longterm commitment of income.

Consider the following hypothetical case. Assume that 2,000 yuan is needed to mechanize each hectare of land and that grain yield is at a respectable level of 2,250 kg/hectare. If by spending this amount of money grain yield can be raised to the higher level of 7,500 kg/hectare, for example, then the annual per hectare revenue from grain sales to the state will be increased by about 1,365 yuan (at 0.26 yuan/kg being the state purchase price). However, the extra revenue <u>cannot</u> be equivalent to extra profit since the total cost of production would also have been increased. Furthermore, the time required to reach the new level of grain yield may take a number of years. Therefore, even under the assumption of a significant increase in grain yield and only modest investment of 2,000 yuan for each hectare (which involves mainly purchases of fixed assets), it would require a relatively long period of time just to pay off the initial outlay.

Hence, while agricultural mechanization has been aimed at improving grain yield, its realization cannot depend on the profits from grain production. Alternative ways for generating the necessary funds had to be found. As discussed earlier, the substantial part of the investment funds for agricultural mechanization raised by the rural collectives did in fact come from non-grain sideline production. Thus, there was some economic justification in advocating a gradual process of agricultural mechanization which was supposed to start from small and less complex machines so that rural collectives could soon start with less expensive machinery which they could afford to purchase without having an unduly long period of accumulation and capital recoupment. On the other hand, it also helped to release critical labour not only for increasing grain output but also to expand non-grain activities. For instance, the use of irrigation and drainage equipment, or processing machines need not be confined to grain production. They could and have in practice been used profitably for the purpose of sideline production. In some extreme cases, hand tractors had been exclusively used for sideline production such as transportation.

Apart from the initial fixed cost component, there were other operating costs associated with agricultural mechanization that a rural collective had to bear. As discussed in Chapter 4, the setting up of county-commune-brigade networks for the repair and manufacture of agricultural machinery had become an integral part of the mechanization process. The establishment of workshops and plants in the brigades and communes required considerable funds. These workshops and plants were being equipped with a range of basic instruments and machine tools which might cost thousands of yuan a piece. For instance, a lathe bed for use in a commune could cost 8,000 yuan (Perkins (ed.), 1977-a, p.279).

Based on data from a number of collectives, some indication of the running cost of agricultural machinery can be obtained. The annual cost of spare parts and attachments was estimated to be 15 yuan for each hectare of cultivated land in Jiangsu Province (Renmin Ribao, December 28, 1973). Cultivation and ploughing cost by tractors averaged 12 to 15 yuan per hectare per year in Anhui Province.[35] Cost of irrigating farmland was 15 yuan per hectare per year in some areas of Henan and Hebei Province.[36] It should be noted that such unit running costs depended, to a large extent, on how effectively the machines had been utilized.

Utilization in turn depended on factors such as the availablity of spare parts and attachments, the conditions of maintenance, the size and the quality of farmland, the availability of fuel and electricity and the possibility of alternative uses of the machines. For example, whereas the amount of work done by one standard tractor was about 190 hectares per year on the national average,[37] it could reach 600 to 800 hectares in the more advanced collectives.[38] While the cost of each standard hectare ranged from 7.5 yuan to 10.5 yuan in the advanced collectives,[39] this cost could be more than doubled for the average collectives (F. Zhang, et al., 1978, p.36).

In summary, the available evidence suggests that grain production, for which agricultural mechanization was to serve, was not a profitable activity for the communes. As such, to finance investment in agricultural development and mechanization, rural collectives had turned to non-grain production. Therefore, as far as the majority of basic accounting units were concerned, there was little immediate financial incentive to engage an all-out effort to mechanize. This does not mean, however that no attempt to mechanize was made, but it does mean that it would have had to be done gradually and selectively under the prevailing economic circumstances. For the better-endowed communes or regions where some initial efforts to mechanize started earlier and have thus spanned over a longer period of time, the case for mechanization on a larger scale seems more promising. This is because of the fact they were more likely to have already diversified their rural economy after achieving an acceptable level of grain yields.

CONCLUSION

Although available information is not sufficient to determine the precise magnitude and direction of the flows of resources between the agricultural and industrial sectors during the period, it is clear that the rural collectives themselves have played a vital part in financing their agricultural development and mechanization efforts. There has certainly been a number of government measures designed to improve the relative position of the agricultural sector over time. However, direct state investments on agricultural development were limited and were relatively small compared with the identifiable and potential flow of funds from the rural sector into agricultural investments and into the state's industrial sector.

Indeed, the indication is that the rural collectives and their members, whether voluntarily or not, have to supply most of the investment funds for acquiring modern inputs to transform their production technology. Based on the available evidence, it appears that the investment funds for agricultural mechanization were basically derived from non-grain production, often through the collective enterprises, and from direct and indirect suppression of the growth of distributable personal income. However, such an approach to the financing of agricultural development was not without its problems.

As discussed earlier, with the primacy placed on grain self-sufficiency, diversification of agricultural production was not politically feasible if the efforts and achievements in grain output were not deemed to be satisfactory. As it was, under the prevailing price structure, grain production was hardly a profitable activity. Hence, production teams were left to rely on their own efforts, basically through increased labour input with selective use of chemical fertilizer and irrigation equipment (when available and affordable), to improve grain output before extensive diversification and the establishment of collective enterprises could really take off. Of course ideally the profitable diversification should start early to promote improvement in grain output, but this appears to have happened only in the better-endowed collectives where grain output was reasonably high.

As long as grain production remained highly labour-intensive, the release of labour for nongrain activities and collective enterprises might not be easily accommodated without the substitution of some mechanized equipment even though the labour engaged in grain production might not be fully employed all year round. Furthermore, the effective demand for the outputs of rural enterprises and diversified production would have been weakened by the constraint imposed on the growth of disposable income and private consumption of commune members and by the self-reliant approach to marketing and production by the rural collectives.

The financing of larger investment in modern inputs such as major agricultural machinery was in general centralized and carried out by the collective administration at the brigade and commune levels. This meant that the brigade and commune levels needed first to build up their financial resources within the commune system. The establishment of collective enterprises and the transferring of resources from the production teams had both been employed as means to strengthen the economic position of the upper levels in the commune system. This gave rise to increased control by the brigade and commune over the economic decisionmaking of the member teams and would thus override the latters' property rights at times. Coupled with the widened control by the government over the activities of the rural collectives as a whole, the institutional and organizational mechanism for maintenance of a high level of accumulation in the collective system was assured. Indeed, as discussed in Chapter 5, the rural credit co-operatives, under the close supervision of the local government, had assumed a major role as supplier of loan funds for productive investment in the rural collectives.

The extensiveness of the direct and indirect control over the economic decision-making of the collective could be viewed as a potentially useful means for directing and concentrating resources into appropriate regions or units where production effects would be optimized. In other words, a thorough and large-scale exercise in building key production units and models could have been implemented. In actual fact, based on the average amount of fixed assets owned by the rural collective and on the various costs (as against the relatively small financial benefits) for mechanizing a unit of land for grain production, it was clear that mechanization had in practice been limited to a few well-off areas and collectives.

However, during the period under investigation, political demands involving the alignment of development strategies to certain favoured socialist orientations still commanded top priority. Thus, the majority of China's collectives were still urged to make preparations for mechanization such as building the three-level network for agricultural machinery repair and manufacture. The First Dazhai Conference put forward ambitious objective but has a hastily drawn up campaign. While placing mechanization as a national programme, it seems to have recognised the dilemma in past mechanization efforts and hence envisaged that actual resources needed to be concentrated in only a selected number of places at any one time in order to gain solid progress. Unfortunately, no serious consideration appears to have been accorded to the overall financial implications of the move nor was there any significant step taken to bring about adjustments which would improve the financial capability of rural collectives in their pursuit of mechanization. Even if the actual mechanization efforts by the government were to be directed initially towards only the selected few key units, there was a need to improve substantially the returns on the main economic activities of the collectives if the eventual modernization of the rural economy was to be achieved by the self-reliant approach.

NOTES

1. See Chapter 1. State enterprises include all economic undertakings by various levels of government. For the purpose of this analysis, private production is left out. As will be shown later, the main sources of finance for mechanization did not come from private economic undertakings. Of course, it does not mean that private economic activities were insignificant in the development of China's economy.

2. As discussed in the preceding chapter, even when specific financial controls were violated, the end use of the funds was basically directed to production investments.

3. The government can of course impose taxation or use pricing policy to extract the investment funds from the rural sector and then presumably put them back into investment projects in the rural sector. The main concern here, however, refers to inducing, or forcing, the rural collectives to devote a desired level of their income to investment.

4. In fact, Paine argued that, 'from the standpoint of analysing economic change, lack of knowledge about the absolute direction of intersectoral resource transfers is not as serious as it might initially seem, since it is information and expectations about net individual

and collective receipts which are relevant for the decision-making process of the peasantry, together with the circumstances of their particular institutional environment'. Paine, 1978, p.700.

5. D. Xu, 1962, p.94. No definition was given for when production should be regarded as developed.

6. Editorial Team of Dazhai Dili, 1975, pp.45. It matters not whether Dazhai's growth rate of total income was genuinely achieved or not, the fact remained that its member's personal income was effectively frozen. This income freeze was indeed one of the main 'attributes' of Dazhai's model status.

7. Reporting Team Stationed in Dazhai, 1977, p.145, p.166. However, there could have been another reason for maintaining a constant value for each workday. It may well be due to the effect of 'labour accumulation' for farmland improvement projects which tended to increase the number of workdays sharing the same amount of total income in a given year (see next section).

8. An economic survey of the Brigade was carried out by staff of Nankai University. The results were published in a book, which contained the most detailed, though still incomplete, economic information on any one production unit in China to have been published and released for many years. See, Editorial Team of Qiong-bang-zi jing-shengfang guang-mang, 1975.

9. Figures are actually available for the years 1955-74, but since there had been several changes in the pattern of ownership in the 1950s and the early 1960s and because our interest is in the 1970s, the figures for the years 1955-68 are left out.

10. It would have been more accurate if the variable of distributed income per unit of labour could be used, but because of the changes in the size and organization in Xipu Brigade and the changes in the coverage of the data of labour force after 1972, the series of figures on units of labour was not comparable and thus cannot be used. For figures on past years not contained in Table 6.3, see Appendix B: (6).

11. Renmin Ribao, December 29, 1977; Dazhai Exhibition Hall, briefing on January 5, 1978.

12. Central Committee of the Chinese Communist Party, The National Programme for Agricultural Development, 1956-1967 (Revised Draft), Article 25. However, the progress had obviously been slow. Even in Xiyang County (a national model), a collective grain reserve in 1976 was only 120 kg per capita. See, Office of Learning from Daqing and Dazhai, Ministry of Commerce (ed.), 1977, p.22.

13. It is beyond the scope of this study to investigate fully the alternatives, the technical soundness and the opportunity costs of engaging in such projects, since it will involve extensive examination, on a macro and micro level, of all those factors for which very little information is available. Furthermore, the whole set of objectives and preferences of the Chinese leadership would have to be evaluated. With the increasing use of modern inputs such as chemical fertilizer, and irrigation equipment, the effect of such projects can

be considerable. There have been reports that indicate a 50-67 per cent reduction in the cost of irrigation alone after completion of such projects. See, <u>Renmin Ribao</u> November 26, 1972; August 16, 1975.

14. In actual fact, some of the plans seem to have been made by the prefecture and county levels while the commune and brigade co-ordinated the execution within their territories. On top of the projects being carried out within the communes, the basic accounting units also contributed a substantial part of their labour to government-managed, large-scale projects which might encompass several counties. In the case of Shandong Province, about 20 per cent of the labour used in agricultural basic construction projects was taken up by these government projects which need not benefit directly the participant teams. See, Bai Rubing, 1978, p.37.

15. Given a pre-determined ratio between W and A, and since $W=Y-C-T-A$ (equations (1) and (2)), expenditures on materials and equipment have to come from either C or A (ultimately A), and if Y and T are constants, then W/Y has to decrease. However, even in accounting manuals and textbooks for production teams, the principle for allocating funds to such projects seems to be ambiguous. See, for example, Department of Agricultural Economics, Liaoning College of Finance and Economics (ed.), 1973, Chapter 3.

16. From the discussions the author had with commune cadres and members, and from the subsequent debate on the appropriate form of agricultural development in the Chinese press since 1977, it seems almost certain that such a limit has been ignored during the 1970s. In fact, even in Xiyang County, such projects had to be curtailed in 1972 after complaints of excessive drafting of labour occurring in previous years. See, Y. Chen, et al., 1975, pp.62-91.

17. During a study tour in China in 1977, the author bought from bookstores in various provinces 'Work Handbook for Commune Member', a kind of logbook for recording and verifying the work-points and workdays each commune member earned to be kept by the individual member. All of them distinguish between production and basic construction works, but they are all added up together for the purpose of income distribution. There is also a provision for the deduction of voluntary labour contribution, but presumably this does not include labour in excess of the permitted limit. See also, Department of Agricultural Economics, Liaoning College of Finance and Economics (ed.), 1973, pp.81-5.

18. According to a report of a county in Guizhou Province, each able-bodied member of the commune devoted 50 workdays each year to such projects for the four years 1971-4. <u>Renmin Ribao</u>, November 3, 1974.

19. The figures were for 1977. Editorial Department of <u>Nongye Jixie</u> (Agricultural Machinery) (ed.), 1978, p.93.

20. <u>Renmin Ribao</u>, September 2, 1971 and February 21, 1975; Bureau of Agricultural Mechanization, 1976, Volume 1, pp.47-8; Shang and Xiao, 1977, p.27. However, this approach may be a difficult one for most collectives. Because for those marginal collectives, which were struggling to cope with self-sufficiency in grain consumption, it is unlikely that their output could be big enough

to earn the premium price for above-quota delivery. Even if the increase in grain output is achieved entirely from sales at premium price paid by the state, the additional cost may be so great that no extra funds can possibly be generated.

21. Article 14 stipulated that the commune could transfer up to 20 per cent of the brigade's public reserve to become the source of public reserve of the commune. Of course, during that time, the production brigades were the basic accounting units, and rural collective enterprises were not developed.

22. See Chapter 3. See also, Wang and He, 1978, pp.16-20.

23. It was reported that, on the average, 20 per cent of the income of commune members derived from family-run sideline production and from private plots. Thus, if private income had been included in the figures of Table 6.7, then the share that could be utilized by the collectives would have been lower, though it is not possible to estimate by how much it could have been reduced due to lack of data. However, it should be noted that during the 1970s, it was not unusual to restrict private economic activities and, in the extreme case, even to eliminate private plots. There were also cases where the collectives imposed an arbitrary surcharge on individual members' private economic activities. See, Zuo Mu, 1979, p.14; Natang zai xue Dazhai zhong kuo-bu qian-jin (Na Tang Brigade Marches Forward in Learning from Dazhai), 1973, p.17; Zhongguo Ciazheng Jingji Chubanshe (ed.), 1977 p.31; Bureau of Agriculture, Revolutionary Committee of Jiangsu Province, 1974, p.28; W. Gan, 1976, p.41.

24. See Chapter 5. See also J. Xie, 1976 pp.45-8; Jingji Guanli (Economic Management), 1979, passim.

25. However, just as in the case of agricultural basic construction projects, there had been brigades and communes that simply drafted the labour from their production teams to work in their enterprises and let the teams continue to pay these workers workpoints and food. One justification that the commune and brigade used was that the enterprises were serving all members of the collectives anyway and thus they have already been compensated indirectly. Renmin Ribao, August 24, 1972 and January 26, October 4, 1978; Hubei Renmin Chubanshe, 1976, pp.87-8.

26. Tianjin College of Finance and Economics 1977, p.180; SWB FE/W739/A1-7, August 29, 1973.

27. In some cases, the incomes from the enterprises were simply split between the controlling units and the enterprises according to an agreed ratio, and all expenditure of the enterprises was paid by the controlling units. It is clear such methods would be used in those collectives where no separate accounts were kept for the controlling unit and for the enterprise. See, Renmin Ribao, October 11, 1975; Jiang and Lu, 1976, p.31.

28. The premium seems to have varied from place to place and at different points in time. In Dazhai Brigade, the author learned from Mr Jia (Deputy Party Secretary of the Brigade, January 1978) that a premium of 30 per cent above the normal price was paid. However, according to Perkins and others, they reported (for 1975) a

50 per cent premium in Dazhai, and a 20 per cent premium for Peking's Red Star Commune. Perkins et al., 1977-a, p.279.

29. See for example, Renmin Ribao, September 10, 1972; Bureau of Rural Finance, People's Bank of China (ed.), 1977, pp.125-9; Department of Economics, Xibei Agricultural College (ed.), 1977, p.14; Department of Agricultural Economics, Liaoning College of Finance and Economics (ed.), 1973, p.125.

30. In notation form

if $P_s > \dfrac{CQ}{Q}$, it does not necessarily imply that

$\quad$ Ps · Q > CQ+W+AT
$\quad\quad$ where $\quad$ Ps $\quad$ = state purchase price of food grains;
$\quad\quad\quad\quad\quad\quad$ CQ $\quad$ = cost of production for food grains, excluding labour remuneration;
$\quad\quad\quad\quad\quad\quad$ Q $\quad\quad$ = grain output;
$\quad\quad\quad\quad\quad\quad$ W $\quad\quad$ = labour remuneration;
$\quad\quad\quad\quad\quad\quad$ AT $\quad$ = Agricultural Tax.

31. According to figures in Sichuan Province in 1978, for collectives with average grain yield, the net profit of rice was only 0.02 yuan/kg while for wheat it was a net loss of 0.01 yuan/kg. Jian Xiuyan, 1979, p.15.

32. Uniformity of prices seems to have been higher among major items of machinery such as large tractors which were being made in only a few centrally managed enterprises. See, Yu Qiuli, 1978; D. Perkins et al., 1977-a, p.279.

33. Renmin Ribao, December 24, 1972; May 17, 1973, August 4, 1978. It is not clear if the quality of the product has any effect on the retail price.

34. This was an average figure considered to be the minimun requirement for 'basic' mechanization in smaller farms of Southern and Eastern China. Mr Li, Cadre of Xinhui Agricultural Machinery Plant, Xinhui County, Guangdong Province, interview on December 23, 1977. Mr Xu, Head of Office of Revolutionary Committee, Huancheng People's Commune, Guangdong Province, interview on December 24, 1977.

35. Bureau of Agricultural Mechanization, 1976, Volume 1, p.52.

36. Briefing at Mengshan Pumping Station (Zhengzhou, Henan Province), December 30, 1977; Renmin Ribao, August 16, 1975.

37. The average figure was for 1977. See, Renmin Ribao, November 25, 1978.

38. Editorial Team of Qiong-bang-zhi jing---, 1975, p.148; Bureau of Agricultural Mechanization, Ministry of Agriculture and Forestry, 1976, Volume 2, p.30; Bureau of Agricultural Machinery Administration, 1975, p.78.

39. Ibid. For definition of standard mu, see note 37 in the previous chapter. One standard hectare is equal to fifteen standard mu.

Chapter Seven

SUMMARY AND CONCLUSION

While the mechanization of China's agriculture could potentially bring about a fundamental technological transformation for raising and sustaining a higher growth rate in agricultural output, the policies and the limited actions attempted have not promoted such a development on an extensive scale. Whether by design or by the demand of economic realities, agricultural mechanization never assumed any national significance in China's development efforts until the First Dazhai Conference in late 1975. Though the production of certain agricultural machines had increased markedly and the formation of the local manufacturing and repairing networks involving the rural communes had started, the effectiveness and the impact of the mechanization efforts were limited and were accompanied by some serious problems in production, management and financing. However, in contrast to the relatively modest contribution made by the state sector towards agricultural mechanization, the costs to the rural collectives were considerable in terms of the sacrifice made in personal consumption to make available finance and labour for investment projects.

It is perhaps not unreasonable to expect that, by policy design, the objective of agricultural mechanization was not and could not have been pursued as an immediate national goal by China's rural communes during the period under investigation. After the question of agricultural machinery ownership had been resolved in favour of the rural collectives during the Cultural Revolution, agricultural mechanization was no longer regarded as a major policy issue. The construction of farmland improvement projects had become the major concern of the Chinese planners. Despite the increasing use of modern inputs such as chemical fertilizer, development in agricultural production was still based on a labour-intensive technology that was geared to achieving grain self-sufficiency at a national and local level. Under the then prevailing political orientation, this labour-intensive technology both necessitated and was perpetuated by an expansion of controls over the activities of the rural collectives.

Considerable efforts were devoted to tackling the existing problems in production organization of agricultural machines and

171

their utilization and management. Indeed, by 1973, the provincial administrations were instructed to restrict and concentrate their resources to equip only selected counties with modern inputs stage by stage. This preferential and gradual approach was certainly not inconsistent with the practice of building models in key production regions and with the emerging desire to apply economic methods in resource allocation. However, apart from the absence of an official policy design, there existed a number of obstacles that rendered the pursuit of agricultural mechanization as a mass movement quite unrealistic and implausible. Based on the evidence and analyses contained in the preceding chapters, some of these obstacles were clearly inherent in the then existing economic situation and many were in fact the results of the prevailing general policies and measures aimed at other economic and political objectives.

One of the more obvious obstacles, for instance, was the apparent low rate of effective utilization of agricultural machinery. The problem could be attributed to the lack of an adequate supply of attachments, spare parts and repair services as well as to the fact that most major machines such as tractors were only designed to serve grain production. The deficiency in accessories was due directly and indirectly to the policy on local industry development. While local industries were given some impetus by the material allocation system under the decentralized administration of economic planning, their development was often constrained by the narrow resource base of the local economy and by the low priority and benefits associated with the production of machinery accessories. With a divergent capacity for local finance and diverse endowment conditions, local efforts to build an effective and workable local manufacturing industry could also easily be frustrated by faults and delays in the planning and distribution process which involved a complex structure of vertical and horizontal control systems.

The primacy on grain self-sufficiency technically and politically restricted the designs and use of most machines to grain production. On the other hand, since grain production was by no means a very profitable activity, there was always incentive to divert agricultural machines to uses other than field operations. The use of tractors as transport vehicles was an outstanding example. However, this would also result in reducing the pressure on local enterprises to produce the 'appropriate' accessories so that the problem was thus further aggravated.

In essence, the most significant obstacle for extending mechanization rapidly lay in the inability of most rural collectives to finance the acquisition and the operation of a comprehensive range of machinery. Even under the institutionalized framework which enforced a high rate of accumulation within the commune system, and in spite of certain concessions made by the state over the years, the majority of rural collectives had great financial difficulty in generating sufficient funds to employ major machinery to increase grain yields. With the then existing pattern of commune ownership where the production teams were the basic accounting units, not only was the purchase of agricultural machinery not a financially viable proposition, but the use of machines also presented difficult problems in their effective management and utilization. The old question arising from the conflict between upholding property rights and achieving efficient management had not been resolved satisfactorily.

The main source for financing the purchase of agricultural machines had been dependent on the income of the collective enterprises run by the brigade and commune administrations. Thus, any advance in the level of mechanization, and indeed agricultural development in general, had to be achieved through a strengthening of the relative economic position of the upper levels in the commune system. The emergence of the four-unification system of machinery management within the commune was a new form of institutional arrangement which reflected the expanding role of the brigade- and commune- level administrations. Such a management system was conceived as a means to circumvent the conflict between property rights and machinery utilization in the hope that no formal change in the pattern of commune ownership was needed.

It was quite clear that, even by the time when the First Dazhai Conference was convened, there were no elements of real urgency, or effective demand from the rural collectives, for pushing through a national programme to achieve basic mechanization within five or ten years. In fact, under the prevailing conditions, one could argue that improvement in the production of a number of appropriate agricultural inputs and machines would have been sufficient to achieve remarkable growth without having to place mechanization as the central task. There was no shortage of labour either in the urban industrial sector or in the collective enterprises that would warrant a massive transfer of labour out of agricultural production. Actually, millions of school leavers from the cities had been transferred to the rural villages and ceilings had been placed on the number of peasants that could be employed in the rural collective enterprises.

It was of course true that mechanization would lighten the toil of the peasants' work in a fundamental way. It was also true that the growth performance in agricultural production, and grain yield in particular, was not up to expectations. However, the reality was that it was beyond the financial and resource ability of the majority of rural collectives to engage in an all-out campaign, given the prevailing conditions and objectives including the self-reliant approach and the primacy of grain, in order to realize agricultural mechanization rapidly. Furthermore, the government appeared to have made no preparations to formulate a comprehensive and realistic programme which would encompass all the relevant variables and constraints and which would offer a good chance of success.

The decision by the First Dazhai Conference to place the mechanization campaign as the central task for the rural sector must be viewed in the context of the general approach which underlay China's development strategy towards the agricultural sector. That was the self-reliant approach imposed onto the rural collectives

173

accompanied by the maintenance of a high level of investment in the share of total collective income. And this had been basically sustained by the institutional structure upon which a continuous socialization process had been built. As stronger emphasis had been given to the need to apply economic methods since 1972, and with the periodic campaigns which promoted the ownership rights of the rural basic accounting units, there was some apparent resistance from certain Chinese planners and from the collectives themselves to accept a higher degree of rural socialization at that stage. On the other hand, there were clearly also some who favoured this development. This was indeed borne out by the fact that the shifting up of basic accounting units to the brigade was guardedly endorsed by the First Dazhai Conference. The significance of the mechanization campaign as proposed by this Conference was that it was a compromise measure, though not a very well-conceived one, attempting to improve the performance in the agricultural sector while at the same time initiating a new stage of rural socialization but without necessarily changing the formal ownership pattern all at once.

The First Dazhai Conference made it an official policy that agricultural mechanization was to be pursued at a quickened pace in only a selected number of counties. Apparently recognizing the economic realities, it formally broadened the concept of agricultural mechanization to include all non-grain production such as animal husbandry, forestry, fishery and other subsidiary production. While the primacy of grain was not in practice challenged, the significance was that in principle it permitted greater scope, in terms of machinery designs and political expediency, for expanding the total income (and thus investment funds) generated by the rural collectives. This move was certainly expected to have a more immediate and greater impact on those collectives or regions where development was already more advanced and which were more likely to be those selected for mechanization first.

With mechanization of agriculture thus intended to be incorporated with diversification of production, conditions for promoting specialization in production within the commune system were created. The emergence of farmland basic construction teams, organic fertilizer collection teams, and the establishment of collective enterprises were examples of the move to specialization. Based on the experiences of the more advanced model units, specialization in production had provided the argument and stimulus for shifting the basic accounting unit to the higher level of the commune system. Indeed, this seemed to be the desirable path as envisaged by the First Dazhai Conference. This was of course also compatible with the traditional ideology which believed that the introduction of specialized modern large-scale production, under the leadership of the Communist Party, would help bring about a higher degree of socialization which was regarded as representing a more desirable form of production relations.

Therefore, while there was no immediate pressure to make agricultural mechanization a top priority objective for <u>all</u> rural collectives, and apparently without much preparation and careful planning and consideration, a national campaign to promote the objective of speeding up agricultural mechanization was launched at the end of the Fourth Five-Year Plan. As discussed in the preceding chapter, for the average rural collective, basic mechanization of agriculture was quite beyond its immediate financial and technical capabilities and in fact this was reflected by the preferential approach that was to be carried out in practice. Hence, the national mechanization campaign promoted within the context of the Learning-from-Dazhai movement was essentially intended to set in train a new stage in the rural socialization process where all rural production units could be involved.

Since striving for mechanization under the existing conditions necessitated the expansion of the economic activities managed by the upper levels of the commune system resulting in a concentration of economic management in the administration at the commune level (as evidenced by the four-unification system), whether there would be an immediate change in the basic accounting unit appears to be less relevant though not unimportant. The already increasing direct and indirect controls over the production, exchange and income distribution decisions of the rural collectives would certainly help to facilitate that process of socialization. Thus, while only a selected number of places would actually be able to proceed towards mechanization at one time, the pressure of the mechanization campaign would sustain and enhance such controls so that the momentum for this stage of the socialization process could be institutionalized.

Though the mechanization campaign in late 1975 was not explicitly linked to the socialization aim, the goals set forth in the First Dazhai Conference did enhance the prospect of shifting the basic accounting unit to the brigade level in selected regions. With its emphasis on the role of mechanization in fully realizing the 'publicness and bigness' of the commune and in advancing socialism, and with the scant attention paid to the practical issues of this pursuit, the mechanization campaign was obviously more an instrument in initiating further institutional and organizational transformations in the rural sector than a pure technical measure to improve production performance.

However, even if only the problems of machinery ownership and utilization were considered, it was by no means certain that they could be automatically resolved by increasing the de facto level of rural socialization formally or informally through the mechanization campaign. A management system based solely on the goodwill and sacrifice for the collective cause of socialism and on rather arbitrary decisions through administrative changes need not produce the desired result. For the anticipated development in rural diversification through and by mechanization, the resultant expansion in commodity exchange needs to be accommodated by a well-considered policy on how this could be facilitated through a more flexible market exchange and planning mechanism. In broader terms, past experiences have amply demonstrated that institutional changes alone cannot always deliver the promised results.

Leaving aside the question of the feasibility of the whole exercise in realizing mechanization within a few years, the decision of the First Dazhai Conference would have meant that some immediate adjustments in operational policies need be adopted. If the strategy for mechanization were to break away from the formerly-held idea of mass movement, and were to be implemented by a preferential approach in practice, then it would have far-reaching implications for the then existing concept of the development of agricultural machinery production, the pattern of material allocation and the financing arrangements for the whole operation.

While the development of self-reliance in the local manufacturing of agricultural machinery might have served as a viable proposition in long-term skill formation and technology transfer under the prevailing social objectives and economic circumstances, its usefulness and its form of operation would need to be re-examined when the pattern of mechanization was to be switched to a selective process limited to only a few places at any one time. The latter was the antithesis to the previous approach where every collective could in principle pursue a varying degree of mechanization at their own pace at any one time. Indeed, this had been used as an important reason for building the extensive framework of local manufacturing capacity and for establishing the massive, though not always effective, networks of repair and manufacturing facilities within the rural communes. The development of a collaborative scheme for local production, however, had demonstrated the inherent difficulties of local manufacturing in agricultural machinery. With the new approach to mechanization, the necessity to introduce appropriate adjustments and rationalization to the industry was clearly quite important. In turn, it would have meant that changes in the material allocation and funding arrangements would have to be made.

It should be noted that, even in the case of collaborative production schemes, their workability had depended very much on suitable adjustments in material and fund allocation, and on the establishment of an appropriate set of organizational framework and price structure. Indeed, the commodity exchange activities (between the rural collectives, and between the rural collectives and the state sector) and the sectoral linkages would be expected to expand greatly given that planned agricultural mechanization was to be financed in the same self-reliant method by the rural collectives, i.e., through diversification of production via their collective enterprises. Therefore, the introduction of more flexible market and planning mechanisms and pricing arrangements to accommodate the expansion of exchanges was necessary.

However, there appears to have been no serious attention given to the more practical and immediate issues such as those discussed above nor were there any programme and action made to examine and deal with the impacts on the derived demand for complementary inputs and on the supply capability that would result from the speeding up of agricultural mechanization. In effect, the 1975 decision on mechanization really epitomized the desire to embark on a faster course of economic modernization while not giving up the basic development concept or the demands for advancing certain perceived principles of socialism.

As subsequent events turned out, this national mechanization campaign was only promoted until late 1978 when it was completely discontinued amidst the review and reform of the whole economic and socialist development concept and strategies. While the four modernizations of agriculture, industry, defence and science and technology are being promoted as the central goal, the mechanization of agriculture is no longer regarded as a prime task with any real urgency. Though discussions on the future course for agricultural development are still continuing among Chinese planners and economists, this policy reversal demonstrates in practical terms that the mechanization objective was indeed an integral part of the policy design for the transformation of the institutional and organizational structure of the economic system. Thus, as the whole economic system and its path for development are currently under review and being changed, the value of agricultural mechanization as an instrument to push through such transformation disappears. Nevertheless, mechanization as a technological reform, in whatever form it will be implemented, will remain an important vehicle to help China's new long march to modernization. The resultant sectoral interdependence between agricultural and industrial production and market demand will be a vital link to sustained economic growth. In this light, an understanding of the issues and problems in the mechanization experience during this recent past will provide some useful perspectives and a basis for studying the present and future course of development.

As a brief postscript, it is interesting to note that at present there is apparently a renewed interest by the peasants themselves in pursuing mechanization. Now that the commune system has been basically abolished all but in name and the peasant households have by 1983 become the effective economic decision-making units in production activities under various forms of the responsibility system, most of the previous problems associated with collective ownership, management and financing are now either absent or irrelevant under the new rural institutional framework and the present leadership's emphasis on development of all agricultural outputs based on a more general principle of economic rationality. While grain production is still one of the most important considerations in the policy makers' planning exercise, it is no longer arbitrarily imposed on all production units (in the present case, the households) regardless of natural considerations and comparative advantage. Equally important is the relaxation (some may argue abandonment) of the central government's concern about income inequality among the peasants. Indeed, freedom for specialization and increasing wealth among sections of the households have even prompted a renewed desire for some form of co-operative or collective organization based on the maximization of economic self-interest. At the same time, the government has reoriented and reformed the state manufacturing industries to produce more modern inputs for the agricultural sector. Peasant households are also allowed to buy and own all kinds of inputs including large machinery such as tractors. Indeed, some economists and no doubt policy-makers in China have been arguing that the present 'decollectivization' is a temporary phenomenon after which the strength of economic progress would generate an inherent demand for rural socialism, only this time it will be initiated entirely by the peasant households on efficiency consideration and for their own interest. Already, there is some evidence that, due to the expansion of ownership and use of large agricultural machinery by households, various new forms of cooperation are being experimented with. Should the present economic policy emphasis continues, it does appear that there would be more voluntary cooperatives or collectives organized as one way to gain economies of scale and more rational management of machines and the scattered land pieces worked by individual households. However, it is clear that increased direct state intervention in the agricultural sector by way of public investment is not the necessary condition for agricultural growth. As the remarkable growth in the last few years has clearly demonstrated, even when direct state investment in the sector has not been raised proportionally (Renmin Ribao, June 30, 1979, December 15, 1981, August 24, 1982), agricultural production can be increased significantly when some of the previous constraints are relaxed and removed. Whether the present policy reforms are sufficient to sustain this growth will pose a constant challenge to the Chinese government which should and could adopt a more flexible approach in dealing with future problems.

APPENDIX A: SOURCE AND NOTES FOR TABLES IN CHAPTER 4

(1)   Sources and Notes for Estimates in Table 4.1

Annual output for the years 1959, 1964, 1966 were K. Chao's estimates, which were based on official claims. Output estimate for 1965 was the average of 1964 and 1966 figures.

1959	=	5,598 (standard unit)
1964	=	21,900
1965	=	23,450
1966	=	25,000

K. Chao, 1970, pp.106-7.

1971:   production estimate derived from 1959 total and the statement that output in 1971 has increased by 15 times since 1959. Wo-men zheng-zai qian-jin (We Are Marching Forward), 1972, p.57.

1972:   production estimate derived from 1971 output and the reported increase of 10 per cent in 1972 over the previous year. Renmin Ribao, February 7, 1973; SWB, FE/W711/A9, February 14, 1973.

1973:   production estimate derived from 1965 output and the statement that output of 1973 was six times that of 1965. Kang Chao, 1970, pp.106-7; SWB, FE/W798/A16, October 23, 1974; SWB, FE/W795/A7, October 20, 1974.

1974:   production estimate derived from 1964 output and the reported increase of 520 per cent in 1974 over 1964. K. Chao, 1970, pp.106-7; Xin Zhongguo er-she wu-nian (New China's 25 Years), 1975, p.42; Perkins, (ed.), 1977, p.119; Khan, 1976, p.18.

1975:   production estimate derived from 1965 output and the statement that output of 1975 increased six times compared to 1965. K. Chao, 1970, pp.106-7; Renmin Ribao, June 16, 1976.

The 1976 production estimate was 131,320 standard units, derived from the 1965 output and the statement that the output of 1976 was 5.6 times that of 1965. K. Chao, 1970, pp.106-7, SWB, FE/W914/A4, February 2, 1977.

Although inconsistent claims on annual output have been scrutinized and dropped in the construction of the series of estimates, an additional consistency check is performed below. It was reported that between 1966 and 1976, production of tractors achieved an average growth rate of 20 per cent (Renmin Ribao, December 24, 1977). Thus, it would mean that output in 1975 should be about 6.1 times that of 1965, that is, output in 1975 should be approximately 145,280 units. Since the 20 per cent was given as an average growth rate, our estimate of 164,150 seems to be acceptable.

(2) Sources and Notes for Estimates in Table 4.2

Unlike the case of conventional tractors, there were no official output figures for annual production for any year up to 1976. It was only in June 1979 that the annual output figures for 1977 and 1978 were released, while information on the past years was still unavailable. However, with this information, an estimation for the physical production figures can be made for the years 1971-6. Only one assumption needs to be made for the production figure of 1976 in order to bridge the index series (1971-6) and the output unit series (1977-8). It is assumed that the output figure in 1976 was 300,000 units, and thus output for 1975 would be 250,000 units according to the production index (see note 9, Chapter 4). The figure for 1975 seems to be realistic, because available disaggregate production figures from only seven provinces in 1975 already totalled 140,000 units. It is not unreasonable to expect that production of 250,000 units could have been reached if output from other provinces and .pamunicipalities such as Shanghai, Peking and Tianjin had been included.

SWB, FE/W871/A9-10, FE/W871/A11, March 31, 1976; Renmin Ribao, September 20, 1975; Renmin Ribao, January 23, 1978; SWB, FE/W799/A16, October 30, 1974; SWB, FE/W823/A23/A4-5, April 23, 1975; SWB, FE/W849/A20, October 22, 1975; SWB, FE/W882/A9, June 16, 1976.

Sources for estimates of the production index:

1971: derived from 1975 figure. It was claimed that production in 1975 was eight times that of 1971. SWB, FE/W871/A8, March 1, 1976.
1973: derived from report that output in 1973 was 32 times that of 1965. SWB, FE/W798/A16, October 23, 1974.
1974: derived from report that output in 1974 was 36 times that of 1965. SWB, FE/W845/A5, September 24, 1975.

1975: derived from report that output in 1975 was 50 times that of 1965. SWB, FE/W914/A1, February 2, 1977.
1976: output in 1976 was 61 times that of 1965, thus the derived estimate annual output in 1976 was 300,000 units. Peking Review, No.9, February 25, 1977, p.15.

Sources for output figures (in units) for 1977 and 1978:

State Statistic Bureau, 1979. Output figures for 1971, 1973, 1974, 1975 were derived from the assumed production of 300,000 units in 1976 and the estimated production index. It is not clear whether the figures given for 1977 and 1978 were in standard units or not. It is also not possible to establish if the claims for output increases, on which the production index had been based, were all referring to standard (15 h.p.) or physical units. However, existing evidence suggests that these figures generally refer to physical units.
As far as overall growth in production was concerned, it was claimed that, between 1966 and 1976, an average annual growth rate of 46.6 per cent was achieved. That would have implied that the 1976 output would be about 66 times that of 1965. This result would differ slightly, but to no significant effect, from the reported claim of only 61 times. See Renmin Ribao, December 24, 1977.

(3) Sources for Estimates in Table 4.3

1960: Guangming Ribao, December 5, 1960.
1965: it was claimed that the machinecultivated area in 1976 was more than twice as large as in 1965. China Reconstructs, February-March, 1977, p.13. It was also claimed in another official news despatch that 40 per cent of the irrigated crop land was machine-ploughed in 1976. The irrigated crop land was said to be about half of total crop land in China. The total crop land was given as 100 million hectares. New China News (Melbourne, Australia), August 23, 1978, p.6; Peking Review, No.39, September 29, 1978, p.18.
1971: Benedict Stavis, 1975-a, pp.47-8.
1974: estimate based on the claim that tractorploughed farmland in 1974 was twice as large as 1965. SWB, FE/W819/A2, March 26, 1975.
1975: derived from 1976 and 1974 estimates. Stavis also gave an estimate equal to this author's. B. Stavis, 1977, p.15.
1976: see notes on 1965.

(4) Sources for Estimates in Table 4.4

(I) Rural electricity consumption based on estimates for 1962 and 1965. Consumption in 1962 was estimated to be 1,550 million kWh, for 1965 it was 3,200 kWh. K. Chao, 1970, p.139.

1971: figure based on the statement that consumption of electricity in the rural sector had increased by six times since 1962. Peking Review, November 10, 1972, p.17.

1973: figure based on the statement that consumption of electricity in countryside was 4.3 times that of 1965. SWB, FE/W756/A13, January 2, 1974.

1975: figure based on the statement that rural electricity consumption rose 4.5 times compared to 1965. SWB, FE/W885/A1, July 7, 1976.

(II)   Number of small hyrdoelectric stations

1971: Wo-men zheng-zai qian-jin (We Are Marching Forward), 1972, p.97.

1972: SWB, FE/W684/A7, August 2, 1972.

1973: SWB, FE/W756/A13, January 2, 1974.

1974: SWB, FE/W795/A11, October 2, 1974.

1975: SWB, FE/W845/A20-21, September 24, 1975.

(III)   Total generating capacity of small hydroelectric stations

1971: Wo-men zheng-zai qian-jin (We Are Marching Forward), 1972, p.97.

1972: SWB, FE/W684/A7, August 2, 1972.

1974: estimate based on the statement that the total number of small hydroelectric stations had an aggregate generating capacity which surpassed China's total electricity generating capacity in 1949. SWB, FE/W795/A11, October 2, 1974. China's total electricity generating capacity was derived from the official figure of total electricity output in 1949, and estimate of utilization rate for small hydro-electric stations by K. Chao. The total national output in 1949 was 4,310 million kWh, while utilization rate for stations was estimated to be 2,000 hours per year (26 per cent). Ten Great Years, p.95; K. Chao, 1970, p.45, p.246, p.254.

1975: estimate derived from output estimate for 1975, see (IV) below.

(IV) Output from small hydroelectric stations

1975: estimate based on statement that electricity output from small hydroelectric stations had exceeded the national electricity output in 1949. Renmin Ribao, September 4, 1975; Ten Great Years, p.95.

(5) Sources for Figures in Table 4.5

Fujiang Province: SWB, FE/W849/A9-10, October 22, 1975;
Hunan Province, Shandong Province, Jilin Province: SWB, FE/W799/A9-10, October 30, 1974;

She County, Chuanan County, Hui County: <u>SWB</u>, FE/W810/A10-11, January 22, 1975.

(6) <u>Sources for Estimates in Table 4.6</u>

1971: based on the statement that total power of irrigation and drainage machinery in 1975 was double that of 1971, and that there were 40 million h.p. in 1975. <u>SWB</u>, FE/W880/A1, June 2, 1976.
1972: <u>Wo-men zheng-zai qian-jin</u> (We Are Marching Forward), 1972, p.92.
1973: <u>SWB</u>, FE/W757/A2, January 9, 1974.
1974: <u>SWB</u>, FE/W819/A2, March 26, 1975.
1975: <u>SWB</u>, FE/W868,A2, March 10, 1976.
1976: <u>Renmin Ribao</u>, December 27, 1977.

(7) <u>Sources for Estimates in Table 4.7</u>

(I) Number of wells sunk in each year

1972: <u>SWB</u>, FE/W706/A4, January 10, 1973.
1973: <u>SWB</u>, FE/W757/A2, January 9, 1974.
1974: estimated figure derived from cumulative total numbers for 1974 and 1973 in column II of the table.
1975: estimated figure derived from cumulative total numbers for 1975 and 1974 in column II of the table.

(II) Cumulative total number of wells

1965: <u>SWB</u>, FE/W819/A2, March 26, 1975.
1971: derived from the estimates for wells sunk in 1972 and the cumulative total number of wells in 1972.
1972: derived from the figure for the cumulative total number of wells in 1973.
1973: <u>SWB</u>, FE/W757/A2, January 9, 1974.
1974: <u>SWB</u>, FE/W801/A6, November 13, 1974.
1975: <u>SWB</u>, FE/W868/A2, March 10, 1976.

(III) Area irrigated by wells

1973: <u>SWB</u>, FE/W757/A2, January 9, 1974.
1974: <u>SWB</u>, FE/W801/A6, November 13, 1974.
1975: <u>Renmin Ribao</u>, June 16, 1976.

(8) <u>Sources for Estimates in Table 4.8</u>

1971: estimated index based on the statement that production of internal combustion engines in 1971 had increased by 3.2 times compared with 1965. <u>Economic Reporter</u>, February 14, 1973.

1972: estimated index based on the statement that engine production in 1972 had increased by 25 per cent compared to 1971. <u>Renmin Ribao</u>, February 7, 1973; <u>SWB</u>, FE/W711/A9, February 14, 1973.

1973: estimated index based on the statement that engine production in 1973 increased by more than seven-fold compared with 1965. <u>SWB</u>, FE/W795/A7, October 2, 1974.

1974: estimated index based on the statement that engine production in 1973 had increased by twelve-fold compared to 1965. <u>SWB</u>, FE/W845/A5, September 24, 1975.

(9) <u>Sources and Notes for Estimates in Table 4.9</u>

(I) Irrigated farmland. Estimates based on the following statements:

(a) During the five years between 1970 and 1974, irrigated acreage increased at the rate of 1.6 million hectares per year.

(b) By 1977, nearly half of the crop land in China had been brought under irrigation.

(c) China's farmland is approximately 100 million hectares.

Assuming that the rate of increase (as given in statement (a)) continued in 1975, 1976 and 1977, the estimated series can thus be reconstructed from a figure of 50 million hectares for 1977. However, it is not clear whether the rate of growth has been an average figure or not. If it was an average growth rate, then the real pattern in the expansion of irrigated acreage cannot be ascertained. Nevertheless, the reconstructed estimate series of Table 4.9 does tally with another independent report of official claim for the years 1972 and 1973. See, Perkins (1975-d), Table 6, Footnote 12, p.360.

Sources for the three statements were:

(a) <u>Peking Review</u>, No.9, February 25, 1977, p.15.

(b) <u>New China News</u> (Melbourne), August 23, 1978, p.6.

(c) <u>Peking Review</u>, No.39, September 29, 1978, p.18.

(II) Source for estimate of effective irrigated area by dams

<u>Renmin Ribao</u>, July 28, 1978.

(III) Area with drainage facilities (or with controlled waterlogging).

1974: area where waterlogging had been controlled. <u>SWB</u>, FE/W801/A6, November 13, 1974.

1977: area of low-lying fields which had drainage facilities. <u>China Reconstructs</u>, July, 1977, p.24.

(IV)   Farmland protected against drought and flooding

1974:   SWB, FE/W789/A16, October 23, 1974; SWB, FE/W814/A15, February 19, 1975.
1975-6: figures derived from 1977 estimate
1977:   Ta Kung Pao, October 29, 1979.

(10) Sources and Notes for Estimates in Table 4.10

Row (I) : Horsepower from tractors per hectare of tractorized farmland

(a)   Total horsepower from tractors calculated by the stocks of all tractors multiplied by their respective horsepower. For conventional tractors, 613,350 standard units (from Note 7 in Chapter 4) give:
        15 h.p. x 613,350 = 9.2 million h.p.

        For hand tractors, the existing stock in 1975 was assumed to be equal to the difference between the stock in 1977 and the output of 1977 and 1976. (See Table 4.2, Note 9 and Appendix A2.) Thus, the stock of hand tractors in 1975 was:
        1,090,000 - 200,000 - 180,000 = 710,000

        It was also assumed that on average, each hand tractor was equivalent to half a standard unit of tractor. Therefore, total horsepower from hand tractors was:
        7 h.p. x 710,000 = 4.97 million h.p.

        Hence, total power from all tractors in 1975 was:
        9.17 + 4.97 = 14.14 million h.p.

(b)   Tractorized acreage was estimated to be 20 million hectares from Table 4.3.

(c)   The estimated figure of 0.7 h.p. per tractorized hectare can thus be found by
        (a)/(b) = 14.14/20 = 0.7

Row (II) : Horsepower from irrigation and drainage equipment per hectare of irrigated land. Estimate series is found by dividing the figures in Table 4.6 by the figures in the first column of Table 4.9.

Row (III) : Horsepower from tractors per hectare of cultivated land. The estimated figure was derived from the figure of 14.14 million h.p. from all tractors calculated above and a total cultivated acreage of 100 million hectares.

Row (IV) : Horsepower from irrigation and drainage equipment per hectare of cultivated land. Estimated series is found by dividing the figures in Table 4.6 by 100 million hectares (for all years).

Row (V) : Horsepower from tractors and irrigation and drainage equipment per hectare of cultivated land. Estimate figure was the sum of figures in Row III and Row IV of Table 4.10.

(11) Sources for Estimates in Table 4.11

Row 1 (Hubei): Bureau of Agricultural Mechanization, 1976, Volume 2, p.44.

Row 2 (Hubei): Hubei Renmin Chubanshe, 1976, pp.91, 93.

Row 3 (Shanxi): Shang and Xiao, 1977, pp.1-2, pp.5-7.

Row 4 (Anhui): Bureau of Agricultural Mechanization, 1976, Volume 1, p.45, p.53.

Row 5 (Hunan): Ibid., pp.37-8.

Row 6 (Jiangsu, Wuxi County): The figure was for the whole county. Hubei Renmin Chubanshe, 1975, p.63.

Row 7 (Hubei): Xinzhou County Communist Party Committee, Hubei Province, 1974, p.84.

Row 8 (Shanghai): Editorial Team of Ren-min gong-she zai yue-jin, 1974, p.115.

Row 9 (Shanghai): Bureau of Agricultural Mechanization, Ministry of Agriculture and Forestry (ed.), 1976, Volume 1, p.29.

(12) Source for Figure 4.1

Renmin Ribao, September 9, 1971; Renmin Chubanshe (ed.), 1972, p.86; Liaoning Renmin Chubanshe (ed.), 1973, p.11; F. Lin, 1976, pp.59-70; Z. Ji, 1977, p.73; SWB, FE/W610/A6, February 24, 1971; SWB, FE/W929/A1, May 18, 1977; SWB, August 29, 1973.

APPENDIX B: SOURCE AND NOTES FOR TABLES IN CHAPTER 6

(1) Source for Table 6.1

1953-70: Liu Suinian, 1979, pp.16-7.
1971-75: He Zhuo, 1979, p.9.

(2) Source for Table 6.2

Row 1: SWB, FE/W884/A1, June 30, 1976.

Row 2: SWB, FE/W798/A17, October 23, 1974.

Row 3: Jiang Xunxin, Lu Xiufeng, 1976, p.5.

Row 4: 1966-75: Zhongguo Caizheng Jingji Chubanshe (ed.), 1977,
       p.39. The figure for increase in total collective income, which
       was for 1964-74, was from: Editorial Team of Dazhai Dili, 1975,
       pp.4-5.

Row 5: SWB, FE/W741/A2, September 12, 1973.

Row 6: Bureau of Agricultural Mechanization,
       Ministry of Agriculture and Forestry (ed.), 1976, Volume 1, p.29.

Row 7: Ibid., p.73.

Row 8: Revolutionary Committee of Fenglai County, Shandong
Province, 1975, p.35.

Row 9: You Jiangwen, Tian Yangzhang, 1976, p.3; Natang zai
       xue Dazhai zhong kuo bu qian-jin (Natang Brigade Marches
       Forward in Learning from Dazhai), 1973, p.7, p.21.

Row 10: SWB, FE/W712/A4, February 21, 1973.

Appendix B

(3) Source and Supplement for Table 6.3

Editorial Team of Qiong-bang-zhi jing-shen fang guang-mang, 1975, p.167, p.170.

Growth of Collective Income and its Distribution in Xipu Brigade, Zunhua County, Hebei Province (1955–1968)

Year	(Y)	(A)	(K)	(H)	(W)	(W/pop.)	(C+T)
1955	52,567 - (100)	2,304 - (4.4)	1,900 - (3.6)	404 - (0.8)	36,659 - (70)	57 - -	13,604 - (25.6)
1956	72,350 +37.7% (100)	2,650 +15% (3.6)	1,750 -7.9% (2.4)	900 +123% (1.2)	50,201 +40% (70)	72 +26.3% -	19,499 +43.3% (26.4)
1957	80,509 +11.3% (100)	4,897 +84.8% (6)	3,297 +88.4% (4)	1,600 +77.8% (2)	57,850 +15% (72)	80 +11.1% -	17,762 -9% (22)
1958	79,771 -0.9% (100)	4,800 -2% (6)	3,520 +6.8% (4.4)	1,280 -20% (1.6)	56,559 -2.2% (71)	76 -5% -	18,412 +3.7% (23)
1959	82,443 +3.4% (100)	5,642 +17.5% (6.8)	3,631 +3.2% (4.4)	2,011 +57% (2.4)	52,289 -7.6% (64.2)	70 -8.6% -	23,912 +30% (29)

Year	(Y)	(A)	(K)	(H)	(W)	(W/pop.)	(C+T)
1960	88,914 +7.9% (100)	3,883 -31.2% (4.4)	2,105 -42% (2.4)	1,778 -11.6% (2)	61,003 +16.7% (68.6)	77 +10% –	24,028 +0.5% (27)
1961	119,149 +34% (100)	8,300 +114% (7)	5,188 +147% (4.4)	3,112 +75% (2.6)	82,844 +35.8% (69.5)	97 +30% –	28,005 +16.6% (23.5)
1962	121,435 +1.9% (100)	9,695 +16.8% (8)	6,071 +17% (5)	3,624 +16.5% (3)	81,861 -1.2% (67.4)	89 -8.3% –	29,879 +6.7% (24.6)
1963	113,556 -6.5% (100)	5,815 -40% (5.1)	4,446 -26.8% (3.9)	1369 -62% (1.2)	75,743 -7.5% (66.7)	81 -8.9% –	31,998 +7.1% (28.2)
1964	97,211 -14.4% (100)	6,280 +8% (6.5)	5,143 +15.7% (5.3)	1,137 -16.9% (1.2)	60,080 -20.7% (61.8)	62 -23.5% –	30,851 -3.6% (31.7)
1965	93,354 -3.9% (100)	6,268 -0.2% (6.7)	4,345 -15.5% (4.7)	1,923 +69% (2)	62,271 +3.6% (66.7)	62 0% –	24,815 -19.6% (26.6)
1966	121,514 +30.2% (100)	16,900 +170% (14)	12,849 +196% (10.6)	4,051 +111% (3.4)	72,998 +17.2% (60)	71 +14.5% –	31,616 +27.4% (26)

Year	(Y)	(A)	(K)	(H)	(W)	(W/pop.)	(C+T)
1967	116,722	17,003	13,739	3,264	65,210	63	34,509
	-4%	+0.69%	+6.9%	-19%	-10.7%	-11.3%	+9.2%
	(100)	(15)	(12)	(3)	(56)	-	(29)
1968	113,765	11,353	8,000	3,353	68,588	64	33,824
	-2.5%	-33.2%	-41.8%	+2.7%	+5.2%	+1.6%	-1.9%
	(100)	(10)	(7)	(3)	(60.3)	-	(29.7)

Y = Total Collective Income
K = Public Reserve
W = Distributable Net Income
(C+T) = Cost and Taxes

A = Public Accumulation of Brigade
H = Welfare Fund
W/Pop. = Income Per Capita

Y = A + W + C + T, and A = K + H.

All percentage figures were rates of increases over the previous year for that variable, all figures in brackets were shares as a percentage of total collective income, all other figures were monetary value expressed in yuan at current prices.

The basic unit of accounting in Xipu has gone through several changes over the years. Between 1953 and 1955, the basic unit of accounting was the elementary producers' co-operative. Between 1956 and 1961, it was the advanced producers' co-operative. In 1962 to 1967, it was the production team whereas for 1968 onwards it was the brigade itself.

(4) Source for Table 6.4

Row 1-Row 3: <u>SWB</u>, FE/W853/A3, November 19, 1975; FE/W861/A5-9, January 21, 1976; FE/W862/A6-9, January 28, 1976.

Row 4-Row 6: <u>SWB</u>, FE/W852/A3-10, November 12, 1975.

Row 7: <u>SWB</u>, FE/W815/A13, February 26, 1975.

Row 8-Row 11: <u>SWB</u>, FE/W815/A7-11, February 26, 1975.

Row 12: <u>SWB</u>, FE/W804/A1, December 4, 1974.

Row 13: <u>SWB</u>, FE/W764/A5, February 27, 1974.

Row 14-Row 15: <u>SWB</u>, FE/W758/A8, January 16, 1974.

Row 16: <u>SWB</u>, FE/W762/A4, February 13, 1974.

Row 17: <u>SWB</u>, FE/W712/A7, February 21, 1973.

Row 18: Jiang and Shu, 1975, p.57.

Row 19: D. Shi, 1975, p.36.

Row 20: Y. Chen, et al., 1975, p.90.

Row 21-Row 26: <u>SWB</u>, FE/W749/A1-2, January 23, 1974.

(5) Source for Table 6.5

Shanghai Rural Suburbs: 1974: <u>Renmin Ribao</u>, September 18, 1975; Hubei Renmin Chubanshe, 1975, p.39. 1977: M. Xue, 1978, p.8.

Peking Rural Suburbs: M. Xue , <u>op.cit</u>.

Tianjin Rural Suburbs: <u>Ibid</u>.

Jiangsu Province: <u>Ibid</u>.

Shandong Province: <u>Ibid</u>.

Wuxi County: 1965: <u>Peking Review</u>, July 29, 1977, p.23. 1975: Xue Xinnong, 1977, pp.61-2.

Wangpo County: Hubei Renmin Chubanshe (ed.), 1976, Volume 2, pp.73-4.

Liangzun Commune: <u>SWB</u>, FE/W904/A2-3, November 17, 1976.

Yantai Prefecture: Hubei Renmin Chubanshe (ed.), 1975, Volume 1, p.36.

(6) Source for Table 6.6

Wuming County: SWB, FE/W878/A3, May 19, 1976.

Haining County: SWB, FE/W825/A4-5, May 7, 1975.

Shangzhuang Commune: Renmin Ribao, February 21, 1975.

Mencheng County: SWB, FE/W800/A9, November 6, 1974.

Licheng County: Department of Water Conservancy (ed.), 1976, p.64.

Xinzhou County: Renmin Ribao, September 6, 1971.

Qingchuan County: SWB, FE/W885/A12, July 7, 1976.

Chuansha County: Hubei Renmin Chubanshe (ed.), 1975, Volume 1, p.42.

Yantai Prefecture: Ibid., p.36.

Xiyang County: Zhongguo Caizheng Jingji Chubanshe (ed.), 1977, p.35.

Natang Brigade: 1971-3: Natang zai xue Dazhai zhong kuo-bu qian-jin (Natang Brigade Marches Forward in Learning from Dazhai), pp.40-4. 1974-5: You and Tian, 1976, p.44.

Fangang Commune: Bureau of Agricultural Mechanization, 1976, Volume 1, pp.47-8.

Taoyuan County: Editorial Team of Taoyuan-xin-mao, 1977, pp.80-1, p.84.

Meixian County: SWB, FE/W709/A7, January 31, 1974.

Luchuan County: SWB, FE/W844/A17, September 17, 1975.

Xinglongjie Commune: Editorial Team of Tao-yuan xin-mao, 1977, pp.80-1, p.84.

(7) Source for Table 6.7

Liuji Comune: Renmin Chubanshe (ed.), 1972, p.54.

Jixing Brigade: Renmin Ribao, August 23, 1972.

Qianan County: Hongqi, No.1, 1972.

Xigou Brigade: Renmin Ribao, January 25, 1972.

Gangyao Brigade: Bureau of Agriculture, Revolutionary Committee of Jiangsu Province, 1974, p.70.

Dongguan County: Renmin Chubanshe (ed.), 1972, p.95.

Tuanpiaozhuang Commune: J. Xie, pp.54-5.

Hunan Province: 1973: SWB, FE/W799/A6, October 30, 1974. 1975-6: Hubei Renmin Chubanshe, 1977, p.47.

Sifang County: SWB, FE/W858/A6, December 31, 1975.

Zhaodong County: SWB, FE/W799/A6, October 30, 1974.

Xiyang County, Peking Red Star Commune, Yangsi Commune, Shanghai July 1 Commune, and Helie Commune: Perkins (et al.), 1977-a, pp.214-5.

(8) Source for Table 6.8

Jiading County: Renmin Ribao, October 19, 1974

Wuxi County: C. Chin, 1977, p.33.

Chuansha County: Renmin Ribao, October 17, 1975.

Malu Commune: Bureau of Agricultural Mechanization, 1976, Volume 1, p.36.

Wuxi County: Hubei Renmin Chubanshe, 1975, p.61.

Hunan Province: SWB, FE/W858/A5, December 31, 1975.

Jinkou Commune: Bureau of Agricultural Mechanization, 1976, p.13.

Lijiazhuang Commune: Bureau of Agricultural Machinery Administration, 1974, p.12.

Caijiajian Commune: Renmin Ribao, February 17, 1975.

(9) Source for Table 6.10

1950: Ta Kung Pao, November 7, 1979.

1957: Peking Review, No.32-33, August 9, 1976, p.26.

1965: Ibid.

1975: Average Price: Perkins (ed.), 1977-a, p.281. Price of Wheat: (0.284 yuan/kg): Ibid., p.279. (0.26 yuan/kg): Peking Review, No.32-3, August 9, 1976, p.26.

1979: Yao Jianhua, et al., 1979, p.26.

(10) <u>Source for Table 6.11</u>

Row 1: J. Yao, 1978, pp.17-8.

Row 2: <u>SWB</u>, FE/W732/A3, July 11, 1973.

Row 3: Reporting Team Stationed in Dazhai, 1977, p.139; Editorial Team of <u>Dazhai Dili</u>, 1975, p.4.

Row 4: <u>Renmin Ribao</u>, September 10, 1972.

Row 5: <u>Ibid.</u>, February 16, 1973.

Row 6: <u>SWB</u>, FE/W754/A3, December 12, 1973.

Row 7: <u>Renmin Ribao</u>, June 29, 1973.

Row 8: <u>Ibid.</u>, August 16, 1975.

Row 9: <u>Ibid.</u>, March 28, 1975

(11) <u>Source for Table 6.12</u>

<u>Tractors:</u>

Gongnong 10	: Mr Li, Cadre of Xinhui Agri- cultural Machinery Plant, Xinhui County, Guangdong Province, interview on December 23, 1977.
10 h.p.	: Perkins (ed.), 1977-a, p.279.
12 h.p.	: <u>Ibid.</u>, p.279, p.280, p.281.
20 h.p.	: <u>Ibid.</u>, p.279.
Dongfenghong 28	: J. Yao, 1978, p.20.
30 h.p.	: Zhongguo Caizheng Jingji Chubanshe (ed.), 1977, p.83.
35 h.p.	: <u>Renmin Ribao</u>, August 4, 1978.

<u>Diesel Engines:</u>

3.5 h.p., 12 h.p., 55 h.p.: Perkins (ed.), 1977-a, p.120, p.280.

<u>Water Pump:</u> <u>Renmin Ribao</u>, December 24, 1972.

<u>Husking Machine:</u> Editorial Team of <u>Ren-min gong-she zai yue-jin</u>, 1974, p.172.

<u>Thresher:</u> <u>China Reconstructs</u>, February-March 1977, p.18.

<u>Boat Cultivator Without Engine:</u> <u>Renmin Ribao</u>, August 20, 1977.

Appendix B

<u>Transplanter:</u>

Manually drawn:

1966 and 1972   :<u>Renmin Ribao</u>, August 17, 1973.
1975   : Perkins (ed.), 1977-a, p.120.

Power-driven : <u>Ibid.</u>

<u>Irrigation Equipment:</u> <u>Ibid.</u>

<u>Transmission Gear:</u> <u>Renmin Ribao</u>, July 12, 1977.

<u>Driver's Cover Compartment:</u> <u>Ibid.</u>, May 17, 1973.

<u>Fuel:</u> Perkins et al. , 1977-a, p.123, p.280.

LIST OF CHINESE PUBLISHERS

Caizheng Chubanshe (Finance Press)
Caizheng Jingji Chubanshe (Finance and Economics Press)

Commercial Press
Dagong Bao She (Dagong Daily Press)
Falu Chubanshe (Law Press)

Foreign Language Press
Kexue Chubanshe (Science Press)
Nongye Chubanshe (Agriculture Press)
Renmin Chubanshe (People's Press)
Renmin Ribao Chubanshe (People's Daily Press)
Shuili Dianli Chubanshe (Hydroelectricity Press)
Xianggang Chaoyang Chubanshe (Hong Kong Chaoyang Press)
Zhongguo Caizheng Jingji Chubanshe (Finance and Economics Press of China)
Zhongguo Qingnian Chubanshe (Chinese Youth Press)

Regional Branches of *Renmin Chubanshe* (People's Press) are not listed.

LIST OF CHINESE PERIODICALS AND NEWSPAPERS

PERIODICALS

Beijing Review (Peking Review, Peking)
Caizheng (Finance, Peking)
China Reconstructs (Peking)
Economic Reporter (Hong Kong)
Hongqi (Red Flag, Peking)
Huaxue Gongye (Chemical Industry, Peking)
Jihua Jingji (Planned Economy, Peking)
Jixie Gongye (Machinery Industry, Peking)
Jingji Yanjiu (Economic Management, Peking)
Nankai Daixue Xuebao (Journal of Nankai University, Tianjin)
Nongye Jixie Jishe (Agricultural Machine Technique, Peking)
Studies on Chinese Communism (Taiwan)
Renmin Shouce (People's Handbook, Peking)
Shehui Kexue Zhangaxian (Frontier of Social Sciences, Zhangchun
                   City, Jilin)
Zhonggong Nianbao (Communist China Yearbook, Taiwan)
Zhonggue Duiwai Maoyi (China's Foreign trade, Peking)
Zhongguo Qinggongye (China's Light Industry, Peking)
Zhongguo Qingnian (Chinese Youth, Peking)

NEWSPAPERS

Dagong Bao (Dagong Daily, Peking)
Gongren Ribao (Workers' Daily, Peking)
Guangming Ribao (Guangming Daily, Peking)
Jiefangjun Ribao (People's Liberation Army's Daily, Peking)
Renmin Ribao (People's Daily, Peking)
Ta Kung Pao (Ta Kung Daily, Hong Kong)

BIBLIOGRAPHY

NOTES

(1) All Chinese names and publication titles, except those originally published in English outside China or in translation series, are romanized according to the Pin-yin system. Geographical names other than Peking and Canton are also romanized by the same system.

(2) Chinese publications with Pin-yin romanized titles appear in their original form. For publications with only Chinese titles, the romanized characters are given in hyphenated forms. All English translations of Chinese titles are the author's.

(3) Speeches and reports by Chinese political leaders are cited by their date of delivery (if known) instead of the publication date (which might lag by several years) for convenience in the identification of their chronological sequence in relation to discussion of policy developments in the text.

Abbott, J.C. (1977), 'Food and Agricultural Marketing In China', Food Policy, No. 4, pp.318-30

Abercrombie, K.C. (1973), 'Agricultural Mechanization and Employment in Latin America', in International Labour Office, Mechanization and Employment in Agriculture : Case Studies from Four Continents, Geneva: International Labour Office

Agricultural Office of Zhejiang Province (ed.) (1977), Ju-qi zhu-gang xue Dazhai: Zhejiangsheng di-er-ci nong-ye xue-Dazhai hui-ye cai-liao xuan-bian (Selected documents from the Second Zhejiang Provincal Conference on Learning from Dazhai), Hangzhou: Zhejiang Renmin Chubanshe

An, Xiang (1976), Dazhai hong-qi piao Dongting (Dazhai's Red Flag Flies Over Lake Dong-ting), Peking: Nongye Chubanshe

An, Xuejiang (1972), 'Must Have Faith in the Mass and in the Party', Hongqi (Red Flag), No.1, pp.11- 8

Ashbrook, A.G. Jr. (1975), 'China : Economic Overview, 1975' in Joint Economic Committee, U.S. Congress, China : A Reassessment of the Economy, Washington, D.C.: U.S. Government Printing Office

Aziz, Sartaj (1973), 'The Chinese Approach to Rural Development', International Development Review, No.4, pp.2-7

Bai, Rubing (1978), 'A Great Socialist Task', Hongqi (Red Flag), No.9, pp.35-40

Ban-hao nong-cun dai-gou-dai-xiao-dian (Do a Good Job in Running Rural Supply and Marketing Shops) (1975), Peking: Caizheng Jingji Chubanshe

Barker, Randolph, et al. (1973), 'Employment and Technical Change in Philippine Agriculture', in International Labour Office, Mechanization and Employment in Agriculture : Case Studies from Four Continents, Geneva: International Labour Office

Berger, Roland (1972), 'The Mechanization of Chinese Agriculture', Eastern Horizon, No.3, pp.7-26

_____ (1975) 'Economic Planning in the People's Republic of China', World Development, Volume 3, Nos. 7 and 8, July-August, pp.551-64

Bergson, Abram (1973), 'Comparative Productivity and Efficiency in the Soviet Union and the United States' in A. Eckstein (ed.), Comparison of Economic Systems, Berkeley: University of California Press

Bhatia, Ramesh (1976), 'Rapporteur's Report On Energy Requirements of Different Farm Systems', Indian Journal of Agricultural Economics, No.3, pp.250-68

Birrell, Robert J. (1970), The Structure of Chinese Communes : 1960-1966 (Unpublished Ph.D. Dissertation, Princeton University)

Blecher, Marc (1976), 'Income Distribution in Small Rural Chinese Communities - A Comment', China Quarterly, No.68, pp.797-816

Bo, Yibo (1957), 'Report on the Implementation Results of the 1956 National Economic Plan and Draft of 1957 National Economic Plan' (Fourth Session of the First National People's Congress, July 1, 1957) in The Fourth Session of the First National People's Congress (Documents) Peking: Renmin Chubanshe, 1957
___ (1964), Socialist Industrialization and Agricultural Collectivization in China, Peking: Foreign Language Press
Borstein, Morris (ed.) (1974), Comparative Economic Systems : Models and Cases (Third Edition), Homewood, Illinois: Richard D. Irwin, Inc.
Breth, Ron M. (1974), The Conflict Within the Chinese Communist Party and its Implications for Agricultural Development : The Case of Collectivization, 1955-56 (Unpublished Master's Thesis in Economics, Monash University)
Broadbent, Kieran (1978), A Chinese/English Dictionary of China's Rural Economy, Farnham Royal, Bucks., England: Commonwealth Agricultural Bureau
Buchanan, Keith (1970), The Transformation of the Chinese Earth, London: G. Bell and Sons, Ltd.
Buck, John L. (1937), Land Utilization in China, Nanking: University of Nanking
Bureau of Agricultural Machinery Administration, Revolutionary Committee of Jinzhong Prefecture Shanxi Province (ed.) (1974), Xiyang da-ban nong-ye ji-xie-hua jing-yan (Experience of Agricultural Mechanization in Xiyang County), Taiyuan: Shanxi Renmin Chubanshe
Bureau of Agricultural Machinery, Yushu County, Jilin Province (1976), 'Take the Party's Basic Line as the Link, Train Technical Teams of Agricultural Machinery Through Three Level System', in Bureau of Agricultural Mechanization, Ministry of Agriculture and Forestry (ed.) (1976), Nong-ye de gen-ben chu-lu zai-yu ji-xie-hua (The Fundamental Way Out for Agriculture Lies in Mechanization), Volume 2, Peking: Nongye Chubanshe
Bureau of Agricultural Mechanization, Ministry of Agriculture and Forestry (ed.) (1976), Nong-ye de gen-ben chu-lu zai-yu ji-xie-hua (The Fundamental Way Out for mriculture Lies in Mechanization), Volumes 1-2, Peking: Nongye Chubanshe
Bureau of Agriculture, Revolutionary Committee of Jiangsu Province (1974), Zong-jie jing-yan kuo bu qian-jin Jiangsu sheng nong-ye xue Dazhai jing-yan xuan-bian (Summarize Experiences and March Forward: Selected Cases of Experience in Learning from Dazhai in Jiangsu Province), Peking: Nongye Chubanshe
Bureau of Agriculture and Forestry, Revolutionary Committee of Shaanxi Province (ed.) (1975), Nong-ye ke-xue ji-shu shou-ce (Handbook of Agricultural Science and Technology), Shaanxi: Shaanxi Renmin Chubanshe
Bureau of Commune and Brigade Enterprise, Hunan Provice (1978), 'Build More Commune and Brigade Enterprises', Hongqi (Red Flag), No.11, pp.53-6

Bureau of Rural Finance, People's Bank of China (ed.) (1977),
Nong-cun ren-min gong-she sheng-chan-dui kuai-ji zhi-shi
(Accounting Knowledge for Production Teams in the People's
Communes), Peking: Zhongguo Caizheng Jingji Chubanshe

Bureau of Water Conseration, Ministry of Agriculture (1966), Shui-li
yun-dong shi-nian 1949-1959 (Ten Years of Water Conservation
Campaign 1949-1959), Peking: Nongye Chubanshe

Burki, S.J. (1969), A Study of Chinese Communes 1965, Cambridge,
Massachusetts: East Asian Research Centre, Harvard University

Cai, Zhang (1971), 'Establish the Attitude that Financial Works Should
Serve Production - Criticize the Pure Financial viewpoint',
Renmin Ribao (People's Daily), February 11

Cassou, P.H. (1976), 'The Chinese Monetary System', Chinese
Economic Studies, No.4, pp.82-97

Central Committee of the CCP (1953-a), 'Decisions on Mutual Aid and
Cooperativization in Agricultural Production' (February 15,
1953), in Chao, Kuo-chun, Agrarian Policies of Mainland China :
A Documentary Study (1949-1956), Cambridge, Massachusetts:
East Asian Research Centre, Harvard University, 1963

_____ (1953-b), 'Decisions on the Development of the Agricultural
Producers' Cooperatives' (December 16, 1953), in Chao,
Kuo-chun, Agrarian Policies of Mainland China : A
Documentary Study (1949-1956), Cambridge, Massachusetts:
East Asian Research Centre, Harvard University, 1963, pp.66-70

_____ (1955), 'Resolution on Agricultural Cooperativization' (October
11, 1955), in Chao, Kuo-chun, Agrarian Policies of Main-land
China : A Documentary Study (1949-1956), Cambridge,
Massachusetts: East Asian Research Centre, Harvard
University, 1963, pp.88-94

_____ (1956), Draft of the National Programme for Agricultural
Development 1956-1967 (in Chinese), Peking: Renmin
Chubanshe, January 1956. (Referred to as the Draft of NPAD.)

_____ (1957-a), 'A Directive on the Rectification of Agricultural
Production Cooperatives' (September 14, 1957), in Renmin
Shouce (People's Handbook), 1958

_____ (1957-b), The Revised Draft of National Programme for Agricultural Development 1956-1967 (in Chinese), Peking: Renmin
Ribao Chubanshe. (Referred to as Revised NPAD.)

Central Committee of the CCP and the State Council (1957-c),
'A Directive on Banning the Blind Outflow of Population from
Rural Villages' (December 18, 1957), in Collected Laws and
Regulations of the People's Republic of China (in Chinese),
Volume 6, Peking: Falu Chubanshe, 1958

_____ (1958-a), 'A Directive on Carrying Out Quickly the Movement
to Improve Farm Tools in Rural Villages' (July 13, 1958), in
Collected Laws and Regulations of the People's Republic of
China, Volume 8, Peking: Falu Chubanshe, 1959

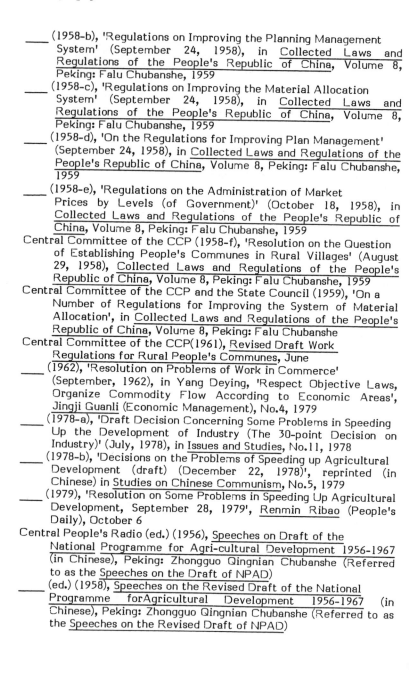

_____ (1958-b), 'Regulations on Improving the Planning Management System' (September 24, 1958), in Collected Laws and Regulations of the People's Republic of China, Volume 8, Peking: Falu Chubanshe, 1959

_____ (1958-c), 'Regulations on Improving the Material Allocation System' (September 24, 1958), in Collected Laws and Regulations of the People's Republic of China, Volume 8, Peking: Falu Chubanshe, 1959

_____ (1958-d), 'On the Regulations for Improving Plan Management' (September 24, 1958), in Collected Laws and Regulations of the People's Republic of China, Volume 8, Peking: Falu Chubanshe, 1959

_____ (1958-e), 'Regulations on the Administration of Market Prices by Levels (of Government)' (October 18, 1958), in Collected Laws and Regulations of the People's Republic of China, Volume 8, Peking: Falu Chubanshe, 1959

Central Committee of the CCP (1958-f), 'Resolution on the Question of Establishing People's Communes in Rural Villages' (August 29, 1958), Collected Laws and Regulations of the People's Republic of China, Volume 8, Peking: Falu Chubanshe, 1959

Central Committee of the CCP and the State Council (1959), 'On a Number of Regulations for Improving the System of Material Allocation', in Collected Laws and Regulations of the People's Republic of China, Volume 8, Peking: Falu Chubanshe

Central Committee of the CCP(1961), Revised Draft Work Regulations for Rural People's Communes, June

_____ (1962), 'Resolution on Problems of Work in Commerce' (September, 1962), in Yang Deying, 'Respect Objective Laws, Organize Commodity Flow According to Economic Areas', Jingji Guanli (Economic Management), No.4, 1979

_____ (1978-a), 'Draft Decision Concerning Some Problems in Speeding Up the Development of Industry (The 30-point Decision on Industry)' (July, 1978), in Issues and Studies, No.11, 1978

_____ (1978-b), 'Decisions on the Problems of Speeding up Agricultural Development (draft) (December 22, 1978)', reprinted (in Chinese) in Studies on Chinese Communism, No.5, 1979

_____ (1979), 'Resolution on Some Problems in Speeding Up Agricultural Development, September 28, 1979', Renmin Ribao (People's Daily), October 6

Central People's Radio (ed.) (1956), Speeches on Draft of the National Programme for Agri-cultural Development 1956-1967 (in Chinese), Peking: Zhongguo Qingnian Chubanshe (Referred to as the Speeches on the Draft of NPAD)

_____ (ed.) (1958), Speeches on the Revised Draft of the National Programme forAgricultural Development 1956-1967 (in Chinese), Peking: Zhongguo Qingnian Chubanshe (Referred to as the Speeches on the Revised Draft of NPAD)

Centre d'etude du sud-est Asiatique et de l'extremeorient, Universite
　　Libre de Bruxelles (ed.) (1972), China After the Cultural
　　Revolution, Bruxelles: Universite Libre de Bruxelles

Chamberlain, Heath B., et al. (1977), 'Impressions of Agricultural
　　Development In a North China County', Pacific Affairs, No.1,
　　pp.667-79

Chang, Fengshi (1963), 'Agricultural Machinery Industries Must Serve
　　Better the Technical Transformation of Agriculture', Gongren
　　Ribao (Workers' Daily), January 5

Chao, Kang (1968), 'Policies and Performance in Industry', in
　　A. Eckstein, W. Galenson, and T.C. Liu (eds.), Economic Trends
　　in Communist China, Chicago: Aldine Publishing Company

＿＿＿ (1970), Agricultural Production in Communist China, 1949-1965,
　　Madison: University of Wisconsin Press

＿＿＿ (1974), Capital Formation in Mainland China 1952-1965,
　　Berkeley: University of California Press

＿＿＿ (1975-a), 'The Growth of a Modern Cotton Textile Industry',
　　in D.H. Perkins (ed.), China's Modern Economy in Historical
　　Perspective, Stanford: Stanford University Press

＿＿＿ (1975-b), 'The Production and Application of Chemical Fertilizers
　　in China', China Quarterly, No.64, pp.712-29

Chao, Kuo-chun (1963), Agrarian Policies of Mainland China : A
　　Documentary Study (1949-1956), Cambridge, Massachusetts:
　　East Asian Research Centre, Harvard University

Chen, Boda (1956), Zhong-guo de she-hui zhu-yi gai-zao (China's
　　Socialist Transformation), Peking: Renmin Chubanshe

Chen, Kuan-I (1976), 'Agricultural Modernization and Industrialization
　　in China', Current History, No. 361, pp.64-67, pp.81-3

Chen, Kuan-I and Tsuchigane, Robert T. (1976), 'An Assessment of
China's Foodgrain Supplies in 1980', Asian Survey, No.10, pp.931-47

Chen, Nai Ruenn (1967), Chinese Economic Statistics, Chicago:
　　Aldine Publishing Company

Chen, Nai Ruenn (1975-a), 'China's Foreign Trade, 1950-1974',
　　in Joint Economic Committee, U.S. Congress, China : A
　　Reassessment of the Economy, Washington, D.C.: U.S.
　　Government Printing Office

＿＿＿ (1975-b), 'An Assessment of Chinese Economic Data :
　　Availability, Reliability and Usability', in Joint Economic
　　Committee, U.S. Congress, China : A Reassessment of the
　　Economy, Washington, D.C.: U.S. Government Printing Office

Chen, Nai Ruenn and Galenson, Walter (1969), The Chinese Economy
　　Under Communism, Chicago: Aldine Publishing Company

Chen, Yonggui (1971), 'Let Revolutionization Lead Mechanization',
　　Renmin Ribao (People's Daily), September 11

Chen, Yonggui, et al. (1975), Chen yong-gui tong-zhi zai Shanxi sheng yi-jiu-qi-si-nian nong-ye xue Dazhai hui-yi shang de jiang-hua: (zhai-yao) (Extracts from Speeches by Chen Yong-guai and Others in the 1974 Shanxi Province's Conference on Learning from Dazhai), Wuhan: Hubei Renmin Chubanshe

Cheng, Chuyuan (1971-a), The Machine-Building Industry In Communist China, Chicago: Aldine Publishing Company

_____ (1971-b), The Economy of Communist China, Ann Arbor: University of Michigan Press

_____ (1973), 'China's Machine Building Industry', Current Scene, No.7

_____ (1974), 'Economic Fluctuations in the PRC : 1949-1972', Current Scene, Volume XII, No.7, July

_____ (1974-b), China's Allocation of Fixed Capital Investment 1952-1957 (Michigan Papers in Chinese Studies No.17), Ann Arbor: Centre for Chinese Studies, the University of Michigan

Cheng, Jinjie (1969), 'Realize Mechanization on the Foundation of Co-operation', Hongqi (Red Flag), No.10, in SCMM, No.666, October 1969

Chiang, Kaiping (1975), Director of Anhwei Provincial Agricultural Machinery Administration, 'Let's Make Up Our Mind and Fight Courageously in the Struggle to Achieve Basically the Mechanization of Agriculture in Five Years', SWB, FE/W858/A10, December 31

Chin, Chichu (1977), 'Farm Mechanization in Wuxi County', Peking Review, August 19

Chin, Steve and Choa, William (1962-64), 'The Mechanization of Agriculture', Contemporary China, Volume VI, pp.1-9

China Institute of Research in Agricultural Mechanization, Capital Worker's Congress, East Is Red Commune (1967), 'Last Ditch Struggle that Courts Self-Destruction - Denouncing the Towering Crimes of China's Krushchev in Opposing Chairman Mao's Wise Decision', Nongye Jixie Jishe (Agricultural Machine Technique), No.5, August 8, 1967, in SCMM, No.613, February 5, 1968

China's Agriculture (1977), Washington: National Council for U.S. China Trade

'China's Farm Machinery Industry Grows by Leaps and Bounds' (1970), Peking Review, No.40, September 30

Chinese Communist Party Committee of Pingshun County (1976), Xigou zai qian-jin (Xingou Is Advancing), Peking: Nongye Chubanshe

Chinn, Dennis L. (1978), 'Income Distribution in a Chinese Commune', Journal of Comparative Economics, No.2, pp.246-65

Clark, Colin (1976), 'Economic Development in Communist China', Journal of Political Economy, No.21, pp.239-64

Class 560, Department of Agricultural Economics, Hubei University (1960), 'The Revolutionary Meaning of the "Eight-Point Charter" for Agriculture', Guangming Ribao (Guangming Daily), August 15

Collected Laws and Regulations of the People's Republic of China
(Zhong-hua ren-min gong-he-guo fa-gui lei-pian) (in Chinese),
(1954-62), Volumes 1-13, Peking: Falu Chubanshe

'Collective Strength of the People's Commune Is Mainstay of
Mechanized Farming' (1968), Nongye Jixie Jishu (Agricultural
Machine Technique), No.2, 1968, in SCMM No.620, July 22

Commentator of Hongqi (1978), 'The Key Is To Speed Up Agricultural
Development', Hongqi (Red Flag), No.9, pp.30-4

'Communique of the Second Plenary Session of the Ninth Central
Committee of the Chinese Communist Party, September 6,
1970' (1970), Peking Review, No.37, September 11, 1970

'Communique of the Tenth Plenary Session of the Eighth Central
Committee of the Chinese Communist Party' (1962), in Renmin
Shouce (People's Handbook), 1963

'Communique of the Third Plenary Session of the Eleventh Central
Committee of the Communist Party of China (adopted on
December 22, 1978)' (1978), Peking Review, No.52, December
29, 1978

Cooper, Charles (ed.) (1973), Science, Technology and Development:
The Political Economy of Technical Advance in Underdeveloped
Countries, London: Frank Cass & Company

'The Correct Way For Speeding Up Agricultural Mechanization'
(1971), Renmin Ribao (People's Daily), September 15

Crook, Frederick W. (1973), 'Chinese Communist Agricultural
Incentive Systems and the Labour Productive Contracts to
Households: 1956- 1965', Asian Survey, No.5, pp.470-81

_____ (1975), 'The Commune System in the People's Republic
of China', in Joint Economic Committee, U.S. Congress, China:
A Reassess-ment of the Economy, Washington, D.C.: U.S.
Government Printing Office

Crook, Frederick W., and Crook, Elizabeth F. (1976), 'Payment
Systems Used in Collective Farms in the Soviet Union and
China', Studies in Comparative Communism, No.3, pp.257-69

Csapo, L. (1974), 'The Hungarian Reform, Towards a Planned, Guided
Market Economy', in Kirschen, E.S. (ed.), Economic Policies
Compared: East and West, Volume 2, Amsterdam and Oxford:
North Holland Publishing Company

Dan, Gang and Hua, Jian (1975), Zhujiang pan shang yu-mi xiang
(The Land of Rice and Fish on the Pearl River), Peking: Nongye
Chubanshe

Dawson, D.L. (1970), Communist China's Agriculture, New York:
Praeger Publishers

Dean, Genevieve C. (1972), 'Science, Technology and Development:
China as a "Case Study"', China Quarterly, No.51, pp.520-34

_____ (1973), 'A Note on the Sources of Technological Innovation
in the People's Republic of China', in Charles Cooper (ed.),
Science, Technology and Development: The Political Economy
of Technical Advance in Underdeveloped Countries, London:
Frank Cass

Deng, Xiaoping (1957), 'Report on the Rectification Campaign'
    (Expanded Session of the Third Plenum, Eighth Central
    Committee of the Chinese Communist Party, September 1957),
    in Collected Laws and Regulations of the People's Republic of
    China, Volume 6, Peking: Falu Chubanshe
___ (1975-a), 'On the General Programme for All Works of the Whole
    Party and the Whole Country (1975)', in Issues and Studies,
    August, 1977
___ (1975-b), 'Some Problems in Speeding Up Industrial Development
    (Draft for Discussion, September 2, 1975) (The 18-points)', in
    Issues and Studies, July, 1977
Deng, Zihui (1957-a), 'Report During the Meeting of Representatives
    of National Agricultural Model Workers' (February 21, 1957), in
    Renmin Shouce (People's Handbook), 1958, pp.507-14
___ (1957-b), 'On the Expanded Reproduction of Agricultural
    Co-operatives and Other Problems' (Speech at the Expanded
    Third Plenum of the Eighth Central Committee of the Chinese
    Communist Party, September 1957), Renmin Shouce (People's
    Handbook), 1958, p.521
Department of Agricultural Economics, Liaoning College of Finance
    and Economics (ed.) (1973), Zen-yan zuo-hao sheng-chan-dui
    cai-kuai gong-zuo (How to Do a Good Job in the Accounting and
    Finance Works in the Production Teams), Shengyang: Liaoning
    Renmin Chubanshe
Department of Agricultural Economics, Xibei Agricultural College
    (1977), Sheng-chan-dui kuai-ji zhi-shi (Accounting For
    Production Teams), Sian: Shaanxi Renmin Chubanshe
Department of Economics, Peking University (1975), Zheng-zhi jing-ji
    xue (Political Economy: Socialism) (unpublished draft for
    comments), April 1973, April 1975
Department of Water Conservancy, Ministry of Hydroelectricity
    (ed.) (1976), Da-gao nong-tian ji-ben jian-she di-san-ji (Exert
    Great Efforts in Agricultural Basic Constructions, Volume 3,)
    Peking: Shuili Dianli Chubanshe
Dernberger, Robert F. (1968), 'The Relationship Between Foreign
    Trade Innovation and Economic Growth in Communist China', in
    Ping-ti Ho and Tang Tsou (eds.), China in Crisis, Volume II,
    Chicago: University of Chicago Press
___ (1974), 'The Transfer of Technology To China', Asia Quarterly,
    No.3, pp.229-52
___ (1977), 'China's Economic Future', in Allen S. Whiting
    and R.F. Dernberger (eds.), China's Future, New York:
    McGraw-Hill Book Company
Diao, Richard K. (1969), Taxation System of Communist China (in
    Chinese), Hong Kong: Union Research Institute
Donnithorne, Audrey (1967), China's Economic System, London:
    George Allen & Unwin Ltd.
___ (1972), 'China's Cellular Economy : Some Economic Trends
    Since the Cultural Revolution", China Quarterly, No.52,
    pp.605-19

_____ (1972-a), The Budget and the Plan in China : Central Local Economic Relations, Canberra: Australian National University Press

_____ (1974), 'China's Antiinflationary Policy', The Three Bank Review, No. 103, pp.1-23

_____ (1976), 'Comment on N.R. Lardy's "Centralization and Decentralization in China's Fiscal Management"', China Quarterly, No.66, pp.328-40

_____ (1977), 'China's Import of Capital Goods and Policy on Foreign Credit 1972-1974', Australian Economic Papers, No.28, pp.1-25

_____ (1978), 'The Control of Inflation in China', Current Scene, Nos. 4 & 5

Doolin, D.J. and Ridley, C.P. (1973), A Chinese-English Dictionary of Chinese Communist Terminology, Stanford: Hoover Institution

Dorner, Peter (ed.) (1977), Co-operative and Commune : Group Farming in the Economic Development of Agriculture, Madison: University of Wisconsin Press

'Draft Decision Concerning Some Problems in Speeding Up the Development of Industry (1978), (The '30-point Decision on Industry'), translated and printed in two parts by Issues and Studies, No.11, 1978 and No.1, 1979

Draft NPAD, see, Central Committee of the CCP(1956)

Ecklund, George (1967), Financing the Chinese Government Budget : Mainland China, 1950-1959, Edinburgh: University Press

Eckstein, Alexander (ed.) (1973-a), Comparison of Economic Systems, Berkeley: University of California Press

_____ (1973-b), 'Economic Growth and Change in China : A Twenty-Year Perspective', China Quarterly, No.54, pp.211-41

_____ (1975-a), China's Economic Development : The Interplay of Scarcity and Ideology, Ann Arbor: University of Michigan Press

_____ (1975-b), 'China's Trade Policy and Sino American Relations', Foreign Affairs, No.1, pp.134-54

_____ (1977), China's Economic Revolution, London: Cambridge University Press

Eckstein, Alexander, Galenson, Walter and Liu, T.C. (ed.) (1968), Economic Trends in Communist China, Chicago: Aldine Publishing Company

Editorial Department of Nanfang Ribao (Southern Daily, Canton) (ed.) (1975) Nong-ye xue Dazhai pu-ji Dazhai xian jiang-hua (On Learning from Dazhai and Popularizing Dazhai-type Counties), Guangdong: Guangdong Renmin Chubanshe

Editorial Department of Nongye Jixie (Agricultural Machinery) (ed.) (1978), Jia-su shi-xian nong-ye ji-xie-hua jiang-hua (Talks on Speeding up the Realization of Agricultural Mechanization), Peking: Renmin Chubanshe

Editorial Team of Dazhai Dili (1975), Dazhai di-li (Geography of Dazhai), Peking: Commercial Press

Editorial Team of Qiong-bang-zhi jing-sheng fang guang-mang (1975),
      Qiong-bang-zhi jing-sheng fang guang-mang: Xipu da-dui de
      jing-ji fa-zhan (The Spirit of Qiong-bang-zhi Shines: the
      Economic Development of Xipu Production Brigade), Peking:
      Renmin Chubanshe
Editorial Team of Ren-min gong-she zai yue-jin (ed.) (1974), Ren-min
      gong-she zai yue-jin: Shanghaishi jiao-qu ren-min gong-she di
      xin jing-yan (People's Communes Are Leaping Forward: The
      New Experiences from People's Communes in the Outskirts of
      Shanghai City), Shanghai: Shanghai Renmin Chubanshe
Editorial Team of (Talk on Political Economy: Socialism) (1976),
      Zheng-zhi jing-ji xue jiang-hua: she-hui zhu-yi bu-fen (Talk on
      Political Economy: Socialism), Peking: Renmin Chubanshe
Editorial Team of Taoyuan xin-mao (1977), Tao yuan xin-mao (The
      New Face of Taoyuan County), Peking: Shuli Dianli Chubanshe
Editorial Team of Xin yu-gong yi-shan ji (1977), Xin yu-gong yi-shan ji
      (The New 'Foolish Old Man Who Moved the Mountain'), Peking:
      Renmin Chubanshe
Eisenstadt, S.N. (1963), Modernization, Growth and Diversity,
      Bloomington: Indiana University Press
_____ (1973), Tradition and Change, and Modernity, New York:
      John Wiley & Sons
Emerson, John P. (1967), 'Employment In Mainland China : Problems
      and Prospects', in Joint Economic Committee, U.S. Congress,
      An Economic Profile of Mainland China, Washington, D.C.: U.S.
      Government Printing Office
'Entering New Phase in Farm Mechanization' (1978), Peking Review,
      No.7, February 17
Erisman, Alva Lewis (1972), 'China : Agricultural Development,
      1949-1971', in Joint Economic Committee, U.S. Congress,
      People's Republic of China : An Economic Assessment,
      Washington, D.C.: U.S. Government Printing Office
_____ (1975), 'China : Agriculture in the 1970's', in Joint
      Economic Committee, U.S. Congress, China : A Reassessment
      of the Economy, Washington, D.C.: U.S. Government Printing
      Office
Etienne, Gilbert (1975), 'China's Agriculture : Present Situation
      and Prospects', in Peter Dorner (ed.), Co-operative and
      Communes : Group Farming in the Economic Development of
      Agri-culture, Madison: The University of Wisconsin Press
_____ (1977), 'Foodgrain Production and Population in Asia : China,
      India and Bangladesh', World Development, Nos.5-7, pp.425-40
Evers, Hans-Dieter (ed.) (1973), Modernization in South-East Asia,
      London: Oxford University Press
Fang, Tsuinong, and Chang, Yihua (1978), 'Strive for Modernization
      of Agriculture', Peking Review, No.23, June 9
FAO, Plant Production and Protective Division (1975), Cereal Seed
      Technology, Rome: Food and Agriculture Organization of the
      United Nations

'Farm Mechanization - Targets for 1980 - An Interview with a Responsible Member of the Office in Charge of Farm Mechanization' (1978), Peking Review, No.8, February 24

Farm Mechanization Promoted by Communes in Hubei's Xinzhou Xian (County)' (1968), in SCMM, No.630, October 14

Farm Mechanization Through Communes' (1968), Nongye Jixie Jishu (Agricultural Machine Technique), No.2, in SCMM, No.620, July 22, 1968

Field, Robert Michael (1973), 'The Chinese Machine-Building Industry : A Reappraisal', China Quarterly, No.54, pp.308-20

_____ (1976), 'Reply to N. Maxwell's "Recent Chinese Grain Figure"', China Quarterly, No.68, pp.819-21

Field, Robert Michael, and Kilpatrick, James A. (1978), 'Chinese Grain Production : An Interpretation of the Data', China Quarterly, No. 74

Field, Robert Michael, Lardy, Nicholas R., and Emerson, John P. (1975), 'Industrial Output by Province in China, 1949-73', China Quarterly, No.63, pp.409-34

_____ (1976), 'Provincial Industrial Output in the People's Republic of China : 1949-75', in U.S. Department of Commerce, Foreign Economic Report, No.12

The First-Five-Year Plan for Development of the National Economy of the People's Republic of China (1953-1957) (Chinese edition) (1955), Peking: Renmin Chubanshe

The First Five-Year Plan for Development of the National Economy of the People's Republic of China in 1953-57 (1956), Peking: Foreign Language Press

Fung, K.K. (1974), 'Output Vs "Surplus" Maximization: The Conflicts Between the Socialized and Private Sector in Chinese Collectivized Agriculture', The Developing Economies, No.1, pp.41-55

Galenson, Walter (1969), Provincial Agricultural Statistics for Communist China, New York: Social Research Journal

Gan, Wu (1976), Dazhai jing-shen zai Wuwei (The Spirit of Dazhai in Wuwei County, Gansu Province), Peking: Nongye Chubanshe

Gao, Xinggao (ed.), (1973), Gong-fei jing-ji wen-ti lun-ji (Collected Papers on the Economic Problems of the Communist Bandits), Taipei: Institute of International Relations

Ge, Jing (1975), 'Develop Agriculture According to the Thoughts of Mao Zedong', Renmin Ribao (People's Daily), July 9

Germai, Gino (ed.) (1973), Modernization, Urbanization and the Urban Crisis, Boston: Little Brown

Gerschenkron, Alexander (1973), 'Ideology as a System Determinant', in A. Eckstein (ed.), Comparison of Economic Systems, Berkeley: University of California Press

Giles, G.W. (1975), 'The Reorientation of Agricultural Mechanization for the Developing Countries', Agricultural Mechanization in Asia, No.2, pp.15-25

Ginsburg, Norton (1977), 'China's Development Strategies', <u>Economic Development and Cultural Change</u>, Volume 25, Supplement, pp.344-62

Gong, Xiaowen (1972), 'Take the Line as Key Link, Establish and Improve Reasonable System of Rules and Regulations', <u>Renmin Ribao</u> (People's Daily), May 31

Gong, Yeping (1973), 'Go All Out and Work Against Time for Speed', SWB, FE/W722/A1-2, May 2, 1973

_____ (1975-a), 'The Correct Way to Develop Small Industries', <u>Renmin Ribao</u> (People's Daily), October 7

_____ (1975-b), 'Strengthen Monetary Management and Control', <u>Renmin Ribao</u> (People's Daily), November 9

Gong, Zheng and Zhao, Jiancheng (1979), 'The Method of Accounting of An Agricultural Machinery Team in the Production Brigade', <u>Jingji Guanli</u> (Economic Management), No. 6, pp.34-6

<u>Gong-ye qi-ye guan-li wen-zuan</u> (1964) (Collected Essays on the Management of Industrial Enterprises), Volume 5, Peking: Zhongguo Gongye Chubanshe

Gray, Jack (1978), 'Mao and the Chinese Rural Economy', <u>World Development</u>, No. 5, pp.567- 81

Great Criticism and Repudiation Group of the First Machine Building Ministry (1977), 'Expose and Criticize the "Gang of Four", Speed Up Agricultural Mechanization', <u>Hongqi</u> (Red Flag), No.1, pp.102-7

Green, Reginald Herbold (1978), 'Transferability, Exoticism and Other Forms of Dogmatic Revisionism', <u>World Development</u>, Volume 6, pp.709-13

Griffin, Keith (1978), 'Efficiency, Equality and Accumulation in Rural China : Notes on the Chinese System of Incentives', <u>World Development</u>, No. 5, pp.603-7

Guoyang County Chinese Communist Party Committee, Guoyang County Revolutionary Committee, Anhui Province (1976), <u>Guoyang da-di pi lu-zhuang</u>, (The Greening of Guoyang County), Peking: Nongye Chubanshe

Gurley, John (1975), 'Rural Development in China 1949-72, and the Lessons to Be Learned from it', <u>World Development</u>, Nos.7 & 8, pp.455-71

_____ (1976), <u>China's Economy and the Maoist Strategy</u>, New York: Monthly Review Press

Hadda, L. (1977), 'Inflation Under Socialism', <u>Australian Economic Papers</u>, No. 28, pp.44-52

Han, Yuanqin and Yin, Xuemi (1963), 'On Economic Accounting of Production Teams', <u>Guangming Ribao</u> (Guangming Daily), April 8

He, Jianzhang (1979), 'On the Current Problems and the Direction of Reform for the Management System of Economic Planning in Our State Sector', <u>Jingji Yanjiu</u> (Economic Research), No.5, pp.35-45

He, Zhuo (1979), 'Readjusting the National Economy: A Strategic Measure to Speed Up Modernization', <u>Jingji Yanjiu</u> (Economic Research), No.5, pp.6- 13

Hirschman, Albert O. (1973), 'Ideology : Mask or Nessus Shirt?',
    in Alexander Eckstein (ed.), Comparison of Economic Systems,
    Berkeley: University of California Press
'History of Struggle ...', See Mass Criticism Unit of Revolutionary
    Great Alliance Commitee, Farm Machinery Management
    Bureau under the Eighth Ministry of Machine-Building (1968),
    'History of Struggle Between the Two Lines'
Ho, Pingti and Tsou, Tang (1968), China in Crisis, Volume II, Chicago:
    University of Chicago Press
Hong, Qiao (1973-a), 'Only When All-Round Arrangements Are Made
    Can All-Round Development Be Achieved', SWB, FE/W715/A5,
    March 14
_____ (1973-b), 'Work to Build Up Grain Reserve', Renmin Ribao
    (People's Daily), December 27
Hou, Xiaochang (1964), 'On the Question of Water Control',
    Guangming Ribao (Guangming Daily), March 30
Hsiao, K. (1971), Money and Monetary Policy in Communist China,
    New York: Columbia University Press
Hsuan, Mo (ed.) (1976), The Collected Comments on Le I-che's Poster:
    A Remark and Notes of Le I-che and Hsien Chi-wen's Posters,
    Taipei, Taiwan: Institute for the Study of Chinese Communist
    Problems
Hu, Changnuan (1979), 'On the Price "Scissors" and the General
    Level of Prices', Jingji Yanjiu (Economic Research), No.6,
    pp.62-9 'Hunan Province Machinery Industries Conference'
    (October 1969), Zhonggong Nianbao (Communist China
    Yearbook), 1969, Section 2, p.163
Hu, Qiaomu (1978-a), 'Observe Economic Laws, Speed Up the Four
    Modernizations', Peking Review, No.45, November 10
_____ (1978-b), 'Observe Economic Laws, Speed Up the Four
    Modernizations', Renmin Ribao (People's Daily), October 6
Hua, Guofeng (1975), 'Summary Report for the National Conference
    on Leaning from Dazhai in Agriculture (October 15, 1975)',
    Renmin Ribao (People's Daily), October 21
Hubei Renmin Chubanshe (1975), Yong Dazhai jing shen gao-hao
    nong-ye ji-xie-hua (Use the Spirit of Dazhai to Do a Good Job in
    Agricultural Mechanization), Volume 1, Wuhan: Hubei Renmin
    Chubanshe
_____ (1976), Yong Dazhai jing-shen gao-hao nong-ye ji-xie-hua
    (Use the Spirit of Dazhai to Do a Good Job in Agricultural
    Mechanization), Volume 2, Wuhan: Hubei Remin Chubanshe
_____ (1977), Yong Dazhai jing-shen gao-hao nong-ye ji-xie-hua
    (Use the Spirit of Dazhai to Do a Good Job in Agricultural
    Mechanization), Volume 3, Wuhan: Hubei Remin Chubanshe
'Hunan Province Machinery Industries Conference' (October 1969),
    Zhonggong Nianbao (Communist China Yearbook), 1969, Section
    2, p.163.
Indian Society of Agricultural Economics (1972), Problems of Farm
    Mechanization, Bombay: Indian Society of Agricultural
    Economics

Industrial Development Organization, United Nations (1969), <u>Planning</u>
<u>For Advanced Skills and Technologies</u>, New York: United
Nations

International Labour Office (1973), <u>Mechanization and Employment</u>
<u>in Agriculture : Case Studies from Four Continents</u>, Geneva:
International Labour Office

Ishikawa, Shigeru (1965), <u>National Income and Capital Formation</u>
<u>in Mainland China</u>, Tokyo: Institute of Asian Economic Affairs
_____ (1967), <u>Economic Development in Asian Perspective</u>, Tokyo:
Kinokuniya Bookstore Company
_____ (1973), 'A Note on the Choice of Technology in China',
in Charles Cooper (ed.), <u>Science, Technology and Development :</u>
<u>The Political Economy of Technical Advance in Underdeveloped</u>
<u>Countries</u>, London: Frank Cass & Company
_____ (1975), 'The Chinese Method of Technological Development :
The Case of Agricultural Machinery and Development Industry',
<u>The Developing Economies</u>, No. 4, pp.430-58
_____ (1977), 'China's Food and Agriculture - A Turning Point',
<u>Food Policy</u>, No.2, pp.90-102

Ji, Li (1975), 'The General Line for Development of Our National
Economy', <u>Economic Reporter</u>, October 29, pp.7-9

Ji, Zhangyu (ed.) (1977), <u>Yushu ren-min xue Dazhai</u> (The People of
Yushu County, Jilin Province, Learn from Dazhai), Peking:
Nongye Chubanshe

Jia, Kecheng and Zhang Yueqing (1979), 'On Price Scissors', <u>Jingji</u>
<u>Yanjiu</u> (Economic Research), No. 1, pp.63-6

Jian, <u>Xiuyan</u> (1979), 'Price Problems in the Adjustment of National
Economy', <u>Nankai Daxue Xuebao</u> (Journal of Nankai
University), No.4, pp.15-9

Jian, Yizhen (1965), 'Actively Promote the Agricultural Scientific
Experiment Movement Centred on Model Fields', <u>Renmin Ribao</u>
(People's Daily), April 5

<u>Jian-ming nong-ye ji-xie-hua ci-dian</u> (Concise Dictionary of
Agricultural Mechanization (1977), Peking: Kexue Chubanshe

Jiang, Han (1973), 'Great Effort Is Needed To Develop Agriculture',
<u>Renmin Ribao</u> (People's Daily), April 17

Jiang, Nongxing and Shu, Huaiqian (1975), <u>Wu-nian de bao-gao: Suqian</u>
<u>xian xue Dazhai gan Xiyang de ji-ben jing-yan</u> (Five-Year
Report: Suqian County's Experience in Learning from Dazhai),
Nanking: Jiangsu Renmin Chubanshe

Jiang, Xunxin and Lu, Xiufeng (1976), <u>Jian-chi dou-zheng xue Dazhai:</u>
<u>Jiangxi sheng Xingzi xian nong-ye xue Dazhai de ji-ben jing-yan</u>
(The Basic Experience of Xingzi County, Jiangxi Province, in
Learning from Dazhai), Peking: Nongye Chubanshe

Jiang, Zhenxing (1979), 'How Do Production Teams Calculate Cost of
Production for Their Products', <u>Jingji Guanli</u> (Economic
Management), No.1, pp.47-51

Jiangsu Provincial Chinese Communist Party Committee (1974),
'Report of Jiangsu Conference on Commerce and Income'
(December 12, 1974),
<u>SWB</u>, FE/W807/A5, January 1, 1975

Johnson, Chalmers (1973), Ideology and Politics in Contemporary China, Seattle: University of Washington Press

Joint Economic Committee, U.S. Congress (1967), An Economic Profile of Mainland China, Washington, D.C.: U.S. Government Printing Office

_____ (1972), People's Republic of China : An Economic Assessment, Washington, D.C.: U.S. Government Printing Office

_____ (1975), China : A Reassessment of the Economy, Washington, D.C.: U.S. Government Printing Office

Kelley, Allen C., Williamson, Jeffrey G., and Cheetham, Russell, J. (1972), Dualistic Economic Development : Theory and History, Chicago: The University of Chicago Press

Khan, Amir V. (1976), 'Agricultural Mechanization and Machinery Production in the People's Republic of China', China Business Review, No.6, pp.17-26

Kirschen, E.S. (ed.) (1974), Economic Policies Compared : East and West, Volume I, Volume II, Amsterdam and Oxford: North Holland Publishing Company

Klatt, W. (1973), 'China's Domestic Economy and Foreign Trade', China Report, Nos. 2 & 3, pp.30-40

Kornai, Janos (1972), Rush Versus Harmonic Growth, Amsterdam and London: North Holland Publishing Company

_____ (1980-a), Economics of Shortage, Amsterdam: North Holland Publishing Company

_____ (1980-b), 'The Dilemmas of a Socialist Economy : the Hungarian Experience', Cambridge Journal of Economics, No.2, pp.147-57

Kuo, Leslie T.C. (1972), The Technical Transformation of Agriculture in Communist China, New York: Praeger Publishers

_____ (1976), Agriculture in the People's Republic of China : Structural Changes and Technical Transformation, London: Martin Robertson & Company

Kuznetz, Simon (1965), Economic Growth and Structure, New York: W.W. Norton & Company

_____ (1973), 'Notes on Stages of Economic Growth as a System Determinant', in Alexander Eckstein (ed.), Comparison of Economic Systems, Berkeley: University of California Press

_____ (1974), Population, Capital and Growth, London: Heinemann Educational Books

Lampton, David (1976), 'The Roots of Inequality in Education and Health Services in China : A First Look at Five Provinces' (Paper Presented at the 30th International Congress of Human Sciences in Asia and North Africa, August, 1976, Mexico City) (Mimeo.)

Lardy, Nicholas R. (1975-a), 'Centralization and Decentralization in China's Fiscal Management', China Quarterly, No.61, pp.25-60

_____ (1975-b), 'Economic Planning in the People's Republic of China : Central-Provincial Fiscal Relations', in Joint Economic Committee, U.S. Congress, China : Reassessment of the Economy, Washington, D.C.: U.S. Government Printing Office

_____ (1975-c), Central Control and Redistribution in China : Central-Provincial Fiscal Relations Since 1949 (Unpublished Ph.D. Thesis, University of Michigan)

_____ (1976-a), 'Reply to A. Donnithorne's Comment', China Quarterly, No.66, pp.340-54

_____ (1976-b), 'Economic Planning and Income Distribution in China', Current Scene, No. 11, pp.1-12

_____ (1978), Economic Growth and Distribution in China, New York: Cambridge University Press

Levy, Marion Jr. (1972), Modernization : Latecomers and Survivors, New York: Basic Books, Inc.

Lewis, W.A. (1954), 'Economic Development with Unlimited Supplies of Labour', Manchester School of Economic and Social Studies, No.22, pp.139-91

Li, Cho-Ming (1962), The Statistical System of Communist China, Berkeley: University of California Press

Li, Fuchun (1957), 'On the Achievements Made in Our First Five-Year Plan, and Our Future Tasks and Direction in Socialist Construction' (Speech at the Eighth National Labour Union, December 7, 1957), in Renmin Shouce (People's Handbook), 1958

_____ (1960), 'Report on the Draft 1960 National Economic Plan' (Second Session of the Second National People's Congress on March 30, 1960) in Second NPC Documents (1960), Peking: Foreign Language Press

Li, Gang and Wu, Jianjun (1978), 'Under the Precondition That the Unified Leadership of the Centre be Strengthened, the Two Initiatives of the Centre and Locality Should be Utilized', Jingji Yanjiu (Economic Research), No.2, pp.25- 30

Li, Qingyu (1956), 'Popularize New Farm Implements', in Central People's Radio (ed.), Speeches on the Draft of the National Programme for Agricultural Development 1956-1967, Peking: Zhongguo Qingnian Chubanshe

_____ (1958), 'Improve Traditional Farm Implements and Popularize New Ones', in Central People's Radio (ed.), Speeches on the Revised Draft of the National Programme for Agricultural Development 1956-1967 (Peking: Zhongguo Qingnian Chubanshe

Li, Xiannian (1957-a), 'Report on Final Accounts for 1956 and Draft Budget for 1957' (Fourth Session of the First National People's Congress), June 29, 1957 in The Fourth Session of the First National People's Congress (Documents) Peking: Renmin Chubanshe, 1957

_____ (1957-b), 'Outline of a Speech Made at the National Meeting of Bureau Chiefs in the Ministry of Finance' (September 7, 1957), in Research Institute of Financial Science (ed.), Shi-nian lai cai-zheng zi-liao hui-bian (A Collection of Documents on Financial Policy in the Past Ten Years), Volume 1, Peking: Caizheng Chubanshe, 1959

_____ (1958), 'Report on the Execution of 1957 Budget and the Draft Budget for 1958' (Fifth Session of the First National People's Congress, February 1, 1958) in Research Institute of Financial Science (ed.), Shi-nian lai cai-zheng zi-liao hui-bian (A Collection of Documents on Financial Policy in the Past Ten Years), Volume 2, Peking: Caizheng Chubanshe, 1959

_____ (1960), 'Report of the Final State Accounts for 1959 and the Draft State Budget for 1960' (March 30, 1960), in Second NPC Documents, Peking: Foreign Language Press pp.49-73

Liang, Zhihui and Zeng Neng (1964), 'How to Carry Out Economic Accounting in Material Supply Works', in Gong-ye qi-ye guan-li wen-xuan (Collected Essays on the Management of Industrial Enterprises), Volume 5, Peking: Zhongguo Gongye Chubanshe

Liang, Zhihui and Zhang, Wenqian (1964), 'How to Establish Co-operative Relations of Fixed-point Supplies Between Enterprises and the Relevant Departments', in Gong-ye qi-ye guan-li wen-xuan (Collected Essays on the Management of Industrial Enterprises), Volume 5, Peking: Zhongguo Gongye Chubanshe

Liao, Luyan (1963), 'Collectivization of Agriculture', Peking Review, No.44

_____ (1956), 'An Explanatory Note on the Draft of the National Programme for Agricultural Development 1956-1967, in Draft of the National Programme for Agricultural Development 1957-1967, Peking: Renmin Chubanshe, January

Liao, Nongge (1968), 'Knock Down China's Krushchev and Completely Discredit by Criticism His Line of State Monopoly', Nongye Jixie Jishu (Agricultural Machinery Technique), No.2, translated in SCMM, No.620, July 22, 1968

Liaoning Renmin Chubanshe (ed.) (1973), Jian-chi gong-ye zi-yuan nong-ye de zheng-que fang-xiang (Holding the Correct Line for Industry to Support Agriculture), Shenyang: Liaoning Renmin Chubanshe

Lin, Chen (1977), 'The Learn From Tachai (Dazhai) Movement : An Analytical Study', Issues and Studies, No.3

Lin, Feng (1976), Hongqiqu pan kai xin-ge (Songs of Joy Along the Red-Flag Canal), Peking: Nongye Chubanshe

Lin, Nan and Liu, Furong (1978), 'A Study into the Specialization and Co-operation in Changzhou City's Production of Hand-held Tractors', Hongqi (Red Flag), No.11, pp.47-52

Lippit, Victor D. (1974), Land Reform and Economic Development in China : A Study of Institutional Change and Development Finance, White Plains, New York: International Arts and Sciences Press Inc.

_____ (1977), 'The Commune in Chinese Development', <u>Modern China</u>, No.2, pp.229-55

Liu, Chengrui, Hu, Naiwu and Yu, Guanhua (1979), 'Link Planning with Market - A Basic Means of Reforming China's Economic Management', <u>Jingji Yanjiu</u> (Economic Research), No.7, pp.37-46

Liu, Guangdi (1979), 'On the Task of the Bank in the New Era', <u>Jingji Yanjiu</u> (Economic Research), No.1, pp.29-35

Liu, Guoguang (1978), 'On the Continuation of High Growth Rate', <u>Jingji Yanjiu</u> (Economic Research), No.2, pp.7-13

Liu, J.C. (1970), <u>China's Fertilizer Economy</u>, Chicago: Aldine Publishing Company

Liu, Pang (1978), 'How to Get High Yield in Agriculture', <u>Peking Review</u>, No.39, September 29

Liu, Suinian (1979), 'Must Consciously Maintain the Balance Between Social Production and Social Needs', <u>Jingji Guanli</u> (Economic Management), No. 3, pp.15-20

Liu, T.C. (1967), 'The Tempo of Economic Development of the Chinese Mainland, 1949-65', in Joint Economic Committee, U.S. Congress, <u>An Economic Profile of Mainland China</u>, Washington, D.C.: U.S. Government Printing Office

Liu, T.C. and Yeh, K.C. (1965), <u>The Economy of the Chinese Mainland : National Income and Economic Development</u>, Princeton: Princeton University Press

_____ (1973), 'Chinese and Other Asian Economies : A Quantitative Evaluation', <u>American Economic Review</u>, No.2, pp.213-22

Long, Yan (1976), <u>Dang de ji-ben lu-xian zhao zheng-tu: Bayang xian xue Dazhai gan Xiyang di jing-yan</u> (The Party Line Lights Our Way: Experience of Bayang County in Learning from Dazhai), Peking: Nongye Chubanshe

Lu, Ruilin (1971), 'Speech on the Yunnan Province Agricultural Work Conference', <u>Zhonggong Nianbao</u> (Communist China Yearbook), 1971, Section 7, pp.66-73

Lu, Wen (1982), 'Further Increase the Economic Efficiency and Results in Farm Production', <u>Nongye Jingjiwenti</u> (Problems of Agricultural Economics), No.2

Lu, Zhanshan (1978), 'Develop County-run and Commune- and Brigade- run Industries, Speed Up the Realization of Agricultural Mechanization', <u>Jingji Yanjiu</u> (Economic Research), No.5, pp.37- 41

Ma, Chuandong and Tian, Jiasen (1978), 'Establish the Four-Unification System', Fully Utilize Agricultural Machinery', <u>Jingji Yanjiu</u> (Economic Research), No.5, pp.42-7

Ma, Hong (1981), 'Questions Concerning the Reform of the System of Economic Management', <u>Jingji Yanjiu</u> (Economic Research), No.7, pp. 11-24

Mah, Feng hua (1961), 'The Financing of Public Investment in Communist China', <u>The Journal of Asian Studies</u>, No.1, pp.33-48

_____ (1971), <u>The Foreign Trade of Mainland China</u>, Chicago: Aldine Publishing Company

'Make Resolution to Achieve Within Five Years' (1975), Renmin Ribao (People's Daily), October 12

Mao, Zedong (1955-a), 'Closing Speech of the Expanded Sixth Plenum of the Seventh Central Committee of the Chinese Communist Party' (September 1955), in Mao Zedong, Mao Zedong Sixiang Wansui (II) (Long Live the Thoughts of Mao Zedong), 1969 (China: s.n.)

_____ (1955-b), 'On Agricultural Co-operativization' (July, 1955), in Mao Zedong, Selected Readings in Mao Zedong's Works (Chinese edition), Peking: Renmin Chubanshe, 1964, pp.397-430

_____ (ed.) (1956-a), Zhong-guo nong-cun de she-hui zhu-zi gao-chao (The Upsurge of Socialism in China's Rural Villages), Volumes 1-3, Peking: Renmin Chubanshe

_____ (1956-b1), 'On Ten Great Relationships' (April 25, 1956), in Mao Zedong, Mao Zedong Sixiang Wansui (II) (Long Live the Thoughts of Mao Zedong), 1969 (China: s.n.)

_____ (1956-b2), 'On Ten Great Relationships', Hongqi (Red Flag), No.1, 1977

_____ (1956-c), 'Speech During the Expanded Session of the Central Political Bureau of the Central Committee of the Chinese Communist Party, April 1956' in Mao Zedong, Mao Zedong Sixiang Wansui (II) (Long Live the Thoughts of Mao Zedong), 1969 (China: s.n.)

_____ (1958), 'Speeches in Chengdu Conference: A Speech on March 22, 1958', in Mao Zedong, Mao Zedong Sixiang Wansui (II) (Long Live the Thoughts of Mao Zedong), 1969 (China: s.n.)

_____ (1959-a), 'Intra-Party Communication' (April 29, 1959), in Mao Zedong, Mao Zedong Sixiang Wansui (II) (Long Live the Thoughts of Mao Zedong), 1969 (China: s.n.)

_____ (1959-b), 'Speech During the Meeting of Party Secretaries from Provinces and Municipalities', (February 2, 1959), in Mao Zedong, Mao Zedong Sixiang Wansui (II) (Long Live the Thoughts of Mao Zedong), 1969 (China: s.n.)

_____ (1964-a), Selected Readings in Mao Zedong's Works (Chinese edition), Peking: Renmin Chubanshe

_____ (1964-b), 'On the Correct Handling of Internal Contradiction Among the People', in Mao Zedong, Selected Readings in Mao Zedong Works (Chinese edition), Peking: People's Press, 1964

_____ (1966-a), 'An Instruction Letter on the Question of Agricultural Mechanization (March 12, 1966)', in Hongqi (Red Flag), No.1, 1978

_____ (1966-b), 'An Instruction Letter on the Question of Agricultural Mechanization (March 12, 1966)', in Mao Zedong, Mao Zedong Sixiang Wansui (II) (Long Live the Thoughts of Mao Zedong), 1969 (China: s.n.)

_____ (1967-a), Mao Zedong Sixiang Wansui (I) (Long Live The Thoughts of Mao Zedong) (China: s.n.)

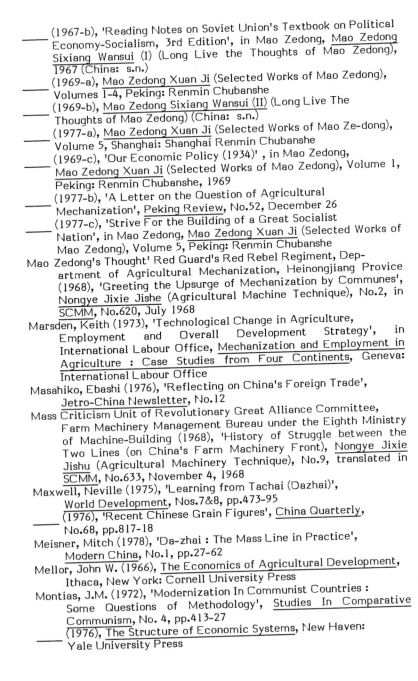

_____ (1967-b), 'Reading Notes on Soviet Union's Textbook on Political Economy-Socialism, 3rd Edition', in Mao Zedong, <u>Mao Zedong Sixiang Wansui</u> (I) (Long Live the Thoughts of Mao Zedong), 1967 (China: s.n.)

_____ (1969-a), <u>Mao Zedong Xuan Ji</u> (Selected Works of Mao Zedong), Volumes 1-4, Peking: Renmin Chubanshe

_____ (1969-b), <u>Mao Zedong Sixiang Wansui (II)</u> (Long Live The Thoughts of Mao Zedong) (China: s.n.)

_____ (1977-a), <u>Mao Zedong Xuan Ji</u> (Selected Works of Mao Ze-dong), Volume 5, Shanghai: Shanghai Renmin Chubanshe

_____ (1969-c), 'Our Economic Policy (1934)', in Mao Zedong, <u>Mao Zedong Xuan Ji</u> (Selected Works of Mao Zedong), Volume 1, Peking: Renmin Chubanshe, 1969

_____ (1977-b), 'A Letter on the Question of Agricultural Mechanization', <u>Peking Review</u>, No.52, December 26

_____ (1977-c), 'Strive For the Building of a Great Socialist Nation', in Mao Zedong, <u>Mao Zedong Xuan Ji</u> (Selected Works of Mao Zedong), Volume 5, Peking: Renmin Chubanshe

Mao Zedong's Thought' Red Guard's Red Rebel Regiment, Department of Agricultural Mechanization, Heinongjiang Provice (1968), 'Greeting the Upsurge of Mechanization by Communes', <u>Nongye Jixie Jishe</u> (Agricultural Machine Technique), No.2, in SCMM, No.620, July 1968

Marsden, Keith (1973), 'Technological Change in Agriculture, Employment and Overall Development Strategy', in International Labour Office, <u>Mechanization and Employment in Agriculture : Case Studies from Four Continents</u>, Geneva: International Labour Office

Masahiko, Ebashi (1976), 'Reflecting on China's Foreign Trade', <u>Jetro-China Newsletter</u>, No.12

Mass Criticism Unit of Revolutionary Great Alliance Committee, Farm Machinery Management Bureau under the Eighth Ministry of Machine-Building (1968), 'History of Struggle between the Two Lines (on China's Farm Machinery Front), <u>Nongye Jixie Jishu</u> (Agricultural Machinery Technique), No.9, translated in SCMM, No.633, November 4, 1968

Maxwell, Neville (1975), 'Learning from Tachai (Dazhai)', <u>World Development</u>, Nos.7&8, pp.473-95

_____ (1976), 'Recent Chinese Grain Figures', <u>China Quarterly</u>, No.68, pp.817-18

Meisner, Mitch (1978), 'Da-zhai : The Mass Line in Practice', <u>Modern China</u>, No.1, pp.27-62

Mellor, John W. (1966), <u>The Economics of Agricultural Development</u>, Ithaca, New York: Cornell University Press

Montias, J.M. (1972), 'Modernization In Communist Countries : Some Questions of Methodology', <u>Studies In Comparative Communism</u>, No. 4, pp.413-27

_____ (1976), <u>The Structure of Economic Systems</u>, New Haven: Yale University Press

Mudra (1975), 'Variety Evaluation', in FAO, Plant Production and Protective Division, Cereal Seed Technology, Rome: Food and Agriculture Organization of the United Nations

'Must Set Up the Necessary Rules and Regulations' (1972), Renmin Ribao (People's Daily), April 4, 5, 19 and May 10, 13, June 16

Nagahiru, Jinzo (1976), 'Agricultural Mechanization Program of China to be Realized in 1980', Agricultural Mechanization in Asia, No.2, pp.20-5

Natang zai xue Dazhai zhong kuo-bu qian-jin (Natang Brigade Marches Forward in Learning from Dazhai) (1973), Nanning: Guangxi Renmin Chubanshe

Nathan, Andrew J. (1976), 'Policy Oscillations in the People's Republic of China : A Critique', China Quarterly, No.68, pp.720-33

National Foreign Assessment Centre (1977), People's Republic of China : Handbook of Economic Indicators, Washington, D.C.: Central Intelligence Agency

New China News Agency (1963), Peking, July 31, 'China Doubles Capital Investment in Farm Machinery Accessories Plants', in SCMM, No.3033, August 6, 1963

'New Development in the Production of Agricultural Machinery' (1963), Gongren Ribao (Workers' Daily), September 24, in SCMM,, No.3089, October 29, 1963

Nove, Alec and Nuti, D.M. (ed.) (1974), Socialist Economics, Harmondsworth, Middlesex: Penguin Books Ltd

Nurkse, R. (1953), Problems of Capital Formation in Underdeveloped Countries, New York: Oxford University Press

Office of Learning from Daqing and Dazhai, Ministry of Commerce (ed.) (1979), Xian-qi shang-ye xue Daqing xue Dazhai qun-zhong-yun-dong xin-gao-chao (Reach New Heights in the Mass Movement to Learn from Daqing and Dazhai in Commerce), Peking: Zhongguo Caizheng Jingji Chubanshe

Orleans, Leo A. (1972), Every Fifth Child : The Population of China, Stanford: Stanford University Press

_____ (1975), 'China's Population : Can the Contradiction Be Solved?', in Joint Economic Committee, U.S. Congress, China : Reassessment of the Economy, Washington, D.C.: U.S. Government Printing Office

'Overcome Resistance, Insist on Letting Commune Operate Machine' (1967), Nongye Jixie Jishu (Agricultural Machinery Technique), No.6, September 8, in SCMM, No.612, January 29, 1968

Paine, Suzanne (1976), 'Balanced Development : Maoist Conception and Chinese Practice', World Development, No.4, pp.277-304

_____ (1978), 'Some Reflections on the Presence of "Rural" or of "Urban Bias" in China's Development Policies 1949-1976', World Development, Volume 6, pp.693-707

Peng Chuncheng (1964), 'A Study on the Question of Priority for Our Country's Technical Transformation in Agriculture', Guangming Ribao (Guangming Daily), March 23

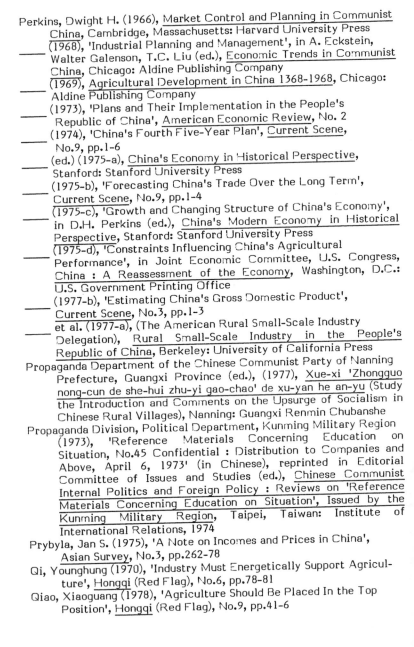

Perkins, Dwight H. (1966), <u>Market Control and Planning in Communist China</u>, Cambridge, Massachusetts: Harvard University Press

———— (1968), 'Industrial Planning and Management', in A. Eckstein, Walter Galenson, T.C. Liu (ed.), <u>Economic Trends in Communist China</u>, Chicago: Aldine Publishing Company

———— (1969), <u>Agricultural Development in China 1368-1968</u>, Chicago: Aldine Publishing Company

———— (1973), 'Plans and Their Implementation in the People's Republic of China', <u>American Economic Review</u>, No. 2

———— (1974), 'China's Fourth Five-Year Plan', <u>Current Scene</u>, No.9, pp.1-6

———— (ed.) (1975-a), <u>China's Economy in Historical Perspective</u>, Stanford: Stanford University Press

———— (1975-b), 'Forecasting China's Trade Over the Long Term', <u>Current Scene</u>, No.9, pp.1-4

———— (1975-c), 'Growth and Changing Structure of China's Economy', in D.H. Perkins (ed.), <u>China's Modern Economy in Historical Perspective</u>, Stanford: Stanford University Press

———— (1975-d), 'Constraints Influencing China's Agricultural Performance', in Joint Economic Committee, U.S. Congress, <u>China : A Reassessment of the Economy</u>, Washington, D.C.: U.S. Government Printing Office

———— (1977-b), 'Estimating China's Gross Domestic Product', <u>Current Scene</u>, No.3, pp.1-3

———— et al. (1977-a), (The American Rural Small-Scale Industry Delegation), <u>Rural Small-Scale Industry in the People's Republic of China</u>, Berkeley: University of California Press

Propaganda Department of the Chinese Communist Party of Nanning Prefecture, Guangxi Province (ed.), (1977), <u>Xue-xi 'Zhongguo nong-cun de she-hui zhu-yi gao-chao' de xu-yan he an-yu</u> (Study the Introduction and Comments on the Upsurge of Socialism in Chinese Rural Villages), Nanning: Guangxi Renmin Chubanshe

Propaganda Division, Political Department, Kunming Military Region (1973), 'Reference Materials Concerning Education on Situation, No.45 Confidential : Distribution to Companies and Above, April 6, 1973' (in Chinese), reprinted in Editorial Committee of Issues and Studies (ed.), <u>Chinese Communist Internal Politics and Foreign Policy : Reviews on 'Reference Materials Concerning Education on Situation', Issued by the Kunming Military Region</u>, Taipei, Taiwan: Institute of International Relations, 1974

Prybyla, Jan S. (1975), 'A Note on Incomes and Prices in China', <u>Asian Survey</u>, No.3, pp.262-78

Qi, Younghung (1970), 'Industry Must Energetically Support Agriculture', <u>Hongqi</u> (Red Flag), No.6, pp.78-81

Qiao, Xiaoguang (1978), 'Agriculture Should Be Placed In the Top Position', <u>Hongqi</u> (Red Flag), No.9, pp.41-6

Raj, K.N. (1973), 'Mechanization of Agriculture in India and Sri Lanka (Ceylon)', in International Labour Office, Mechanization and Employment in Agriculture : Case Studies from Four Continents, Geneva: International Labour Office

Rao, R.V. (1967), Cottage and Small Scale Industries and Planned Economy, Delhi: Sterling Publishers

Rawski, Thomas G. (1973), 'Chinese Industrial Production, 1952-1971', Review of Economics and Statistics, No.2, pp.169-81

_____ (1975-a), 'The Growth of Producer Industries, 1900-1971', in D.H. Perkins (ed.), China's Modern Economy in Historical Perspective, Stanford: Stanford University Press

_____ (1975-b), 'Problems of Technology Absorption in Chinese Industry', American Economic Review, No.2, pp.383-388

_____ (1976-a), 'Chinese Economic Planning', Current Scene, No.4

_____ (1976-b), 'Discussion : On the Reliability of Chinese Economic Data', Journal of Development Studies, No.4, pp.438-41

'Relying on the Masses to Build Power Stations With Local Resources - Investigation on How Small Hydro-Electric Power Stations are Being Built in Hilly Areas of Yungchun County in Fujiang Province' (1970), Peking Review, No.10, March 6

Ren, Luosun (1980), 'Changes in China's Economic Management', Beijing Review, No.5, February 4

Renmin Chubanshe (ed.) (1972), Yan-zhou Mao zhu-xi zhi-yin de nong-ye ji-xie-hua dao-lu qian-jin (Advance Along the Road of Agricultural Mechanization Guided by Chairman Mao), Peking: Renmin Chubanshe

Reporting Team Stationed in Dazhai (1977), Dazhai jing-yan (The Experience of Dazhai), Taiyan: Shanxi Renmin Chubanshe

Research Institute of Financial Science (ed.), (1959), Shi-nian-lai cai-zheng zi-liao hui-bian (A Collection of Documents on Financial Policy in the Past Ten years), Volumes 1-2, Peking: Caizheng Chubanshe

Research Office of Agricultural Policy (ed.) (1982), Zhongguo nong-ye jing-ji gai-yao (Outline of China's Agricultural Economy), Peking: Nongye Chubanshe

Revised NPAD, see, Central Committee of the CCP (1957-b)

Revolutionary Committee of Fenglai County, Shandong Province (1975), Tie-bi yin-chu huan xin-tian (Iron Arm and Silver Hoe Change a New Sky), Peking: Nongye Chubanshe

Revolutionary Criticism and Repudiation Group of the Daqing Oilfield Workers (1970), 'The Politics of Proletariat Dictatorship Must be Stressed and Stressed and Stressed Again - Criticize and Repudiate Nonsense of "Political Work Should Serve the Purpose of Production"', Guangming Ribao (Guangming Daily), February 1

Revolutionary Great Alliance Headquarters and Revolutionary Great
    Criticism and Repudiation Group of Organizations under the
    Eighth Ministry of Machine-Building (1968), 'Two Diametrically
    Opposite Lines in Agricultural Mechanization', Nongye Jixie
    Jishe (Agricultural Machine Techniques), No.9, in SCMM,
    No.633, November 4, 1968

Revolutionary Great Criticism and Repudiation Writing Group, Anhui
    Province (1970), 'Grasp Better the Class Struggle in the Realm
    of Agricultural Economy', Hongqi (Red Flag), No.2, pp.20-6

Revolutionary Worker's Criticism and Repudiation Group of Peking
    Knitting General Factory (1970), 'Criticism and Repudiation of
    Sun Yefang, The Struggle, Criticism and Transformation in the
    Economic Front', Renmin Ribao (People's Daily), February 24

Reynolds, Bruce L. (1978), 'Two Models of Agricultural Development :
    A Context For Current Chinese Policy', China Quarterly, No.
    76, pp.842-72

Reynolds, Lloyd G. (1971), The Three Worlds of Economics, New
    Haven: Yale University Press
    _____ (1975), 'China as a Less Developed Economy', American
    Economic Review, No.3. pp.

Richman, Barry (1969), Industrial Society in Communist China,
    New York: Random House
    _____ (1975), 'Chinese and Indian Development : An Inter-
    disciplinary Environment Analysis', American Economic
    Review, No. 2

Riskin, Carl A. (1969), Local Industry in Chinese Economic Develop-
    ment, 1950-57 : The Case of Kwangtung Province (Unpublished
    Ph.D. Thesis, University of California, Berkeley)
    _____ (1969-b), 'Local Industry and Choice of Technique in Planning
    of Industrial Development in Mainland China', in Planning for
    Advanced Skills and Technologies, United Nations: Industrial
    Development Organization
    _____ (1971), 'Small Industry and the Chinese Model of Development',
    The China Quarterly, No.46, pp.245-73
    _____ (1975-a), 'Surplus and Stagnation in Modern China' in
    D.H. Perkins (ed.), China's Economy in Historical Perspective,
    Stanford: Stanford University Press
    _____ (1975-b), 'Workers' Incentives in Chinese Industry', in Joint
    Economic Committee, U.S. Congress, China : A Reassessment
    of the Economy, Washington, D.C.: U.S. Government Printing
    Office
    _____ (1978-a), 'China's Rural Industries : Self Reliant Systems
    or Independent Kingdoms', China Quarterly, No.73, pp.77-98
    _____ (1978-b), 'Political Conflict and Rural Industrialization
    in China', World Development, Volume 6, pp.681-92

Robinson, Joan (1969), The Cultural Revolution in China,
     Harmondsworth, Middlesex: Penguin Books Ltd.
_____ (1975), Economic Management In China, London: Anglo-Chinese
     Educational Institute
Rong, Zihe (1958), 'A Few Problems in Improving Financial
     Management System', Caizheng (Finance), No. 1
Ruttan, V.W. (1968), Growth Stage Theories, Dual Economy Models
     and Agricultural Development Policy, Guelph: University of
     Guelph
Schickele, Rainer (1968), Agrarian Revolution and Economic Progress
     : A Primer For Development, New York: Praeger Publishers
Schram, Stuart R. (ed.) (1973), Authority, Participation and Cultural
     Change in China : Essays by a European Study Group,
     Cambridge: Cambridge University Press
Schran, Peter (1969), The Development of Chinese Agriculture,
     1950-1959, Urbana: University of Illinois Press
_____ (1977), 'China's Price Stability : Its Meaning and Distributive
     Consequences', Journal of Comparative Economics, No.4,
     pp.367-88
Schultz, Theodore W. (1964), Transforming Traditional Agriculture,
     New Haven: Yale University Press
_____ (1968), Economic Growth and Agriculture, New York: McGraw-
     Hill Book Company
Schurmann, Franz (1968), Ideology and Organization in Communist
     China, Berkeley: University of California Press
Second NPC Documents, see, Second Session of the Second National
     People's Congress of the People's Republic of China
     (Documents) (1960), Peking: Foreign Language Press
Second Session of the Second National People's Congress of the
     People's Republic of China (Documents) (1960), Peking: Foreign
     Language Press
Sen, A.K. (1969), 'Choice of Technology : A Critical Survey of a
     Class of Debates', in Planning for Advanced Skills and
     Technoologies, United Nations: Industrial Development
     Organization
_____ (1975), Employment, Technology and Development, Oxford:
     Clarendon Press
'Shaanxi Rural Work Conference' (1972), SWB, FE/3878/B15, January
     3, 1972
Shang, Yuli and Xiao Yaozhang (1977), Dazhai cha-shang jin chi-bang
     (Dazhai Has Got Golden Wings), Peking: Nongye Chubanshe
Shanghai Renmin Chubanshe (ed.) (1974), She-hui zhu-yi xin nong-cun
     (Socialist New Villages), Shanghai: Shanghai Renmin Chubanshe
Shen, Dixiao (1976), Xiaoxian da-bu gan Xiyang (Xiao County Is
     Catching Up With Xiyang), Peking: Nongye Chubanshe

Shi, Di (1975), Du-jiang-ji : Hebei sheng Zhengding xian ren-min xue Dazhai gan Xiyang de jing-yan (Crossing Yangtze - Experience of Learning from Dazhai in Zhengding County, Hebei Province), Peking: Nongye Chubanshe

Sigurdson, Jon (1972), 'Rural Industry - A Traveller's View', China Quarterly, No.50, pp.315-37

_____ (1973), 'Rural Industry and the Internal Transfer of Technology', in Stuart R. Schram (ed.), Authority, Participation and Cultural Change in China : Essays by a European Study Group, Cambridge: Cambridge University Press

_____ (1975), 'Rural Industrialization in China', in Joint Economic Committee, U.S. Congress, China : A Reassessment of the Economy, Washington, D.C.: U.S. Government Printing Office

_____ (1977), Rural Industrialization in China, Cambridge, Massachusetts: Harvard University Press

_____ (1978), 'Rural Industrialization : A Comparison of Development Planning in China and India', World Development, Volume 6, pp.667-80

60-Articles, See , Central Committee of the CCP (1961)

Smerden, Ernest T. (1971), 'Some Critical Steps in Achieving Agricultural Mechanization in Developing Countries', Agricultural Mechanization in Asia, Volume 2, Autumn

Speeches on the Draft of NPAD, Speeches on the Revised Draft of NPAD, See Central People's Radio (ed.)

Spencer, D.L., and Woroniak, A. (ed.) (1967), The Transfer of Technology to Developing Countries, New York: Praeger Publishers

Sprague, G.F. (1975), 'Agriculture In China', Science, No.4188, May 9

State Council (1955), 'Draft Model Regulations for the Agricultural Producers' Cooperatives', (November 10, 1955) in Chao, Kuo-chun, Agrarian Policies of Mainland China : A Documentary Study (1949-1956), Cambridge, Massachusetts: East Asian Research Centre, Harvard University, 1963, pp.95-102

_____ (1957-a), 'Resolution on Further Improving the Works in Relieving Natural Calamity', (Issued on September 16, 1957), in Collected Laws and Regulations of the People's Republic of China, Volume 6, Peking: Falu Chubanshe, 1958

_____ (1957-b), 'Regulations on Improving Industrial Management System' (November 14, 1957) in Research Institute of Financial Science (ed.), Shi-nian-lai cai-zheng zi-liao hui-bian (A Collection of Documents on Financial Policy in the Past Ten Years), Volume 1, Peking: Caizheng Chubanshe, 1959

_____ (1957-c), 'Regulations on Improving Commercial Management System' (November 14, 1957) in Research Institute of Financial Science (ed.), Shi-nian-lai cai-zheng zi-liao hui-biao (A Collection of Documents on Financial Policy in the Past Ten Years), Volume 1, Peking: Caizheng Chubanshe, 1959

_____ (1957-d), 'Regulations on Improving Financial Management System' (November 14, 1957), in Research Institute of Financial Science (ed.), <u>Shi-nian-lai cai-zheng zi-liao hui-bian</u> (A Collection of Documents on Financial Policy in the Past Ten Years), Volume 1, Peking: Caizheng Chubanshe, 1959

_____ (1958-a), 'Regulations on Improving Financial Management System for Basic Constructions' (July 5, 1958), in <u>Collected Laws and Regulations of the People's Republic of China</u>, Volume 8, Peking: Falu Chubanshe, 1959

_____ (1958-b), 'On the Works of Credit Departments of the People's Communes and Regulations of Working Capital of State Enterprises (December 20, 1958)', in <u>Collected Laws and Regulations of the People's Republic of China</u>, Volume 8, Falu Chubanshe, 1959

_____ (1962), 'On the Resolution To Reestablish and Establish Specialized Corporations at All Levels in the Commercial System' (May 5, 1962), in <u>Collected Laws and Regulations of the People's Republic of China</u>, Volume 13, Peking: Falu Chubanshe, 1962

_____ (1963), 'Motion for the Establishment of State Bureau of Material Management (March 23, 1963)', (passed by Standing Committee of the National People's Congress on May 25, 1963), in <u>Collected Laws and Regulations of the People's Republic of China</u>, Volume 13, Peking: Falu Chubanshe,

State Statistics Bureau (1960), <u>Ten Great Years</u>, Peking: Foreign Language Press

State Statistics Bureau (1979), 'Report on the Results of the 1978 National Economic Plan (June 26, 1979)', <u>Renmin Ribao</u> (People's Daily), June 28

Stavis, Benedict (1975-a), <u>Making Green Revolution : The Politics of Agricultural Development in China</u> (Rural Development Monograph No.1), Ithaca, New York: Cornell University Press

_____ (1975-b), 'How China Is Solving Its Food Problem', <u>Bulletin of Concerned Asian Scholars</u>, No.3, pp.22-38

_____ (1976), 'A Preliminary Model for Grain Production in China, 1974', <u>China Quarterly</u>, No.65, pp.82-96

_____ (1977), 'Speech in Conference on China's Agriculture, St. Louis. Missouri, November 18, 1976' in <u>China's Agriculture</u>, Washington: National Council for U.S. China Trade

_____ (1978-a), <u>The Politics of Agricultural Mechanization In China</u>, Ithaca, New York: Cornell University Press

_____ (1978-b), 'Agricultural Research and Extension Services in China', <u>World Development</u>, Volume 6, pp.631-45

Steidlmayer, Paul K. (1976), 'What is to Be Learned from Dazhai?', <u>Asian Profile</u>, No.6, pp.481-503

Stewart, Frances (1973), 'Choice of Techniques in Developing Countries', in Charles Cooper (ed.), <u>Science, Technology and Development : The Political Economy of Technical Advance in Under-developed Countries</u>, London: Frank Cass & Company

Strassmann, W. Paul (1968), Technological Change and Economic Development, New York: Cornell University Press

Strong, Anna Louise (1964), The Rise of the Chinese People's Communes and Six Years After, Peking: New World Press

Su, Xing (1965), 'The Struggle Between Socialist and Capitalist Roads in China After the Land Reform', Jingji Yanjiu (Economic Research), No.7

____ (1976), Wo-guo nong-ye de she-hui zhu-yi dao-lu (Our Socialist Way In Agriculture), Peking: Renmin Chubanshe

____ (1979), 'On a Few Problems in Raising the Labour Productivity in Agriculture', Jingji Yanjiu (Economic Research), No.2, pp.37-43

Sun, Gangruo (1978), 'Systems of Material Supply', Renmin Ribao (People's Daily), December 7

Swamy, S. (1973-a), Economic Growth in China and India 1952-1970 : A Comparative Appraisal, Chicago: University of Chicago Press

____ (1973-b), 'China's Economic Growth 1966- 1972', China Report, No.6

Tan, Chenlin (1960), 'Strive for the Fulfilment, Ahead of Schedule, of the National Programme for Agricultural Development' (A Report Delivered at the Second Session of the Second National People's Congress on April 6, 1960), in Second NPC Documents, Peking: Foreign Language Press

Tan, Feng (1975), 'Speed up the Pace of Agricultural Mechanization', Hongqi (Red Flag), No.11, pp.21-5

Tan, Renpu (1971), 'Speech on the Yunnan Province Agricultural Work Conference', (September 1969), Zhonggong Nianbao (Communist China Yearbook, Taipei), Section 7, pp.58-66

Tang, Anthony (1968), 'Policy and Performance in Agriculture', in A. Eckstein (ed.), Economic Trends in Communist China, Chicago: Aldine Publishing Company

Tang, Qinghong (1979), 'Reform of Supervisory Patterns of Bank Credit', Jingji Yanjiu (Economic Research), No.8, pp.45-51

Tao, Zhu (1964), 'The People's Communes Forge Ahead', Renmin Shouce (People's Handbook), Peking: Dagong Bao She

Ten Great Years, See State Statistics Bureau (1960)

Text of the 1970 Draft of the Revised Constitution of the People's Republic of China' (1971), in Studies in Comparative Communism, July, pp.100-6

Tianjin College of Finance and Economics (1977), Nong-cun she-dui qi-ye he-suan yu guan-li (Accounting and Management for Rural Collective Enterprises), Tianjin: Tianjin Renmin Chubanshe

Timmer, C.P. (1976), 'Food Policy in China', Food Research Institute Studies, Volume XV, pp.53-69

'To Support Production Is a Fundamental Duty of Socialist Bank' (1971), Renmin Ribao (People's Daily), September 19

Tobin, James (1974), 'The Economy of China : A Tourist View', Current Scene, No.5

Tsiang, S.C. (1967), 'Money and Banking in Communist China', in Joint Economic Committee, U.S. Congress, An Economic Profile of Mainland China, Washington, D.C.: U.S. Government Printing Office

U.S. Department of Agriculture (1978), People's Republic of China : Agricultural Situations, Washington, D.C. Department of Agricultire

U.S. Department of Agriculture (1976), 'The Agricultural Situation in the People's Republic of China and Other Communist Asian Countries', Foreign Agricultural Economic Report, No.124

Uchida, Genko (1966), 'Technology in China', Scientific American, No.11

Vanek, Jaroslav (1975), 'Introduction' in J. Vanek (ed.), Self Management, Harmondsworth, Middlesex: Penguin Books Ltd

'Vigorous Development of Small Local Industry' (1970), Peking Review, February 6

Walker, Kenneth R. (1965), Planning in Chinese Agriculture : Socialization and the Private Sector, 1956-1962, London: Frank Cass & Company

_____ (1966), 'Collectivization in Retrospect : The Socialist High Tide of Autumn 1955-Spring 1956', China Quarterly, No.26, pp.1-43

_____ (1977), 'Grain Self-sufficiency in North China, 1953-1975', China Quarterly, No.70, pp.555-90

Wang, Gengjin, and He, Jianjiang (1978), 'On a Few Problems in Realizing Rural Economic Policies', Jingji Yanjiu (Economic Research), No.8, pp.16- 20

Wang, Gengjin, et al. (1979), 'For Faster Growth In Agricultural Production, More Attention Must Be Paid to the Material Interest of the Peasants', Jingji Yanjiu (Economic Research), No.3, pp.26- 8

Wang, K.P. (1975), The People's Republic of China : A New Industrialized Power with a Strong Mineral Base, Washington, D.C.: Bureau of Mines

Wang, Mengkui, Dong, Yusheng, and Xing, Junfang (1979), 'On Co-operationAmong Specialized Departments in Industrial Production', Jingji Yanjiu (Economic Research), No.10, pp.43-50

Wang, Shichu (1968), 'Nothing Can Stand in the Way of Mass Enthusiasm for Farm Mechanization', Nongye Jixie Jishu (Agricultural Machine Technique), No.2, in SCMM, No.620, July 1968

Wang, Shouan (1979), 'An Examination on the Question of Reforming the Material System', Shehui Kexue Zhangxian (Frontier of Social Science), No.2

Wang, Shuchun (1964), 'Investigating Problems of Water Control', Jingji Yanjiu (Economic Research), No.1

_____ (1978), 'The Policy of Concentrating Forces to Fight Battle of Annihilation Must Be Adhered to in Basic Construction', Jingji Yanjiu (Economic Research), No.11, pp.28-34

Wang, Sikui (1964), 'The Question of Stable Co- ordination and Fixed-point Supplies for Industrial Enterprises', in Gong-ye qi-ye guan-li wen-zuan (Collected Essays on the Management of Industrial Enterprises), Volume 5, Peking: Zhongguo Gongye Chubanshe, pp.29-36

Wang, Wei (1963), 'Modernization of China's Agriculture', Peking Review, No.9, March 1

Wang, Xin (1964), 'Co-ordination and Sharing Is an Important Method in Doing a Good Job in the Supply Work', in Gong-ye qi-ye guan-li wen-zuan (Collected Essays on the Management of Industrial Enterprises), Volume 5, Peking: Zhongguo Gongye Chubanshe

Warriner, Doreen (1969), Land Reform in Principle and Practice, Oxford: Clarendon Press

Wei, Min (1975), 'China's Tax Policy', Peking Review, No.37, September 12

Weisskopf, T.E. (1975), 'China and India : Contrasting Experiences in Economic Development', American Economic Review, No.2

Wen, Yin and Liang, Hua (1977), Tachai: The Red Banner, Peking: Foreign Language Press

Wheelwright, E.L., and McFarlane, Bruce (1970), The Chinese Road to Socialism, New York: Monthly Review Press

Whiting, Allen S., and Dernberger, R.F. (1977), China's Future, New York: McGraw-Hill Book Company

Whitson, W.W. (1973), 'China's Quest For Technology', Problems of Communism, No. 3

Whyte, Martin King (1975), 'Inequality and Stratification in China', China Quarterly, No.64, pp.684-711

Winkler, Edwin A. (1976), 'Policy Oscillations in the People's Republic of China : A Reply', China Quarterly, No.68, pp.734-50

Wo-guo nong-ye de she-hui zhu-yi gai-zao, (The Socialist Transformation of Our Country's Agriculture) (1977), Shanghai: Shanghai Renmin Chubanshe

Wo-men zheng-zai qian-jin (We Are Marching Forward) (1972), Peking: Renmin Chubanshe

Wong, John (1973), Land Reform in the People's Republic of China : Institutional Transformation in Agriculture, New York: Praeger Publishing Company

_____ (1976), 'Some Aspects of China's Agricultural Development Experience : Implications For Developing Countries in Asia', World Development, No.4, pp.485-97

_____ (1977), 'Communization of Peasant Agriculture : China's Organizational Strategy for Agricultural Development', in Peter Dorner (ed.) (1977), Co-operative and Commune, Group Farming in the Economic Development of Agriculture, Madison: The University of Wisconsin Press

Worker-Peasant-Soldier Students of Class 71, Department of Political Economy, Wuhan University (1976), Zue-dian zheng-zhi jing-ji xue, she-hui zhu-yi bu-fen, xiu-ding-ben (Learning Political Economy, On Socialism, Revised Edition), Wuhan: Hubei Renmin Chubanshe

World Bank (1982), World Development Report 1982, New York: Oxford University Press

Wortman, Sterling (1975), 'Agriculture In China', Scientific American, No.6

Writing Group of the First Ministry of Machine-Building (1971), 'Advance Along the Road to Agricultural Mechanization as Directed by Chairman Mao', Renmin Ribao (People's Daily), September 17

Writing Group of the Heilongjiang Provincial Revolutionary Committee (1970), 'Develop Local Industry in a Bigger, Faster, Better and More Economical Way', Hongqi (Red Flag), No.6, pp.82-8

Writing Group of the Henan Provincial Revolutionary Committee (1970), 'Road Forward for China's Socialist Agriculture', Hongqi (Red Flag), No.2, pp.5-15

Writing Group of the Jilin Provincial Revolutionary Committee (1970), 'The Class Struggle in the Sphere of Socialist Construction and Economics - Criticizing the Revisionist Economic Theory of Sun Yefang', Hongqi (Red Flag), No.2, pp.52-63

Writing Group of the Ministry of Finance (1972), Zai zi-li-geng-sheng qin-jian-jian-guo de dao-lu-shang (On the Road to Build the Country with Self-Reliance and Diligence), Peking: Renmin Chubanshe

Writing Group of the Revolutionary Criticism and Repudiation Group of the Ministry of Textile (1970), 'The "Profit Principle" is Capitalist Principle - Criticism of Anti-Revolutionary Element Sun Yefang's Investigation Report (1961) on Shanghai First National Cotton Textile Factory', Guangming Ribao (Guangming Daily), January 23

Writing Group of the State Capital Construction Commission (1970), 'Simultaneously Develop Big and Small and Medium Enterprises', Peking Review, No.48, November 27

Wu, Jiapei (1978), 'The Experience of Changzhou City in Organizing Production by Co-operation Along A "Dragon-Line" Is Good', Jingji Yanjiu (Economic Research), No.7, pp.25-31

Wu, Waisong and Chen Guanghan (1978), 'An Expansion on Marx's Theory of Reproduction', Jingji Yanjiu (Economic Research), No.1, pp.21-5

Wu, Wei (1964), 'The Multiple Utilization of Agricultural Labour Force', Guangming Ribao (Guangming Daily), January 6

Wu, Yuanli (1965), The Economy of Communist China, London: Pall Mall Press

_____ (1967), 'Planning, Management, and Economic Development in Communist China', in Joint Economic Committee, U.S. Congress, An Economic Profile of Mainland China, Washington, D.C.: U.S. Government Printing Office

_____ (1967-b), The Spatial Economy of Communist China, New York: Praeger Publishers

_____ (1970), The Organization and Support of Scientific Research and Development In Mainland China, New York: Praeger Publishers

229

_____ (1971), 'Food and Agriculture in Mainland China', Current
History, No.419, pp.160-4

Xiao Dezhan (1960), 'Increase the Labour Productivity of Our
Agriculture', Guangming Ribao (Guangming Daily), March 7

Xiao, Han (1978), 'The Only Road to Realize Agricultural
Mechanization', Jingji Yanjiu (Economic Research), No.3,
pp.26-8

Xie, Junhua (1976), Kao qiong-bang-zi jing-shen ban nong-ye ji-xie
hua (Depend on the Spirit of 'Qiong Bang Zi' to Carry Out
Agricultural Mechanization), Peking: Nongye Chubanshe

Xin, Tianshan and Zhu, Changcheng (1976), Tian-shanjiao-xia zhan
xin-tu: Wusu xian nong-ye xue Dazhai (A New Picture Under
Tianshan Mountain: Wusu County Learns from Dazhai), Peking:
Nongye Chubanshe

Xin Zhongguo er-shi-wu nian (New China's 25 Years) (1975), Hong
Kong: Xianggang Chao Yang Chubanshe

Xinzhou County Communist Party Committee, Hubei Province (1974),
Xinzhou nong-ye ji-xie-hua (Agricultural Mechanization in
Xinzhou County), Peking: Nongye Chubanshe

Xu, Dixin (1962), Zhongguo guo-du shi-qi guo-min jing-ji de fen-xi
(1949-1957) (An Analysis of the Economy of China During Her
Transitory Period, 1949-1957), Peking: Renmin Chubanshe

_____ (1963), 'The Role and Position of Agriculture in the National
Economy', Renmin Shouce (People's Handbook), Peking:
Dagong Bao She

Xu, He, et al., (ed.) (1975), Zheng-zhi jing-ji xue ming-ci jie-shi
(Dictionary of Political Economy), Urumqi: Xinjiang Renmin
Chubanshe

Xue, Muqiao (1978), 'On the Collective Ownership System of
Socialism', Jingji Yanjiu (Economic Research), No.10, pp.2-9

_____ (1979), 'On the Question of Reforming the System of Economic
Management', Hongqi (Red Flag), No.8

Xue, Xinnong (1977), Guang-ming can-lan de xi-wang:Jiangsu Wuxi
xian she-dui gong-ye de fa-zhan (Bright Hope: Development of
Commune and Brigade Enterprises in Wuxi County, Jiangsu
Province), Shanghai: Shanghai Renmin Chubanshe

Yang, Deying (1979), 'Respect Objective Laws, Organize Commodity
Flow According to Economic Areas', Jingji Guanli (Economic
Management), No.4, pp.11-3

Yang, Heng, et al. (1968), 'The People's Commune Can Achieve
Mechanization with Greater, Faster, Better and More Economic
Results', Nongye Jixie Jishe (Agricultural Machine Technique),
No.8, August, in SCMM, No.629, September, 1968

Yang, Jianbai (1964), 'The Internal Relationship Between Agriculture
and Industry', Guangming Ribao (Guangming Daily), April 27

Yang, Jun and Wang Songpei (1962), 'An Attempt to Discuss a Few
Economic Problems in Agricultural Mechanization', Guangming
Ribao (Guangming Daily), October 15

Yang, Peixin (1963), 'The Question of Finance During the Process
of Agricultural Modernization in Our Country', Jingji Yanjiu
(Economic Research), No.6

_____ (1979), 'Lenin's Thought on Socialist Banking Lights the Way for Our Country's Banking Works', Jingji Yanjiu (Economic Research), No.3, pp.45-54

Yao, Jianfu (1978), 'Strengthen Research on the Techniques and Economics of Agricultural Mechanization', Jingji Yanjiu (Economic Research), No.12, pp.17-22

Yao, Jianhua, et al. (1979), 'What Does Fluctuation in Peanut Production Tell Us?', Jingji Guanli (Economic Management), No.5, pp.25-6

Yao, Jinguan (1978), 'On a Few Problems in the Price Scissors of Industrial and Agricultural Goods', Jingji Yanjiu (Economic Research), No.12, pp.32-6

Yayami, Y. and Ruttan, V.W. (1971), Agricultural Development : An International Perspective, Baltimore: John Hopkins University Press

Yeh, K.C. (1968), 'Capital Formation', in A. Eckstein, W. Galenson and T.C. Liu (ed.), Economic Trends in Communist China, Chicago: Aldine Publishing Company

Yeh, K.C., and Roll, Charles R., Jr. (1975), 'Balance in Coastal and Industrial Development', in Joint Economic Committee, U.S. Congress, China : A Reassessment of the Economy, Washington, D.C.: U.S. Government Printing Office

Yi, Cai (1965), 'The Question of Raising the Economic Efficiency of Model Field Production', Guangming Ribao (Guangming Daily), September 13

Yi, Hongren (1979), 'On the Control System for Working Capital', Jingji Yanjiu (Economic Research), No.8, pp.40-4

Yin, H. (1970), Economic Statistics of Mainland China 1949-1957, Michigan: University Microfilm

Yong Dazhai jing-shen ban cai-zheng jin-rong (1977) (Use the Spirit of Dazhai to Carry Out Works in Finance), Peking: Zhongguo Caizheng Jingji Chubanshe

You, Jianwen and Tian, Yangzhang (1976), Lai-zi Zhuang-xiang de bao-gao (Report from a Zhuang Village), Peking: Nongye Chubanshe

Yu, C.L. (1971), 'The Local Industry and Its Impact on Agricultural Development in China', Asia Quarterly, No.4, pp.321-41

Yu, Qiuli (1978-a), 'Speech at the Third National Conference on Agricultural Mechanization', Renmin Ribao (People's Daily), January 26

_____ (1978-b), 'Summary Report to the Third National Conference on Agricultural Mechanization (January 26, 1978)', Collected Documents and Materials of the Third National Conference on Agricultural Mechanization, Peking: Renmin Chubanshe

Yuan, Baohua (1978), 'Place Product Quality In First Priority', Hongqi (Red Flag), No.6, pp.51-5

Yunker, James A. (1975), 'A Survey of Market Socialist Forms', Annals of Public and Co-operative Economy, No.2, pp.131-62

Zhan, Wu (1979-a), 'Take the Chinese Road of Agricultural Modernization', Jingji Guanli (Economic Management), No.9, pp.11-17, p.58

____ (1979-b), 'Take the Chinese Road of Agricultural Modern-
ization (Part II)', Jingji Guanli (Economic Management), No.10,
pp.4-9

Zhang, Chunqiao (1975), 'On Exercising All-round Dictatorship
Over the Bourgeois', Hongqi (Red Flag), No.4, pp.3-12

Zhang, Fushan, et al. (1978), 'The Great Directive for Developing
Agricultural Mechanization in a Faster, Better and more
Economical Way', Jingji Yanjiu (Economic Research), No.3,
pp.29-36

Zhang, Fushan, Wang Songpei, and Zhang Siqian (1979), 'Place
Agricultural Mechanization in Its Deserved Position in
Agricultural Modernization', Jingji Yanjiu (Economic Research),
No.11, pp.22-9

Zhang, Gensheng (1979), 'Interview with Zhang Gensheng', Economic
Reporter, October 17

Zhang, Jingfu (1979), 'Report on the Results of 1978 State Budget
and Draft Budget for 1979', Renmin Ribao (People's Daily),
June 25

Zhang, Shushan (1979), 'A Few Ideas on Reforming the System of
Material Management', Jingji Guanli (Economic Management),
No.8, pp.15-8

Zhang, Yang, et al. (1976), Shou-fu tuo-la-ji de gou-zao yu shi-yong
(The Construction and Use of Hand-held Tractors), Peking:
Renmin Chubanshe

Zhang, Yongjia (1965), 'A Preliminary Inquiry Into the Accumulation
of Labour by the Collective Economy of the People's
Commune', Jingji Yanjiu (Economic research), No.11, November
20, in SCMM,, No.508, January 24, 1966

Zhao, Fengnian (1972), 'Fully Realize the National Programme For
Agricultural Development', Renmin Ribao (People's Daily),
September 23

____ (1974), 'Further Develop Our Socialist Agriculture', Hongqi
(Red Flag), No.12, pp.67-71

Zhao, Liufu (1963), 'The Proper Development of Agricultural
Machinery in Our Country', Guangming Ribao (Guangming
Daily), December 9

Zhao, Tianfu and Zhu Daohua (1964), 'A Few Problems in Building
High and Stable Yielding Farmland', Guangming Ribao
(Guangming Daily), August 24

Zhao, Xue (1956), 'Report on the Proposed Second FiveYear Plan
for Development of Our National Economy - Section on
Finance' (September 16, 1956), in Research Institute of
Financial Science (ed.), Shi-nian lai cai-zheng zi-liao hui-bian,
(A Collection of Documents on Financial Policy in the Past Ten
Years), Volume 1, Peking: Caizheng Chubanshe, 1959

____ (1957), 'Problems of Agricultural Mechanization', Jihua
Jingji (Planned Economy), April

Zhao, Yushen (1973), 'The Communist Bandits Step UpWorks on
Agricultural Mechanization', in Gao Xiang-gao (ed.), Gong-fei
Jing-ji Wen-ti Lun-ji (Collected Papers on the Economic
Problems of the Communist Bandits), Taipei,

Zheng-zhi jing-ji-xue jiang-hua : she-hui-zhu-yi bu-fen (Talks on
  Political Economy: Socialism) (1976), Peking: Renmin Chubanshe
Zhong-hua ren-min gong-he-guo xian-fa (Constitution of the People's
  Republic of China) (adopted on January 17, 1975 by the Fourth
  National People's Congress) (1975), Peking: Renmin Chubanshe
Zhongguo Caizheng Jingji Chubanshe (ed.) (1977), Yong Dazhai
  jing-shen-ban cai-zheng jin-rong (Use the Spirit of Dazhai to
  Carry Out Financial Works), Peking: Zhongguo Caizheng Jingji
  Chubanshe
Zhou, Enlai (1957), 'Report on Government Works' (Fourth Session
  of the First National People's Congress, June 26, 1957), in The
  Fourth Session of the First National People's Congress
  (Documents), Peking: Renmin Chubanshe, 1957
——— (1959), 'Report on Government Works' (First Session of the
  Second National People's Congress, April 18, 1959), Peking: in
  The First Session of the Second National People's Congress
  (Documents), Peking: Renmin Chubanshe, 1959
——— (1962), Ten Point Program (April, 1962) reprinted in
  E.L. Wheelwright and B. McFarlane, The Chinese Road to
  Socialism, New York: Monthly Review Press, 1970
——— (1965), 'Report on Government Works', in Collected Documents
  of the First Session of the Third National People's Congress of
  the People's Republic of China, Peking: Renmin Chubanshe
——— (1973-a), 'Report to the Tenth National Congress of the Chinese
  Communist Party' (August 24, 1973), in Collected Documents of
  the Tenth National Congress of the Chinese Communist Party,
  Peking: Renmin Chubanshe
——— (1973-b), 'Report to the Tenth National Congress of the Chinese
  Communist Party', Renmin Ribao (People's Daily), September 1
Zhou, Jin (1976), 'How State-run Factories Are Managed', Economic
  Reporter, October 1
Zhou, Shujun (1955), 'Material-Technical Supply Plan', Jihua Jingji
  (Planned Economy), No.10, pp.30-3, translated in Chinese
  Economic Studies, Volume X, No.3, Spring, 1977, p.63
Zhou, Zijian (1978), 'Organize Well Specialized Production in
  Machine Building Industries For High-speed Development',
  Hongqi (Red Flag), No.11, pp.43-7
Zhu, Daohua, et al. (1963), 'On the Relationship Between Agricultural
  Mechanization, Intensive Farming and Raising Per Unit Yields',
  Guangming Ribao (Guangming Daily), September 16
Zhu, Fulin and Xiang, Huaicheng (1979-a), 'Some Views On the Reform
  of Financial and Fiscal System', Jingji Guanli (Economic
  Management), No.5, pp.16-9
——— (1979-b), 'Questions on Expanding the Financial Power of
  Enterprises', Jingji Guanli (Economic Management), No.6,
  pp.14-17, p.42
Zimmerman, L.J. (1975), 'Non-monetary Capital Formation and Rural
  Development', World Development, No.6, pp.411-9
Zuo, Mu (1979), 'On "Getting Ahead"', Jingji Yanjiu (Economic
  Research), No.7, pp.14-7